BEST

OF

THE

WEST

BEST OF THE WEST

EDITED
BY

MURRAY
MEDNICK

BILL
RADEN

CHERYL
SLEAN

BEST OF THE WEST
© 1991 by Padua Hills Press

ISBN: 0-9630126-2-2

Printed in the United States of America.

For those who may be strangers to the Padua Hills Playwrights' Workshop/Festival, it's important to remember that there's no actual Padua theatre, at least in the sense of an auditorium. Neither is there a lighting booth, producer's suite, box office, lobby or parking lot. For nine months out of the year, in fact, the most concrete manifestation of the Padua Hills Playwrights' Workshop/Festival might well be this collection of plays. This is because Padua is a playwright's theatre. In an era in which TV has dislodged theatre from the center of American cultural life, it's hard to exaggerate the importance of that distinction. Unlike the average repertory company, Padua's sole mission is the cultivation of new American voices for the stage. It stands for a reassertion of the playwright's authority in a theater where, too often, experimentation and the freedom to explore an original voice is shackled by the institutional pressures of the box office and subscription drive.

For fourteen summers now, Padua has gathered on the outskirts of Los Angeles like some fantastic, itinerant circus, setting up its stages and lights under the stars, and inviting the surrounding community to witness the results of the previous four weeks of workshops and rehearsals. It is no coincidence that the past fourteen years of plays and playwrights have produced some of the most important and original works in Los Angeles and, arguably, in the country. Culled from the 1989 and 1990 seasons hosted by California State University at Northridge, this book is a small sampling of those accomplishments. Though there is no consistent style represented here, these pages all share in a respect for the spoken word which is at the heart of the Padua philosophy. They act on an artistic tradition passed down from Artaud, and through such Off-Off-Broadway hothouses as the Judson Poet's Theatre and Theatre Genesis, which stakes theatre's future on its unique difference from television or movies. These plays reflect a process that, even when it aggressively confronts the limits of language and dramatic form, is carried out in a spirit of rigorous inquiry. Most importantly, these plays represent the vital belief of writers committed to the idea that theatre still has a meaningful and responsible role to play in our cultural life.

Bill Raden
Los Angeles, June, 1991.

BONDAGE

BY

SUSAN

CHAMPAGNE

Bondage was first performed at the 1990 Padua Hills Playwrights Festival with the following cast:

Toots	Molly Cleator
Chita	Roxanne Rogers
Eddie	John Pappas
Dash	Dan Sullivan
Man #1	Jeff Levy, Douglas Heller
Understudy for Toots	Thea Constantine
Director	Susan Champagne
Lighting Design	Jason Berliner
Set Design	Nick Flynn, John Kippen, Margaret Dunn
Stage Manager	Hillary Fox

Scene 1

(The Ink Spots singing "Do I Worry" plays over the following: an iris slowly opens revealing CHITA and TOOTS standing near a bus stop bench. Toots wears a simple dress suit and sneakers. Chita wears a very nice dress suit and expensive high heals. Toots stares at some gum stuck at the bottom of her shoe. She holds Chita's shoulder for support. Chita holds her briefcase and stares out confidentially. The pose is broken when the iris is fully open. The song continues to play as Chita and Toots involve themselves in a ritual transforming themselves from working women to . . . women. They sit at the bus stop bench. An awkward Toots takes the lead from Chita. Chita teases her hair. Toots fixes her hair neatly. Chita pulls out a pocket knife and applies lipstick using the knife as a mirror. Toots looks at her dainty compact to apply her lipstick. Chita changes her shoes to sneakers which she pulls out of her very nice briefcase. She simultaneously takes big, aggressive but tidy bites in her hot dog. Toots eats her hot dog and looks at the sky. She tries to be neat, but spills mustard and ketchup on herself as it falls out of the hot dog. Chita pulls a nose ring out of her briefcase and puts it on her nose. Chita and Toots look at the sky—it's gray—a ready-to-rain sky. The iris fades out and lights come up. The song ends.)

TOOTS: I'm doubting myself.

CHITA: *(Short, deadpan)* Yeah?

TOOTS: I don't know why it is that I'm doubting myself, but I'm doubting myself.

CHITA: Yeah?

TOOTS: I think it's in relation to other people. I'm fine when I'm in relation to myself. I get along with myself fine, but when I'm with other people, I—I tend to read people's minds.

CHITA: You're a mind-reader?

TOOTS: Incorrectly and then assuming they're judging me and that they're reading my mind and my judgements of them.

CHITA: Yeah. It's a real salt-shaker you're tripping on.

TOOTS: Yeah. It probably has to do with Catholicism and, you know, the death thing.

CHITA: Oh yeah, what's that?

TOOTS: The last 4 people I've known personally that have died? I got the death thing beforehand and then, you know, they did it. So when I feel anything that I can't place my finger on, I think it's a harbinger of impending doom.

(Chita looks at her during the following:)

TOOTS: It's usually I just drink too much coffee, but sometimes—

CHITA: Don't look at me.

(Toots looks away.)

TOOTS: O.K.

CHITA: If you ever have those feelings about me—

TOOTS: I won't tell you.

CHITA: You've had them recently then?

TOOTS: *(Smiling)* Of course not.

CHITA: You worry too much about what people think and what they think you think and what you think they think. Too much thinking. Are you a Libra?

TOOTS: You know better than that.

CHITA: Oh, that's right. You're a Capricorn.

TOOTS: Libra rising.

(Toots smiles at Chita. Chita smiles back.)

TOOTS: Wanna walk back with me?

CHITA: I've gotta buy some rope. *(She smiles.)*

TOOTS: Why don't you wait here a minute? I think it's gonna rain.

(Chita leaves, looking at the sky and yelling:)

CHITA: DON'T RAIN!

(She smiles at Toots.)

CHITA: It won't.

(Toots looks at the sky fearfully and stands under the bus stop waiting area. A man approaches. He's a little funny-looking. He could be harmless, but—)

EDDIE: Nice watch. What time is it?

TOOTS: It's 4:35.

EDDIE: Where are you going?

TOOTS: Home.

EDDIE: Where do you live?

TOOTS: Not far from here.

EDDIE: Not far from here?

TOOTS: Not too close though.

EDDIE: Are you waiting for the bus?

TOOTS: YES. NO. I'm waiting for my friend in the CAR.

EDDIE: If it's so close, why are you waiting for the bus?

TOOTS: I'm afraid of the rain.   EDDIE: You're afraid of the rain.

EDDIE: I don't have any bad kind of intention.

TOOTS: I know your intention.

Scene 2

(Some time later. Eddie and Toots are in Toots' bed. They both have big smiles on their faces.)

TOOTS: I thought, "Why not?"

EDDIE: Sure.

TOOTS: No mental energy. No worry. *(Pause)* No worry, right?

EDDIE: Me? no. Look at me. *(Laughs, pause)* No worry to me?

TOOTS: Me? No. *(Pause, dejected—)* No concern.

EDDIE: No concern?

TOOTS: No. *(She looks at him and melts—)* Yes. *(Pause)* Maybe.

(She smiles at him, he at her. They shyly look away. Pause.)

EDDIE: Hey, can we eat something now?

TOOTS: OK. Yeah. In my refrigerator, I have some plums. Why don't you bring us back a few?

(Eddie looks at her.)

TOOTS: Oh, you want me—you, you want us to—to go out *there* and eat something—out there.

EDDIE: No it's not that, it's just—

TOOTS: You want more than plums.   EDDIE: I want more than
                                                                                    plums.

(After a longing, they kiss. Then he holds her from behind.)

TOOTS: My second name is Marilyn after Marilyn Monroe, but I don't look anything like her and when I was four, I wet the bed and my sister caught me—

(She looks at him.)

EDDIE: Any trouble since then?

TOOTS: No.

EDDIE: *(He caresses her)* You've got fine child-bearing hips.

TOOTS: Large.

EDDIE: Large enough to bear a child.

EDDIE: We didn't just conceive a   TOOTS: We didn't just conceive a
          child?   child.

TOOTS: *(Sadly)* No.

(A beat. He holds her in his arms.)

TOOTS: My mother's friend Doris Jalopsky had a lobotomy and all she did all day was build things out of popsicle sticks. She made her daughter Nadine a beautiful playhouse for her dolls, but Nadine stuck it up her butt or s-somehow it got stuck up there. One of the sticks.

EDDIE: You're trembling.

TOOTS: *(On the verge of tears)* S-she was a victim of her mind and then her mind made her a victim. They h-had to get a doctor to pull it out. And Doris h-had her head like this and cried and cried. It was such a nice doll's house before Nadine ripped it up and stuck it up her butt. *(Beat)* I'm afraid of my MIND!

EDDIE: I am too.

Scene 3

(Eddie is sitting on a chair. Toots is standing and adjusting a new gray sweater she's put on him.)

TOOTS: I was crocheting it for my brother and then he almost jumped off this building but someone pulled him back into the building on time but ever since then he's developed an aversion to gray because that's the color of pavement and that's what he would have smashed into and his guts would have splattered on if he succeeded with the jump. Gray looks good on you though.

(She smiles.)

EDDIE: I'm not planning on jumping off anything.

TOOTS: I'm glad.

(He wants to kiss her, but he's apprehensive. He wants to again, but is apprehensive. By the third time, he feels it's O.K. and he kisses her.)

EDDIE: *(A joke)* Anybody else in your family, you know—jump off anything?

TOOTS: Oh, no.

(He's relieved until—)

TOOTS: My uncle shot himself. But that was before I was born. It was really sad I guess. It was a secret. Some of my cousins are 50 and they don't know about it. They think he fell off a horse. My parents told me he got stepped on by a horse and I believed them for a while. I don't know why they told me that.

EDDIE: Why did he do it?

(He looks at her. She looks away. Beat.)

TOOTS: Sit on my lap.

EDDIE: Why?

TOOTS: It's the thing to do.

(He sits on her lap.)

EDDIE: Is anyone in your family a comedian?

TOOTS: I am.

(He laughs a lot.)

TOOTS: But I got booed off the stage at the—the Improv cause I talk too softly so I *write* comedy.

EDDIE: You don't seem funny.

TOOTS: Oh, I'm not. But my mind is when I let it have fun.

EDDIE: Maybe I should massage your brain.

TOOTS: O.K.

EDDIE: Sit on *my* lap.

TOOTS: *(She does)* O.K.

EDDIE: I'm a comedian.

TOOTS: You are?

EDDIE: Yes.

TOOTS: Maybe I've laughed at you before.

EDDIE: Lots of people have. Look at this face. UG-LY. Perfect laugh
material.

(He smiles.)

TOOTS: I don't think it's ugly.

(They kiss and fall off the chair. The chair falls on top of them.)

Scene 4

Eddie and Toots are on the couch. They watch T.V.

TOOTS: Eddie I love you so much, I'm gonna write you an ode to
Eddie. (She sings—)

> Eddie La lala lala la Eddie.
> La la la Eddie La Ed la la la—die,
> la you la me!

How was it?

EDDIE: Are you gonna put words in it?

TOOTS: Those were the words. It's a personal ode. You're supposed
to guess the LAs. It's the subtext. I'm enjoying life much more now.

(Pause)

EDDIE: I hate David Letterman.

TOOTS: He's so cynical.

EDDIE: He makes lots of money. He doesn't have to sell used cars.

TOOTS: I know it's hard on you, honey.

EDDIE: And they're not even good cars. They're American.

TOOTS: I'm sorry.

EDDIE: Where's Chita?

TOOTS: *(Lying)* She's at the bank cashing her check.

(Chita enters aggressively.)

TOOTS: Here she comes. Hi Chita.

CHITA: Hi Toots. Hi Ed-DIE.

(Chita throws her purse at Eddie. It's heavy and it hurts his arm. She goes into her room and closes the door.)

EDDIE: I don't think Chita likes me.

TOOTS: I don't think she does either.

(They look at each other, then look at her door.)

Scene 5

Eddie and Toots are still on the couch. Toots is in the middle of the story. She sometimes looks toward Chita's door which is behind them.

TOOTS: Well, she used to sniff glue when she was in the third grade. That started it. When she was in seventh grade, she had a baby. When she was in ninth grade, she went to juvenile hall for armed robbery. When she came out, she got her GED. She went to UC Berkeley undergrad and to Harvard Law School.

EDDIE: *She's* a lawyer?

TOOTS: Yes. And I'm her legal secretary.

(Toots smiles proudly. Then we hear a man's scream from within Chita's room.)

TOOTS: Oh no. It's happening. She's doing it. Let's go to my room. *(They almost go, when—)* It's too late. We have to stay here or it'll look like we're sneaking out cause we noticed it.

CHITA: *(From off-stage)* I SAID GET THE HELL OUT OF HERE NOW. YOU SON-OF-A-BITCH! NOW!

(A frightened man runs out of the apartment from Chita's room. Chita comes out of her room. She guzzles from a gatorade bottle. She is sweaty. She wears

big black leather boots that go up to her hips and a one-piece leather bathing suit with Viking breast cups. She laughs and climbs over the couch from behind it to sit in between the loving couple. She laughs hysterically. She looks at the David Letterman show on T.V.)

CHITA: Did he roll anything over or drop anything from the roof?

EDDIE: No.

CHITA: Oh. Who's on?

TOOTS: Michael J. Fox and Betty White.

CHITA: *(Disgusted)* No. No, definitely not. Way past my bedtime. Catch you later. I have to be in court in 7 hours.

(Chita goes in her room and slams her door shut. Toots and Eddie look at her door and then look at each other.)

Scene 6

Chita, Toots, and Eddie are covered with mud. They have just come in from the rain. Toots and Eddie take their raincoats off. They have on terry-cloth bathrobes. Toots has bunny slippers. Eddie has bare feet. Chita has her Viking outfit on underneath her London Fog which she opens up but doesn't take off.

CHITA: Now I don't have a car. It's stuck. I have to have a car.

TOOTS: You can take the bus. I can show you how to do it.

CHITA: I can't take the bus. My time's too precious. *(To Eddie—)* You can take the bus. I can take *your* car.

(Eddie looks at Chita. After a beat, he gives her his car keys. She leaves.)

EDDIE: She just took my car.

TOOTS: You let her take it.

EDDIE: She drives like a maniac.

TOOTS: She knows where she's going. She's the person in my whole life who most knew where she's going. She knocks obstacles down with her fist.

EDDIE: That's not all she knocks down.

TOOTS: She's in control of her life.

(Toots smiles and watches out the window as Chita speeds away. Eddie looks out the window in fear and disbelief.)

Scene 7

(Eddie has just come from work. Chita has too. Eddie and Chita enter the apartment as the scene begins. Eddie expects to find Toots, but . . . Chita takes out her nose earring, eats something, and reads the Wall Street Journal *as she talks to Eddie.)*

CHITA: She's out of control. Way overboard. Do you hear how much she talks? She's not in control of her mind. It's a separate entity. Floating in the cosmos like a little lost goose. La la la. *My* mind is a wonderful thing. Every second I can use my mind, I use it well. Everything I do is timed. Every time I have has a predetermined function. I make us of all my time. I'm not an idle talker. I'm not a drinker, smoker, drug-user. I am not an artist, hippie, or friend. *I* am a professional. I WON MY CASE.

(She kisses him strongly on the lips.)

CHITA: Don't kiss me back.

EDDIE: *(Timidly, after a beat)* Can I have my car back now?

CHITA: *(Of her nose ring)* I was thinking about a hoop. About this big.

EDDIE: I need my car. I have a comedy gig.

CHITA: *(Mocking him)* "Comedy gig."
    I need your car.
    I'm a lawyer.
    Law isn't funny.
    Law is serious.

(He looks at her. She stares at him and slowly melts. She kisses him again passionately. They roll off of the couch onto the floor. She breaks the kiss.)

CHITA: Why did you do that?

(She slaps him. She runs into the other room. He manages to pick himself up as he sees her coming out of her room with a rope and handcuffs. He runs for the door. He bumps into a man in an Armani suit who carries a briefcase. Chita smiles and holds the rope and handcuffs up to the new man so that Eddie can see this. The new man smiles. Eddie runs out as Chita's smile slowly fades.)

Scene 8

(Eddie and Toots sit at the dining room table. She wears a slip. He wears his boxer shorts. We hear the loud sound of a walker moving slowly outside. We hear the rain.)

TOOTS: That lady across the street? Her husband died in a car wreck. She was left a cripple. But she uses her walker and she takes the bus and buys things. She's proud she can do that. *(She smiles)* She must have gone when the rain let up. Now she's caught in it. She's all alone. I'm afraid of being all alone like that. I'm afraid of lots of things.

EDDIE: I'm afraid of lots of things too.

TOOTS: I'm afraid of earthquakes, spontaneous combustion, my own anxiety —

TOOTS: Death.	EDDIE: Death.
Life.	Life.

TOOTS: But I like it even though I'm afraid of it.

(They kiss. They fall onto the floor and get tangled up in the tablecloth. They get even more tangled up as they make out and roll all over the floor. Chita enters the apartment. She is very dishevelled in what she's wearing and how she's acting. Her blouse is buttoned the wrong way and her hair is a mess. She sees them and is shy. They are scared and embarrassed. They stay wrapped together in the tablecloth, but they manage to stand up and sit on the couch.)

TOOTS: Hi Chita.

CHITA: *(Shyly)* Hi Toots. *(Not looking at him)* Hi Eddie.

EDDIE: *(Not looking at her)* Hi Chita.

(Chita walks downstage and looks out the "window." We hear the walker coming closer to the building. Then, the walker stays put and we hear the woman with the walker yell:)

WOMAN: Chita! Chita! Chita!

CHITA: I don't hear anything. *(Covers her ears)* La la la la. It doesn't exist.

(She smiles until her smile falls off. They stare at her. She catches them staring. They look away. She looks away and looks toward the window as the lights fade.)

Scene 9

(Chita and Toots enter the apartment. They are both dressed somewhat nicely—evening-wear, not office-wear. Chita is softened, a little vulnerable. Toots is elated.)

TOOTS: So you think he did good, Chita?

CHITA: Everyone laughed.

TOOTS: Everyone laughed a lot. You did, too. I'm glad. They like my stuff. They like him.

CHITA: They do.

TOOTS: He really does a good Arnold Schwarzenegger impression, too.

CHITA: The best I've seen. And Maria Shriver.

TOOTS: Hey, I'm not doubting myself any longer.

CHITA: You're not?

TOOTS: No. That thing you told me about worrying about what people think and what they think I think, all that stuff? It helped. I'm trying not to be a victim of my own mind. I'm trying to just respect it.

CHITA: Good.

TOOTS: Do you like Eddie's friend Dash? We're trying to set you up
with him.

CHITA: He's O.K.

(Eddie and Dash enter.)

TOOTS: Hi Eddie. We were just talking about you.

(Toots kisses Eddie.)

TOOTS: *(To Chita)* Didn't you like Eddie?

CHITA: Loved him.

(She kisses him awkwardly on the cheek.)

DASH: We bought some champagne so we all could have a little
toast.

TOOTS: We have to go.

(Toots and Eddie sneak out leaving Chita and Dash alone.)

DASH: Nice watch. What time is it?

CHITA: 11:35.

DASH: 11:35?

CHITA: You have to go somewhere?

DASH: No. Unless you want me—

CHITA: No.

WOMAN WITH WALKER: Chita! Chita!

DASH: Want me to go answer it?

CHITA: NO. It's some crazy old lady trying to sell me a subscription to
Vanity Fair.

DASH: At 11:35?

CHITA: She's Crazy.

(Pause. They smile at each other, then shyly look away.)

CHITA: You're not wearing a suit.

DASH: I don't like suits.

CHITA: What do you do for a living?

DASH: I'm a carpenter.

CHITA: Oh.

DASH: What, do you wear suits all the time?

CHITA: Yes.

DASH: What, are you a lawyer or something?

CHITA: Yes.

(He laughs.)

CHITA: What's so funny?

DASH: You don't seem bitchy enough.

CHITA: *(A roar—)* I'M PLENTY BITCHY.

(A long awkward pause.)

CHITA: I'll put on some music?

(He nods. Chita leaves the room and puts on Marlene Dietrich singing "Falling in Love Again." She returns and sits with Dash.)

CHITA: I love her so much.

DASH: Yeah?

CHITA: When I was little, I used to go to Sears and Roebuck and hide inside a walnut-panelled home entertainment center/wall unit that was across the aisle from the colored TVs and I'd watch her movies.

DASH: You didn't have a T.V. at your home?

CHITA: I had a T.V.

CHITA: I didn't have a home.   DASH: You didn't have a home?

CHITA: Sort of.

DASH: Yeah. I mighta seen you there myself. I wasn't home much either. Once I was watchin' the Partridge Family—I was really into Susan Dey at the time—and my old man switched over to wrestling cause he was into Lou Albano. *(Pause)* We had some words.

CHITA: Yeah?

DASH: Yeah. He bashed me in the head with a baseball bat. I got a permanent dent in my skull. Wanna feel it? It's O.K. I don't mind.

(She reluctantly and then tenderly touches his dent.)

DASH: I forgive him though.

CHITA: You do?

DASH: It took me a while though. Growing up, I was a terror. I'd bash the headlights offa cars and kill pigeons with my bow and arrow and feed 'em to my dog. I hated everything and everybody cause my old man was a sicko and had control of the T.V. and everything and everybody. So I developed my own system of control and in it, I was the meanest and the toughest person. I could take everything so I'd go searchin' for the hardest things to take. Nobody could make me feel anything unless I let 'em. And I never let 'em cause when I felt 'em get near, I could hear that baseball bat bashing into my brain. So—I—I used to sniff glue when I was in third grade. By ninth, I was in juvenile jail for armed robbery.

CHITA: *(Smiling big)* I was too.

DASH: What ?

CHITA: Nothing.

(A moment. They slowly melt toward each other. He almost kisses her when she turns her head. Marlene's off. The Ink Spots are on now. We hear "If I Didn't Care" followed by "We Three" as —)

CHITA: Marlene's off. This music of hers is on the same tape. I don't have the energy to move from laughing so much tonight.

DASH: You have a nasty ass laugh. I had fun with you tonight.

(She's bashful, but she smiles at him anyway and he at her. He grabs the champagne bottle, but she goes to grab it to be on top of things. He pours the champagne.)

DASH: I may be a carpenter, but I'm a gentleman.

CHITA: Jesus was a carpenter and he gave all those people fish.

(They toast and drink. Dash stands up.)

DASH: Give me your hands and your hips.

CHITA: Ha?

DASH: Come here.

CHITA: Excuse me?

DASH: You wanna dance with me don't you?

CHITA: Two big adults dancing in a small room by themselves at night?

DASH: Yeah.

(She dances with him, awkwardly for a while. Finally, he dips her. She feels vulnerable as they end up this close to one another at the end of the dip. So—)

CHITA: I better go to bed. I can't think straight. I'm acting silly. I'm not in control of my mind.

DASH: Do you control your mind or does your mind control you?

CHITA: Let me sit down.

(She almost collapses in his arms as she sits.)

CHITA: You don't seem like you were ever hateful.

DASH: I gave up on it. You can't keep tryin' to control what people think about you and how they act toward you. You can't keep thinkin' that every time someone tries to get close to you, they've got a bat behind their back. Or you won't let anything good happen, you know?

(She looks at him and touches the spot on his head.)

CHITA: It'll never go away?

(He shakes his head. He kisses her on the cheek. They almost kiss when—)

CHITA: Wanna play a game?

(He nods. She smiles and runs to her room. She comes back with her handcuffs.)

CHITA: The game starts with me putting these on you and then I tell you to say things and do things and then you do them. I'll go to the other room and put my costume on.

(He laughs at her. A lot. He takes her hands. He dances with her.)

DASH: Save it. Let's ditch these things.

(Chita is scared and nervous as he throws the handcuffs behind his back.)

DASH: And you don't need to tell me what to do and what to say. The game goes *both* ways and it's not a game. It's you and me and we play it by ear.

(They kiss.)

CHITA: When I was in 7th grade, I had a baby, but I gave her up for adoption and now she wants to see me and my great–aunt who lives across the street and walks with a walker—she doesn't sell Vanity Fair—she keeps tryin' to give me my kid's address, but I—I don't want to see her cause I don't know what would happen and I can't live with that, you know? Not knowing what will happen?

(The other lights fade and we are left with a spotlight on the two.)

DASH: You can't?

CHITA: No. Pretend you didn't hear that.

DASH: No. I heard it. *(Pause)* You're O.K.

CHITA: I don't know what your intention is.

DASH: I don't either.

(They dance as the iris slowly closes on them.)

END

Our Witness

by

Martin Epstein

Our Witness was first performed at the 1990 Padua Hills Playwrights Festival with the following cast:

Annabel	Ann Marie Baldwin
Richard	Dave Higgins
Cat	Dendrie Taylor
Director	Martin Epstein
Assistant Director	Ki Gottberg
Set Design & Costumes	Naomi Shohan
Lighting Design	Jason Berliner
Stage Manager	Hillary Fox

CHARACTERS:

RICHARD (Early 40's.)
ANNABEL (Late 30's.)
CAT (Delicious.)

SCENE:

Their living room, New York City. Down right, a baby grand piano
and a music stand. Left, a liquor cart, several bottles of good stuff,
together with a cordless phone and a phone machine. In front of cart, a
chair, its back toward wall, left. A Persian or Oriental imitation carpet
covers much of the floor. Left of center, a microphone and stand.
Down left-center, a love seat. Rear wall right, a barred window, open,
with outside catwalk, a view of neighboring roof and fragmented
Manhattan buildings in distance. Up left, against back wall, a sofa. Up
right, a door to the outside. Up let, a door to the bath and bedrooms.

TIME:

Summer, late afternoon, then evening. July.

Scene 1

Their living room, late afternoon, July.

A duet for piano and violin begins in the darkness. The lights come up on the performers, who are obvious beginners. The man, in his forties, at the piano: graceful and casually dressed. The woman, mid to late thirties, on the violin: she is attractive, wears a summer dress. They play several measures. (The piece is "La Cinquantaine" by Gabriel Marie.) He stops. She stops.

WOMAN: Why have we stopped?

MAN: Do you hear what we sound like?

WOMAN: I told you when we began I was tone deaf.

MAN: Um.

WOMAN: Shall we take it from the top?

MAN: Let's rest a bit.

(She lowers violin, holds it by its neck.)

WOMAN: My teacher thinks I'm making remarkable progress.

MAN: Does she?

WOMAN: She says it's no easy thing to start an instrument as difficult as the violin at the age of thirty-five.

MAN: The piano isn't exactly a kazoo, Annabel.

WOMAN: I never said it was. But you've been playing it since the age of seven, Richard, and musically speaking, you're not that much better than me.

MAN: I took lessons at the age of seven. I stopped when I was twelve.

WOMAN: That still gives you a five year start.

MAN: Those five years didn't count.

ANNABEL: Why not?

RICHARD: Because I was just pretending.

ANNABEL: What?

RICHARD: Pretending, Annabel. My parents wanted me to play, so I went through all the motions. But the whole while I sat there, crucified to the keyboard, my real self was far far away.

(*Pause.*)

ANNABEL: Richard?

RICHARD: Hm?

ANNABEL: Why are we playing this stupid duet?

RICHARD: Why?

ANNABEL: My teacher told me I wasn't ready for duets, but you insisted. Okay. So I sacrifice her wisdom and my own pride, and I accompany you in what turns out to be a sado-masochistic re-enactment of some childhood trauma, and I would like, yes, to know why.

(*Pause.*)

RICHARD: Well, Annabel . . .

ANNABEL: Well, Richard . . .

RICHARD: I suppose I grieve for the loss of passion between us. (*A beat.*) And since there's so little else we seem to share these days, I had hoped by playing duets, beginners though we are, we might recover some of the rapture we experienced in the early days of our relationship.

ANNABEL: (*A beat.*) Richard, when you speak to me like that, directly, and from your heart, there is nothing I wouldn't do for you. Absolutely nothing.

(*They regard each other.*)

RICHARD: Shall we take it from the top?

(She nods.)

RICHARD: One and two and . . .

(They play. Much the same as before, only harder, more frenetic: A musical abyss. He stops. She continues a moment, stops.)

ANNABEL: Why have we stopped?

RICHARD: Because we're finished.

ANNABEL: With the rapture or with the relationship?

RICHARD: With the rapture, Annabel. The relationship, as we both well know, has been over for ages.

ANNABEL: *(A beat.)* What am I supposed to do with a remark like that?

RICHARD: A woman with any imagination would pack her bags and go.

ANNABEL: *(A beat.)* Richard?

RICHARD: Hm?

ANNABEL: Are you actually saying these horrible things, or am I only imagining you're saying them?

RICHARD: What difference does it make?

ANNABEL: *(A beat.)* Richard?

RICHARD: What?

ANNABEL: If, as you say, or I imagine, our relationship has been over for ages, why are we still living under the same roof?

RICHARD: Because we're both too smart to think it could be significantly different with anyone else.

ANNABEL: I'm sorry, but I don't think that's reason enough to stay together.

RICHARD: Fine. Let's end it, then.

ANNABEL: End it? Just like that?

RICHARD: If you want papers, Annabel, we can always spend ten thousand dollars and get a divorce.

ANNABEL: *(A beat.)* Richard, we can't possibly divorce.

RICHARD: Why not?

ANNABEL: Because to the best of my recollection, we're not married.

RICHARD: *(Looks at her.)* Oh, come on.

ANNABEL: Never had a service that I can remember.

RICHARD: We've been together more than seven years . . .

ANNABEL: Never summoned our friends or family together, or a single witness for that matter . . .

RICHARD: Common-law something: if we share the same bed and/or domicile for seven years or more . . .

ANNABEL: We were never ever married, Richard!

RICHARD: *(Kindly.)* Well, it's too late now, don't you think?

ANNABEL: Yes, that's exactly what I think! *(Puts violin in case and closes it.)* But I should like to know why?

RICHARD: Why what?

ANNABEL: Why, even in the throes of our early rapture, you never so much as suggested the possibility?

RICHARD: I almost asked you once.

ANNABEL: Oh?

RICHARD: Five years ago. You probably wouldn't remember. We were driving on the San Diego freeway and we heard the clanking of cans behind us. This "Just Married" couple passed us in the next lane. . .

ANNABEL: . . .a sixty-five white Volvo covered with pink carnations, go on. . .

RICHARD: Everyone around us began honking.

ANNABEL: You louder than all the rest, continue . . .

RICHARD: There was this Mexican guy in a red Chevy on my left. We waved and smiled to each other. And I thought: Hey, this guy would probably beat the shit out of me if I walked into his neighborhood bar, but because of this anonymous "bride and groom", we're suddenly friends.

ANNABEL: Yes, you both stepped on the gas and we became their personal escort as far as Sepulveda Blvd.

RICHARD: That's when I wanted to ask you.

ANNABEL: But you never said a word.

RICHARD: No.

ANNABEL: Why not?

RICHARD: I don't know. I just didn't.

(She doesn't take her gaze off him.)

RICHARD: Okay, I'll tell you. When I tried to imagine the two of us, standing at some altar, with our friends and family looking on, I felt . . .

ANNABEL: What?

RICHARD: . . . ashamed.

ANNABEL: Ashamed of who, Richard?

RICHARD: Of myself.

(Silence.)

RICHARD: It's not an easy thing to talk about.

ANNABEL: Try.

RICHARD: I felt they would all look at me and know . . .

ANNABEL: What?

RICHARD: That it wasn't the real me standing there.

ANNABEL: Excuse me, Richard, but this "real you" you keep talking about, just where does this personage hang out?

RICHARD: To be honest, Annabel, it's been so long since I've had any direct contact with him, I'm not even sure he exists.

ANNABEL: Richard . . .

RICHARD: Hm?

ANNABEL: Why didn't you tell me any of this when me met?

RICHARD: Wouldn't it have killed the rapture?

ANNABEL: The rapture died anyway, you putz.

(Silence. She looks around.)

ANNABEL: What's this microphone doing here?

RICHARD: I have no idea.

(She takes microphone from stand, turns it on, blows.)

ANNABEL: *(Miked.)* Testing. One two. Testing. . . Okay, Richard, I am ready to admit this disgusting conversation could only be taking place inside my own head. . .

RICHARD: You don't have to let me off the hook so easily, you know.

ANNABEL: *(Miked.)* Who's letting you off the hook? I just want to change the subject, okay?

RICHARD: Please.

ANNABEL: *(Miked.)* So how's your work going?

RICHARD: My work?

ANNABEL: *(Miked.)* They all love you on the job, don't they?

RICHARD: I'm good at what I do and people tend to respect that, yes.

ANNABEL: *(Miked.)* A few of the women you hang out with would just love to fuck you, wouldn't they?

RICHARD: A few of the men, too, Annabel.

ANNABEL: *(Miked.)* I get my share of propositions.

RICHARD: I should hope so.

(Silence.)

ANNABEL: *(Miked.)* So tell me, Richard . . .?

RICHARD: Tell you what, Annabel?

ANNABEL: *(Miked.)* Why are you feeding that cat?

RICHARD: Why am I feeding what cat?

ANNABEL: *(Miked.)* You know very well what cat. *(Crossing to the piano, she leans against it.)* That filthy flea-infested piece of orphaned shit that's been hanging around our window, and who we both agreed we would not feed or let into the apartment for any reason, you remember making such an agreement with me, Richard?

RICHARD: Yes.

ANNABEL: *(Miked.)* Then why have you broken it?

RICHARD: I haven't broken our agreement, An . . .

ANNABEL: *(Miked.)* I do the shopping, Richard. I know how many cans of gourmet tuna I buy for myself, and how many I eat. This week I bought three, I ate one, where did the other two go?

RICHARD: Annabel, I have not been feeding that cat.

ANNABEL: *(Miked.)* Liar.

RICHARD: Annabel, I have not been feeding that cat.

ANNABEL: *(Miked.)* Liar!

RICHARD: Annabel. . .

ANNABEL: *(Miked.)* Liar! Liar! Liar!

RICHARD: Alright, for the sake of argument, let's say I took pity on this piece of orphaned shit and I fed the son of a bitch, so what?

ANNABEL: *(Miked.)* So what?

RICHARD: Yes. So what?

ANNABEL: Since you have such a short memory, it's useless for me to tell you "so what". *(She turns to the house, addressing the audience, miked.)* I met him a little over seven years ago. I had just broken from a long, hopelessly impossible relationship, and I was seriously thinking about living alone for the rest of my life.

RICHARD: Annabel..?

ANNABEL: *(Miked.)* I was going to work hard, save my money, and buy a little cottage on the Cape, where I could finish off my days with the three things I loved most in the world: the ocean, my garden and my cats. My two cats.

RICHARD: Annab . . .

ANNABEL: *(Miked.)* Shhh! Don't interrupt! Listen! Listen to what you should know!

RICHARD: *(To audience.)* I'd like to know who it is she thinks she's talking to?

ANNABEL: *(Miked.)* She's talking to all those she knows and loves who are not going to be at her wedding, Richard! Now shut up and listen! *(A beat.)* Where was I?

RICHARD: Your two cats. . .

ANNABEL: Right. *(Miked.)* She had it all figured out. Never again was she going to sacrifice her privacy for the little erotic intimacies that come with sharing her bathroom with an absolute stranger. But she had not, as yet, met him. *(She turns toward Richard. He plays a soft chord.)* They were fixed up by a mutual friend . . .

RICHARD: Lonnie Melrose, god bless 'm.

ANNABEL: *(Miked.)* But after talking with him for ten minutes, she couldn't have been less interested.

RICHARD: Oh, come on, Annabel . . .

ANNABEL: *(Miked.)* In a good anonymous lay, perhaps . . .

RICHARD: Which she got.

ANNABEL: *(Miked.)* Which she never got! Though he did come on like one of the greatest singles ads of all time, flooding her with the history of a "pretend self" she swallowed hook, line and sinker!

RICHARD: *(To audience, stoic.)* She never for a moment suspected how tired I was of telling my story.

ANNABEL: *(Miked.)* Ladies, beware. Beware the man who reveals and reveals. Beware the man who lays siege to your solitude!

RICHARD: *(To audience.)* I wasn't even going to call her for a second date!

ANNABEL: *(Miked.)* The man who phones all hours of the day and night, leaving cryptically obscene messages on your machine . . .

RICHARD: *(To audience, a wordless gesture.)*

ANNABEL: *(Miked.)* The man who hand delivers two and three letters a week full of quotes from Henry James and Emily Dickenson . . .

RICHARD: *(To audience, a wordless gesture.)*

ANNABEL: *(Miked.)* But most of all, beware the man who parks his fucking car in your garage after the fourth date and takes off to New York for two weeks.

RICHARD: *(To audience.)* She offered me her garage!

ANNABEL: *(Miked.)* Liar!

RICHARD: *(To audience, in his defense.)* Every night, the last thing he'd hear before he fell asleep, "Richard, I love you." *(Plays piano chord.)* Every morning, first thing he'd hear, *(Piano chord as he speaks.)* "Richard, I love you . . ."

ANNABEL: I couldn't think of anything else to say.

RICHARD: Get on with it, on with it.

ANNABEL: *(Miked.)* For almost a year, packing their toothbrushes, they chase each other back and forth across the Bay Bridge. *(He imitates chase on keys.)* Until he decides it's time for her to meet his mother. *(Chord spasm.)* Only his mother doesn't want to meet another of his women, so she has a stroke and dies while they're somewhere over the great Kansas night. (*He starts to pick out funeral march.*) So that when they land, they do not, as planned, go to the Russian Tea Room, but begin the two week ordeal of burying her and cleaning out her apartment. (*She slams keyboard cover down, he pulls his hands away.*)

RICHARD: It wasn't my fault my mother died, Annabel.

ANNABEL: (*Miked.*) I know. It was mine. Wanna describe what happened on the way back to California?

RICHARD: I asked her to move in with me.

ANNABEL: Oh come on, you can do better than that.

RICHARD: I'm not gonna cry in public, Annabel.

ANNABEL: Just make the gesture, Richard.

(*Richard makes a little house with his fingers.*)

ANNABEL: Now say the words.

RICHARD: (*Holding the house.*) Annabel, would you like to move in together?

ANNABEL: And she's so moved she says "Oh my . . ."

RICHARD: (*Still holding the finger house.*) "Oh my . . ."

ANNABEL: (*Miked.*) And so they move into a beautiful seven room flat with a panoramic view of the city, only they're not in that house a full half hour, when he starts huffing and puffing and gasping for air . . .

RICHARD: (*To audience.*) His old asthma condition. He thought it was benign.

ANNABEL: (*Miked.*) So she takes him to SF Emergency, where they inject him with steroids, and bring him, thank god, back to life, but the good doctor of respiratory ailments tells her she must choose between him and her cats.

RICHARD: I felt very bad about that, Annabel.

ANNABEL: (*Miked.*) Max and Isabel, my two beautiful cats, whom I have raised from kittenhood and who, over the years, have given me more consistent rapture than any man I've ever known. And I must choose between these two furry creatures and a presumptuous stranger who has admittedly spent the greater part of his pretend existence sitting on a piano bench, and I don't hesitate for a moment.

RICHARD: She really doesn't.

ANNABEL: (*Miked.*) Because if I did, I would have chosen the cats!

RICHARD: (*To audience.*) You see how she puts me in an impossibly beholden position?

ANNABEL: (*Miked.*) Nor am I going to mention what not having a garden does to me, or having to leave the natural beauty of Northern California to follow him to New York, so he could continue to pursue his idiotic professional obligations!

RICHARD: (*To audience.*) Returning to New York was very important for both of us.

ANNABEL: (*Miked.*) Yes. This is where the energy is.

RICHARD: It's true. The energy is here . . .

ANNABEL: (*Miked.*) Here, in this mecca of filth and insecurity, this Big Apple of provincial fatuousness!

RICHARD: That too.

ANNABEL: (*Miked.*) This Cockroach heaven, this cesspool of hype and sublimated incest fantasies . . .

RICHARD: Sublimated what?

ANNABEL: (*Miked.*) This thoroughly unsensual asexual rent inflated work-a-holic pit of yuppified slime; this masturbatory maze of well dressed rats whose favorite color is black . . .!

RICHARD: Don't you think you're over doing it a bit?

ANNABEL: (*Miked.*) No . . . I'm not going to linger on how out of place, how morally destroyed, how offended I am by everyone and everything I see around me. Not to mention the absolute spitefulness of the weather. I'm only talking now about my two cats, Max and Isabel, and how I gave them up to live with him! (*Turns, regards him.*) And how I would hope, and expect, that he would at least have the decency not to feed the first stray flea infested piece of orphaned shit who comes begging at our window, particularly with my white albacore tuna, which he does not even bother to replace!

RICHARD: (*To audience.*) Once again, I have not now or ever fed that cat!

ANNABEL: BULLSHIT!

RICHARD: I have been eating it myself, okay!

ANNABEL: Oh, have you?

RICHARD: For my lunch, yes!

ANNABEL: Why didn't you come right out and say so?

RICHARD: I felt silly.

ANNABEL: (*Miked.*) Richard?

RICHARD: What?

ANNABEL: (*Miked, low.*) Fuck you.

(*She puts the microphone back in the holder. She exits, left.*)

RICHARD: (*Alone.*) All this fuss over a stupid cat.

(*He opens the keyboard, begins to play his part of the duet. Annabel re-enters, belting her trench coat.*)

RICHARD: Going somewhere?

ANNABEL: I'm leaving you, Richard.

RICHARD: What about your things?

ANNABEL: I'll be back for them.

RICHARD: You're not going very far, then?

ANNABEL: Just far enough to give you the time you'll need to make contact with your real self.

RICHARD: (*Stops playing.*) I beg your pardon?

ANNABEL: Before I leave you forever, Richard, you are going to do us both the satisfaction of making contact with your real self!

RICHARD: Oh Annabel . . .

ANNABEL: Because when I come back through that door, I expect to find that self and no other waiting in this room with a sincere and genuine proposal!

RICHARD: Oh Annabel . . .

ANNABEL: Not that I will ever accept it! I just want you—and us both—before we never have to see each other again, to have had the privilege of hearing what it sounds like.

RICHARD: How do I know you'll refuse?

ANNABEL: You don't. But even if I say yes, I promise I will do everything in my power to crush whatever dreams of rapture may still be thrashing around inside either of us.

RICHARD: You're not giving me much of a choice, Annabel.

ANNABEL: I'm not giving you any choice, Richard.

RICHARD: And if I refuse?

ANNABEL: (*A beat.*) I wouldn't do that if I were you.

RICHARD: I'm not afraid of you, Annabel.

ANNABEL: Oh yes you are. (*Looks at her watch.*) You've got twelve to fifteen minutes to complete this task. (*She picks up the violin.*) Do you understand what it is you have to do?

RICHARD: Yes, I think so.

ANNABEL: Please repeat it to me.

RICHARD: Sometime in the next twelve to fifteen minutes, I'm to make contact with my real self, and come up with a proposal for our raptureless future together, which you may or may not accept.

ANNABEL: That's it. Good luck.

RICHARD: Thanks. Why are you taking the violin?

ANNABEL: (*She regards him, opens door, her hand on the knob.*) Listen: I'd like to give you some advice that will keep you from trivializing this whole experience.

RICHARD: Please.

ANNABEL: As soon as I'm gone, don't start drinking.

RICHARD; Okay.

ANNABEL: And don't call your ex-wife for sympathy or comic relief.

RICHARD: Okay.

ANNABEL: And don't call one of your old girlfriends and propose.

RICHARD: (*A half smile.*) Okay.

ANNABEL: And stop picking your cuticles, it's driving me crazy!

(*He puts his hands in his jacket pockets.*)

RICHARD: Is that it?

ANNABEL: Yes.

(*She exits, slamming the door behind her. A beat. The door opens.*)

ANNABEL: (*Off.*) And don't feed that cat!

(*She slams the door. A long pause.*)

RICHARD: Twelve to fifteen minutes to make contact with my real self. (*Sighs. Looks over at liquor cart.*) Hey, Real Self, what do you say to six or seven fingers of some very fine Scotch? (*Voice of real self.*) "Don't mind if I do." (*He rises.*) Incredible sensation: I'm actually on my feet. (*He crosses to liquor cart, pours himself a huge drink, swabs the juice around in the glass.*) This is too easy. Besides, I can feel her watching me through the walls. (*Sets drink down. He turns, moves toward microphone, takes microphone from holder, switches it on, blows: speaks.*) Annabel, I want to be worthy of a struggle, here, but the truth is—as soon did you left the room, my Real Self materialized. Now, regarding that proposal for our raptureless future together, the answer is no. No. (*He puts the microphone back into holder. Leans in.*) I'm sorry. (*Switches it off. He checks his watch. Slips his hands back into his jacket pockets. To audience.*) Well, now that the task is accomplished, and I still have twelve or so minutes to kill, I think I'll feed that cat.

(*He withdraws a can of tuna, together with a large red handled can opener.*)

RICHARD: (*Opening the can.*) I lied when I told her I wasn't feeding it. A long while back I learned in any argument with a woman, there's no right or wrong, there's only accusation and denial. (*He sets the can of tuna through the bars on the catwalk and taps bars with opener.*) Here, kitty kitty— Here, Puss puss puss. . . (*An afterthought.*) And no matter how stupid or false your own case may be, you've got to deny and deny until she's completely overwhelmed by her own outrage, loathing and disgust. That's when she usually gives up. (*Taps bars.*) Hey, puss puss puss . . .

(*Enter Cat, from right. It is huge, for a cat: a completely costumed thing, furry and feline, with a long tail.*)

RICHARD: (*Dropping can opener.*) Jesus Christ . . .

(*Cat pushes the tuna can with her paw, picks it up, turns it over, shakes tuna free, tosses can back into the house. She dabs her paw in tuna, lifts it to her mouth. Richard, backing slowly away from the window, turns, half addressing audience.*)

RICHARD: This is not the cat I've been feeding for the last three weeks. The cat I've been feeding was . . . (*He shows its size.*) This is obviously some other cat.

(*Cat rubs the bars with her body, croons: meoow.*)

RICHARD: This is some altogether "different" cat.

(*Turning, Cat rubs the bars with the other side of her body, croons: meeoow.*)

RICHARD: (*Looks at his watch.*) She'll be back any moment.

(*Cat sits, one paw through bars. She rubs her head against them, croons:*

meeooow.)

RICHARD: If I don't want trouble, I should get rid of this cat immediately.

(*Cat rubs head, gets grip on bars with all its paws, lifting itself onto the bars. croons: meeow.*)

RICHARD: Speak to me, Real Self! What should I do? (*Richard takes mike.*) "Richard, if you don't let this wonderful creature into the house immediately, I will never speak to you again!" (*Off mike.*) What if Annabel walks in? (*Miked.*) Deny. (*Off.*) Deny? (*Miked.*) Tell her it's all in her head, what she sees is impossible, and if she can't live with it, she should have herself committed. (*Off.*) What about my allergies? (*Miked.*) What about them? (*Off.*) If I can't last more than a thirty minutes with a little cat, or two little cats, what do you think a cat this size will do to me? (*Miked.*) That's just what we're going to find out, Richard, how long you can last with a really big cat. What's the alarm code? (*Off.*) Hey, wait. . . (*Miked.*) Relax, Richard. Your Real Self knows exactly what has to be done.

(*He punches in the code. A little tune. He pulls the gate back, locking it into a snap on the wall. Cat clinging to bars, lets herself drop onto sofa.*)

RICHARD: (*Miked.*) Well done, Puss.

(*Cat watches him, then explores the sofa. He moves toward her, mike in hand. Cat backs away, left. He stops. Cat stops. He sits on sofa, right. Cat sits, left. They look at each other.*)

RICHARD: (*Checks his watch.*) If the woman I live with walks in, I'm going to deny you. Otherwise, I don't see why we can't be friends. Provided I don't have a fatal reaction . . . (*He moves toward the Cat. It leaps off sofa, explores the room.*) I guess I'll have to earn your trust. (*Checks watch.*) You move well, Cat. It's a kick just to sit here and watch you . . . But there's a limit to the voyeur in each of us . . .

(*He slides to the floor on his knees, moves on all fours toward the Cat. Cat moves. He moves. Cat moves, meows. He moves, meows. Cat moves, he remains motionless, meows. Cat becomes interested, approaches him. He meows. Cat comes close, sniffs. He sniffs. They nuzzle. Cat raises paw to his head. He brings his hand to Cat's head.*)

RICHARD: We've both got great hair.

(*They spar. He pushes Cat over on its side, collapsing beside it, laughing. Cat purrs.*)

RICHARD: Tell you a secret, Puss. If I were Annabel, I'd have never given a creature like you up for a creature like me. (*He strokes it.*) And you're not gonna make me sick, are you, Puss? Nohoho. . . Nohoho. . .

CAT: (*Licks his face.*) Meow. . .

RICHARD: (*Laughs.*) Oh come on. . .

CAT: (*One paw over him, licks several times.*) Meow. . .

RICHARD: (*Laughing.*) Okay . . .Okay . . .Okay, Cat, enough . . . Enough, hey . . . Listen, fur-ball, this is fun, but we need to talk . . . (*Cat croons.*) I need to talk . . .

CAT: Meow . . .

RICHARD: (*Grabbing Cat's fur.*) Shhh. Be still now. Listen. This is the real me talking to you, Cat. The real Richard is talking. (*Cat listening.*) Puss, I am in a raptureless relationship with a woman who thinks she is imagining all this . . . But I know for a fact she is much too—pragmatic—to ever come up with a creature like you . . .

CAT: Meow . . .

RICHARD: Which leads me to suspect that I'm the one imagining her.

CAT: Meow . . .

RICHARD: But if I'm the one imagining her, why do I permit her to go on thinking she's the one imagining me? (*A beat.*) And why have I installed her in here (*Indicates his head.*) like a personal guard who judges every single move I make?

CAT: Meow. . .

RICHARD: O Cat, I don't feel good about myself when she's around.

CAT: Meow . . .

RICHARD: Cat, I'm lonely, I'm sad, I'm loveless, I feel like my real life is having an affair with someone else behind my back!

CAT: Meow . . .

RICHARD: And on top of it all, she wants a sincere and genuine proposal!

CAT: Meow . . .

RICHARD: Goddamn couples! The curse of Couples! The horrible horror of couples! (*He shudders.*) Cat, you don't know how lucky you are to get it in the alley twice a year and then have done!

CAT: Meow . . .

RICHARD: (*Intimate, a generous grip of fur.*) O Cat, if only you knew how long it's been since I've had a quality type fantasy about another woman!

CAT: Meow. . .

RICHARD: And even when she looked at me and said she would do anything, absolutely anything, why couldn't I tell her what it was I really wanted!

CAT: Meow . . . (*Sounds like "why."*)

RICHARD: Because I couldn't imagine what I wanted in her presence, Cat!

CAT: Meow . . . (*Sounds like "why."*)

RICHARD: Because I was afraid.

CAT: Meow . . . (*Sounds like "why."*)

RICHARD: BECAUSE I WAS AFRAID! (*Cat, a bit startled, tries to ove away. He holds onto it.*) Shhh, it's okay, Kitty, I'm sorry, I didn't mean to shout like that, Shhhh, it's Annabel I was afraid of, not you, not you, nohoho, Shhh, there's a good cat, a pleasure cat, a cuddle cat, I'm not afraid of you, shhhh, shhhh . . . (*He leans over, whispers.*) Listen, Cat: another secret, just between us, Puss . . . The rapture is still alive . . .

CAT: Meow . . .

RICHARD: *(Miked.)* The rapture is alive.

CAT: Meow . . .

RICHARD: *(Miked.)* The rapture is alive, and it owes its life to you, Cat. . .

CAT: Meow . . .

RICHARD: *(Miked.)* To you, Puss, to you, yes, to you . . . *(Cat purrs. He holds microphone and picks up purr.)* O Cat, I'd marry you in a second! But you don't give a shit about any of that stuff, do you? *(He draws the microphone down Cat's stomach. Purring louder.)* No, of course not. Rapture doesn't need to marry, rapture doesn't need a witness. *(Richard and Cat are spread out together, they share the mike.).*

CAT: *(Miked.)* Meow . . .

RICHARD: *(Miked.)* Rapture goes where it wants to go . . .

CAT: *(Miked.)* Meow . . .

RICHARD: *(Miked.)* Rapture does want it wants to do . . .

CAT: *(Miked.)* Meow . . .

RICHARD: *(Miked.)* Rapture is lively, *generous* . . .

CAT: *(Miked.)* Meooow . . .

RICHARD: *(Miked.)* Rapture wants to play, Puss . . .

CAT: *(Miked.)* Meooooow . . .

RICHARD: *(Miked.)* Meoooooow . . .

CAT: *(Miked.)* Meooooooow . . .

RICHARD: *(Miked.)* Meooooooow . . .

CAT: *(Miked.)* Meoooooooooooow . . .

BOTH: *(Miked.)* MEOOOOOOOOOOOOOOOOOOOOOOOOOOW . . .

(*Outside buzzer, loud. Richard and Cat freeze.*)

ANNABEL: (*Off, miked.*) Richard . . . ?

RICHARD: (*Miked.*) She's back.

ANNABEL: (*Off, miked.*) I forgot my keys. Would you buzz me in, please?

RICHARD: (*To Cat.*) She wants me to buzz her in.

CAT: Meow . . .

RICHARD: I'm sorry, Puss, you'll have to go.

CAT: (*Preoccupied with microphone cord.*) Meooow . . .

RICHARD: Listen, Cat, weekdays she leaves at eight, doesn't get back till six, I'll rap on the bars, we can have the whole day . . .

CAT: (*Miked.*) MEOOOOOOOOOO!

(*Buzzer.*)

RICHARD: Cat, it's been fun, but you really have to go!

ANNABEL: (*Off, miked.*) Richard . . ?!

RICHARD: Hold your horses, I'm on the toilet, for Chrissake! (*Cat has wound the cord around her neck as she continues to purr into it. Richard tries to unwind it.*) Come on now, Puss, enough!

(*Cat thinks he is playing and takes up the game, twisting itself even more.*)

RICHARD: Jesus, Cat! Untangle yourself, come on, untangle!

(*Cat purrs loudly into microphone. Richard tries to untangle it.*)

ANNABEL: (*Buzzing hard.*) Richard!

(*Richard seizes the Cat by a paw and drags it to the window.*)

RICHARD: Okay, asshole, let's go!

(*Cat twists and rakes his forearm with its free paw.*)

RICHARD: (*Releases Cat.*) Son of a bitch!

(Cat springs back to microphone, falls over playfully, picks it up and croons: meooow. Cat looks back at Richard, who is holding his arm.)

(Buzzer.)

ANNABEL: *(Off, Miked.)* Richard, if I have to ring one more time, I'm calling the police!

RICHARD: *(Frantic.)* She's going to call the police!

CAT: *(Miked.)* Meoooooooooooow!

(Richard grab the Cat by the scruff of its neck, lifting and dragging it to the window.)

CAT: *(Shrieks.)* MEOOOOOOOOOOW!

RICHARD: I SAID I WANT YOU OUT OF HERE!

(Cat whirls around, sinking its teeth into the side of Richard's face. He screams, wrestles with Cat. They both go down, roll, Richard screaming, the Cat shrieking. He disengages himself, grabs the twisted end of the chord and the microphone and pulls.)

RICHARD: I SAID I WANT YOU OUT OF HERE! OUT! OUT! OUT!

(Cat jerking wildly. Cat hangs limp. Buzzer.)

ANNABEL: *(Off, Miked.)* Richard. . .

RICHARD: *(Punctuating the air with his finger.)* Buzz! Buzz! Buzz! *(To audience, holding Cat.)* It'll take her exactly eighty-seven seconds to come through that door. I've timed it. *(To Cat, angry, pulls on microphone.)* Why did you bite me? Why? Why? *(Cat limp.)* Cat . . .? *(He releases it, it slumps to the floor.)* Oh Jesus, Jesus—*(He unwinds microphone, puts it back in holder, grabs Cat under its armpits, lifts, looks out at house.)* Not me, I didn't do this. The real me did not do this. *(Dragging Cat to the bathroom door.)* This is the act of the pretend me, the real me doesn't strangle cats! Where are you going, idiot, first place she'll go is the bathroom, it's her only privacy!

ANNABEL: *(Off, knocks on door, weary.)* Richard . . .

RICHARD: One moment, Annabel, I'll be right with you. *(To himself.)* Gotta move, Pronto! *(He drags the Cat downstage, lifts and seats it on the*

piano bench, letting it support itself against the front of the keyboard. To
Cat.) Don't move! (To audience.) If she says anything, I'll just deny.

(Knocking on door.)

RICHARD: Hey, Annabel?

ANNABEL: (In tears, off.) I forgot my keys . . . !

RICHARD: Sweetheart, I'm opening the door, but I want you to count
to ten before you come in, and I don't want you to ask me why,
okay? (Silence.) Annabel?

ANNABEL: (Off.) Two . . . three . . . four . . .

RICHARD: (Backing toward bathroom door.) Slower, Annabel.

ANNABEL: (Slower.) Five . . . six . . . seven . . .

RICHARD: Slower . . . slower . . .

(He exits, slamming and locking the door behind him.)

ANNABEL: Eight . . . nine . . . ten . . .

(Annabel enters. She is carrying the violin. Sound of running water in
bathroom. She takes in the room, focusing on the tuna can. She picks it up,
puts it on the piano. Sees the can opener. Picks it up, puts it next to the can.
She looks at the Cat. She turns, crosses to the liquor art, discovers Richard's
old drink, lifts it, drinks.)

RICHARD: (Off.) Everything okay out there?

ANNABEL: Everything's just fine! (Sits, holding the glass in one hand
and the violin across her lap.)

(Richard enters. In trying to wash the blood off, he has smeared it all over his
hands, face, neck and shirt.)

RICHARD: You have a good walk?

ANNABEL: It was alright. (Looks at him.) You're covered with blood.

RICHARD: I cut myself shaving. What are you drinking?

ANNABEL: (Looks at glass.) Scotch.

RICHARD: Mind if I join you?

ANNABEL: It's a free country.

RICHARD: (*Pours himself a glass.*) Believe it or not, Annabel, this is the first distraction I've allowed myself since your departure. Cheers.

(*She lifts her glass, doesn't drink.*)

RICHARD: I guess you'd like to know if I made contact?

ANNABEL: Who with?

RICHARD: My real self.

ANNABEL: Oh yeah. How'd it go?

RICHARD: It went well, Annabel. It went very well.

ANNABEL: Glad to hear it.

RICHARD: I couldn't have done it without your help.

ANNABEL: Sure you could.

RICHARD: No. If you hadn't urged me to it, as well as left the house . . . Anyway, I made contact, and my real self and I had a good heart to heart . . .

ANNABEL: I can't marry you, Richard.

RICHARD: What?

ANNABEL: I said I can't marry you. I'm sorry. Thanks anyway for asking.

RICHARD: Well . . . Why can't you marry me, Annabel?

ANNABEL: Because I'm insane.

RICHARD: (*A beat.*) You're certainly acting more depressed than usual . . .

ANNABEL: Don't try to lighten my load, Richard. I said, "I'm insane!"

RICHARD: What makes you think you're insane, Annabel?

ANNABEL: You don't see the giant cat sitting at the Steinway, do you?

RICHARD: (*Looking.*) The giant cat..?

ANNABEL: Sitting at the Steinway . . .

RICHARD: (*Looking.*) Sitting at the Steinway?

ANNABEL: You don't see it, do you?

RICHARD: (*Looking.*) No.

(*Cat falls over, its body slamming the keys. Annabel spasms.*)

ANNABEL: Didn't hear that, either, I suppose?

RICHARD: Hear what, Annabel?

ANNABEL: (*Teary.*) Well, you know, I'm really glad, Richard.

RICHARD: Annabel . . .

ANNABEL: I'm glad you don't see or hear what I do, because if you did, they'd have to put us both away, and they don't have asylums for couples, do they?

RICHARD: I don't think so, no . . .

ANNABEL: (*Crying, she takes his hand.*) Oh Richard, I really do love you, you know. You're such a sweetheart, and I've always thought of you as my ideal mate . . .

RICHARD: (*His other hand on her head.*) Annabel . . .

ANNABEL: If I withold myself sometimes in your presence, it's because I'm afraid of being overwhelmed by the power my feelings . . .

RICHARD: (*Moved.*) Annabel . . .

ANNABEL: (*Sobbing.*) The moment I'm away from you, I really miss you, Richard . . .

RICHARD: Annabel . . .

ANNABEL: And I'm sorry I've put you through so much over the years, I'm so sorry . . .

RICHARD: Annabel . . .

ANNABEL: (*Kissing his hand, holding it to her cheek.*) Richard, I can't bear the thought of living apart from you . . .

RICHARD: Annabel, listen, maybe we can work something out.

ANNABEL: No, no. Even if I didn't see that monster cat sitting at the Steinway, I still couldn't live with you anymore.

RICHARD: Why not?

ANNABEL: (*Sobbing.*) Oh Richard . . .

RICHARD: (*Alarmed.*) What is it, Annabel, what's going on?

ANNABEL: There's this other man . . .

RICHARD: What other man?

ANNABEL: This man . . .

RICHARD: Annabel, are you having an affair?

ANNABEL: (*Shakes head.*) In the street just now, this black man . . . He may have been white, but he was so covered with filth, I couldn't tell what he was. Oh Richard, his hair was all matted and sticky, and he had no shirt or shoes. All he had on was a Hefty bag.

RICHARD: (*Genuine.*) No styrofoam cup?

ANNABEL: He was finished begging. He passed me like a zombie . . .

RICHARD: I don't understand, Annabel. What's this man got to do with our living together?

ANNABEL: Seeing him reminded me of the other one.

RICHARD: What other one?

ANNABEL: In my dream, last night, this other man came up to me in the street and poured gasoline all over my hair!

RICHARD: (*Relieved.*) Oh, in your dream . . .

ANNABEL: Yes. In my dream. This complete stranger come up to me on the street and poured gasoline all over my head. Then he began fumbling in his pocket for matches . . .

RICHARD: (*Trying to lighten it.*) So where the hell was I?

ANNABEL: You were right there, Richard. You were less than five feet away, and you just stood there, watching. Even when he got the matches out and struck one, you didn't lift a finger . . .

RICHARD: (*Defensive.*) It was your dream, Annabel.

ANNABEL: (*Losing it.*) My dream, your dream, who gives a shit whose dream it is: Richard, I'm about to spontaneously combust, and I can't even count on you to piss on the flames!

RICHARD: (*Useless.*) Annabel . . .

ANNABEL: WHERE ARE THE REAL MEN, GOD?

RICHARD: Annabel . . .

ANNABEL: (*Over the edge.*) Call the A Team! Call the B Team! Call the C Team! Call the D Team!

RICHARD: (*Grabs and shakes her shoulders.*) Annabel . . . !

ANNABEL: That's my name. Why are you shaking me like that You're making me nauseous . . . !

RICHARD: Annabel you're not insane I do see that cat!

ANNABEL: Oh Richard . . .

RICHARD: I see her as clearly as I see you . . .

ANNABEL: Richard, please, you do not have to sacrifice your own sanity!

RICHARD: It's no sacrifice! Look! Look! (*He grabs the Cat's head and pulls it into an upright position.*) Look, Annabel! (*She looks.*) Now listen! Listen! (*Standing a little to the side, he takes the Cat's two paws and begins pounding the keys: bang bang bang.*) You hear that,

Annabel? (*Bang bang bang.*) It's music, Annabel! Music! (*Bang bang bang.*) Commere, Annabel! COMMERE! (She approaches.) Touch it, Annabel! GO ON, TOUCH IT!

ANNABEL: (*Touching its head, shudders.*) Ugh, it has texture!

RICHARD: It's dead texture, Annabel! Dead! (*Bang.*) Dead! (*Bang.*)

ANNABEL: (*In a daze.*) How'd it die?

RICHARD: I strangled it! (*Bang.*) I didn't mean to strangle it, but it wouldn't leave when I wanted it to. It wouldn't leave and it clawed my hand and bit my face so I strangled it! (*Bang.*) I strangled it! (*Bang.*) I strangled it! (*Bang bang bang.*)

ANNABEL: (*Her hands to her ears.*) Richard!

RICHARD: (*Bang bang bang.*) What?

ANNABEL: STOP IT!

RICHARD: (*Still.*) It wouldn't leave. (*Sad, he leans in, his cheek to its head.*) It wouldn't go away.

ANNABEL: How'd it get into the house?

RICHARD: (*Stroking it.*) I was feeding your white albacore tuna to one of the local strays, and this monster cat showed up instead. I wasn't going to let it in, but my real self said he would never speak to me again if I didn't.

ANNABEL: Your real self . . . ?

RICHARD: You should have never asked to make contact, Annabel. My real self doesn't give a shit about anything except his own perpetual gratification. (*Stroking Cat.*) We were having such a good time . . . such a good time . . .

ANNABEL: Richard . . .

RICHARD: Hm?

ANNABEL: (*Miked.*) We're not real, are we?

RICHARD: What?

ANNABEL: (*Miked.*) You and I, we don't belong to the world out there.

RICHARD: (*Stroking Cat.*) What world is that, Annabel?

ANNABEL: (*Miked. Looking at audience.*) Out there. The normal ones, the successful ones. The ones who marry, have children, pay their bills on time . . . (*Weepy.*) The ones who really love and accept their lives and each other as something to be cherished . . .

RICHARD: (*Looking at audience.*) I have no idea who these people are you're talking about.

ANNABEL: (*Looking at audience.*) The ones who seem to be taking so much pleasure in our desperate unhappiness, don't you see them, Richard?

RICHARD: (*Looking.*) No.

(*Annabel crosses to love seat, sits. She holds her forehead with her hand.*)

RICHARD: (*Behind her, to audience.*) Whenever she holds her forehead like that, it means she's in her hopeless mode. Next stop, bubbles from the nose and complete catatonia!

ANNABEL: (*Holding her forehead.*) God, he's so cruel . . .

RICHARD: (*To audience.*) Yes, I'm cruel. Because she knows exactly what the sight of her like that does to me!

ANNABEL: (*Still holding.*) It reminds him of his mother . . .

RICHARD: (*Overlap.*) . . . she wants to eat me alive with her despair!

ANNABEL: Hey, Mr. Psychology, what if my suffering has NOTHING to do with you or your goddamn mother?!

RICHARD: (*Overlap.*) THE SHEER HELPLESSNESS OF HER SITTING HERE LIKE THIS MAKES ME WANT TO FUCKING KILL HER!

ANNABEL: SO KILL ME BASTARD WHAT ARE YOU WAITING FOR KILL ME KILL ME KILL ME JUST LIKE YOU KILLED THAT POOR CAT!

RICHARD: WITH A LOT MORE PLEASURE THAN I KILLED THAT CAT!

(*He drops cord coil around her neck.*)

ANNABEL: THE FIRST TIME I SET EYES ON HIM I KNEW HE WAS A MURDERER I KNEW I KNEW I TOLD MYSELF WATCH OUT ANNABEL DON'T LET THIS KILLER IN!

RICHARD: THE FIRST TIME I LAID EYES ON HER I KNEW SHE WAS AN ALBATROSS A SWAMP A PIT OF BOTTOMLESS SORROW I SAID TO MYSELF RUN RICHARD RUN . . .

ANNABEL: BUT HE GOT IN ANYWAY MR. NICEGUY THE KILLER PRETENDED TO BE A NEEDY SENSITIVE SOUL AND I LET DOWN MY GUARD AND HE GOT IN . . .

RICHARD: BUT I GOT MY DIRECTIONS ALL MIXED UP AND I RAN TOWARDS HER INSTEAD OF IN THE OPPOSITE DIRECTION . . .

ANNABEL: AND NOW HE'S GOING TO DO TO ME WHAT HE DID TO THAT POOR CAT . . .

RICHARD: AND NOW I'M GOING TO DO TO HER WHAT SHE'S DONE TO MY WHOLE GODDAMN LIFE!

(*He pulls the cord taut.*)

ANNABEL: (*Her hands to her throat.*) Richard . . . !

(*The phone rings.*)

(*Richard and Annabel freeze. The phone rings three more times. Answering machine picks up.*)

RICHARD'S VOICE: (*Friendly.*) Hi. Neither Richard or Annabel can come to the phone right now . . .

ANNABEL'S VOICE: But we really want to hear from you . . .

RICHARD'S VOICE: So leave a message of any length . . .

ANNABEL'S VOICE: At the sound of the beep . . .

BOTH VOICES: And we'll get back to you as soon as possible.

ANSWERING MACHINE: BEEP.

(*A masculine voice laughs softly, then: click.*)

RICHARD: (*Still holding mike and cord.*) Who was that?

ANNABEL: The man with the matches, probably . . .

(*Eyes closed, she holds her forehead. Richard lets go of mike and cord. He sits opposite her on the love seat. He closes his eyes and holds his forehead.*)

(*A long pause.*)

(*Cat falls over on keys. Startled, Annabel and Richard jump into each other's arms.*)

RICHARD: Annabel . . . !

ANNABEL: Richard . . . ?

(*They kiss. They kiss. They kiss again.*)

RICHARD: Annabel . . .

ANNABEL: Richard . . .

(*They kiss. They kiss. They kiss again.*)

RICHARD: I love you, Annabel.

ANNABEL: Oh Richard . . .

(*They rise, kiss, stumble about, more kisses.*)

RICHARD: Marry me, Annabel.

ANNABEL: Fuck me, Richard.

(*They kiss, moving about. They kiss, sinking to their knees. They kiss, clinching and rolling over.*)

RICHARD: Annabel . . .

ANNABEL: Love me, darling . . . love me . . . love me . . .

(*The Cat at the piano flicks her tail, revives. She looks at Richard and Annabel, completely engaged in their rhapsodic embrace. Cat turns back to piano and plays a two pawed cacophonous rhapsody: climaxing at the same time as the couple on the floor.*)

(*Blackout.*)

Scene 2

Almost immediately, Richard's miked breathing in darkness. Lights up, dim. Richard and Annabel entwined. Outside the window, night. A few speckled stars. Moonglow. The whole room is darkly radiant, alive with the constant din of a New York summer night. Richard sits up, turns off mike. He kisses Annabel. She sighs, rolls over. He moves off on all fours toward the piano.

ANNABEL: Sweetheart?

RICHARD: (*Rising, he sits on the piano bench. He is breathing hard.*) Yes, dear?

ANNABEL: Are you alright?

RICHARD: (*Coughing.*) My chest's a bit tight . . .

ANNABEL: Should we turn on the air-conditioner?

RICHARD: No, I'll be alright . . .

(*He sits, tries to breathe.*)

ANNABEL: Richard . . .

RICHARD: Yes?

ANNABEL: (*Unwinding microphone.*) I accept . . .

RICHARD: What?

(*Lights come up slow.*)

ANNABEL: Your proposal. (*Pause.*) You did propose, or did I just dream you proposed?

RICHARD: (*Pause.*) No, Annabel, I proposed . . .

ANNABEL: Good. For a moment, there, I was afraid . . . When would you like to set the date?

RICHARD: Whenever . . .

ANNABEL: It's July. Most of our friends won't be back in the city until the end of summer. How does late August sound?

RICHARD: (*Coughing, breathing hard.*) Late August sounds fine.

ANNABEL: Good. Would you like to call someone?

RICHARD: Now? (*Checks watch.*) It's after ten.

ANNABEL: I think it would be a good idea if we called and told someone immediately, yes.

RICHARD: Okay. Why don't you call someone, then.

ANNABEL: I think it would be a good idea if *you* made the call.

RICHARD: Okay. (*He rises, crosses to phone, picks it up.*) Got any preferences?

ANNABEL: How about Lonnie Melrose?

RICHARD: (*A beat.*) I don't feel like talking to Lonnie right now.

ANNABEL: Choose someone else, then.

RICHARD: Gottisman . . .

ANNABEL: Who?

RICHARD: Richard Gottisman. We went to camp together.

ANNABEL: How come you never mentioned him?

RICHARD: I didn't much like him. He was huge and oily and a bit effemminate, and he played a very dirty game of basketball. But between us, we ran the bunk for five, six summers. Everyone called us "the two Dicks."

ANNABEL: Why him, Richard?

RICHARD: Because he was the first guy I personally knew to lose his virginity.

ANNABEL: Oh?

(*He dials.*)

RICHARD: Hi. Name is Gottisman, Richard. G-o-t-t-i-s-m-a-n. Lawyer. Forest Hills somewhere. Thank you. (*Listens. Dials.*) This is going to be quite a shock for ole Dicky. I always suspected he thought I was a fag. (*As though to a child.*) Oh hi, I hope I'm not keeping you up past your bed time, but I'm an old friend of your daddy's from Camp Onnekonda. I have some very good news for him. Is he home? (*A beat. Whispered.*) I hate people who let the baby answer the phone! (*On phone.*) Oh, hello, Mrs. Gottisman? Yes, well, I'm an old friend of your husband's from Camp Onnekonda, could I speak with him, please? (*A beat.*) What? (*A beat.*) Oh Jesus! (*He shuts phone off, tossing it away.*)

ANNABEL: What's wrong?

RICHARD: He's dead.

ANNABEL: Dead? What of?

RICHARD: I forgot to ask. God, God, God, Richie . . .

ANNABEL: I thought you said you couldn't stand him.

RICHARD: I must have lied. (*Breathing hard.*) I really feel his loss . . .

ANNABEL: Richard . . .

RICHARD: (*Pressing his head with his hands.*) Try to understand this, Annabel: one moment two sixteen year old guys go up for the same rebound, twenty years later only one of them comes down . . .

ANNABEL: (*Picks up phone.*) But which one of you has the ball?

RICHARD: (*Breathing hard.*) We were the two Dicks . . .

ANNABEL: (*Dials.*) Speaking of dicks, Richard, did you ever have one up your ass?

RICHARD: (*Dazed.*) What?

ANNABEL: You should try it some time, it might surprise you. (*Hands him the phone.*) Here.

RICHARD: Who am I talking to?

ANNABEL: Our witness.

RICHARD: Hello? (*A beat.*) Oh, hi Duff. This is Richard. Richard! Your daughter Annabel's boy friend.

ANNABEL: What a pleasure it's going to be to kiss that loathsome word goodbye.

RICHARD; Well, I'll tell ya, Duff: Annabel and I have decided to take the plunge, and being a gentleman of the old school, I told her we shouldn't make any plans until we checked it out with you. (*Cover receiver.*) He says, "That's fine."

ANNABEL: Thank him.

RICHARD: Thanks, Duff. Here, I'll let you speak with her. (*Extends phone to her.*)

ANNABEL: (*Turning away.*) I don't want to speak to him.

RICHARD: (*On phone.*) Annabel says she'll catch you later, Duff. Yeah, I guess I am breathin' a little hard, ha ha. Okay, Duff, talk to ya soon. (*Shuts phone off. Breathing hard. Annabel watches him.*). Well, I guess this is it, huh?

ANNABEL: (*Picks up microphone, switches on.*) Richard?

RICHARD: What?

ANNABEL: (*Miked.*) I hate you. I really hate you. I wish you were dead, and I wish I was far far away. (*She lays microphone down between them.*)

RICHARD: Well, Annabel—(*He picks it up, miked.*)—as long as you're not indifferent. (*He lays it down.*)

(*He rises, crosses to window. Closing the bars slowly over the frame, he rests his full weight on the iron gate. He is breathing hard, unable to catch his breath. He moves downstage, holding and following the curve of the piano.*)

ANNABEL: (*Quiet.*) You want me to get your medicine?

(*Richard, breathing hard, begins to cry. Annabel rises, crosses to him, leans herself over his back, encircling his body with her arms.*)

(*Mozart sonata for violin and piano fades in, specifically, "Sonata in G." Outside the window, an enormous blood-yellow moon crosses slowly from right. Or rather, is floated in by the Cat, who remains mostly hidden behind it: i.e., with just the tips of her claw-fingers showing. Moon still. The lights dim, leaving Annabel and Richard in a coupled silhouette against the bars. Cat looks out at them.*)

END

Oscar

and

Bertha

BY

MARIA

IRENE

FORNES

An earlier version of *Oscar and Bertha* was presented as a work in progress at the State University of New York - New Paltz, the Guthrie Theatre Lab, and at the 1989 Padua Hills Playwrights Festival. The cast of the Padua Hills presentation was as follows:

Eve	Molly Cleator
Pike	Laura Fanning
Bertha	Mary Forcade
Oscar	Pamela Gordon
Director	Maria Irene Fornes
Assistant Director	Connie Monaghan
Lighting Design	Jason Berliner
Steven Heller's *Tarantella* performed by	Valerie Gordon

CHARACTERS:

OSCAR (45 years old.)
BERTHA (His sister. 43 years old.)
EVE (A servant. 40 years old.)
PIKE (A man. 40 years old.)

SET:

Upstage, extending across the stage, is a corridor that leads on the right to the main door and on the left to the kitchen and other rooms. On the downstage of the corridor there is a wall. On the center of this wall there is the entrance way to a hallway that runs perpendicular to the corridor. On each side of the hallway there are walls. On the upstage side of each wall there is a door. These doors lead: on the right, to Bertha's room; on the left, to Oscar's room. The downstage walls of these rooms are abot eighteen inches high. The downstage area is to the right, the dining room; to the left, the living room. In Bertha's bedroom there is a single bed against the right and down walls and a night table against the right wall. There is a small picture of a landscape in the back wall. Oscar's bedroom mirrors Bertha's bedroom. In the dining room there is a sideboard against the right wall and a table and three chairs to the left of the sideboard. In the living room there are two stuffed chairs and a side table. On the side table in Bertha's room there is paper and pencil. On Oscar's side table there is a paper and pencil, a comic book, and a newspaper. In the drawer of the side table there is a plate of food. On the sideboard there is a cup of water. On the dining table there is a newspaper. In the table drawer there is a newspaper. On the left stuffed chair there is a newspaper. On the right stuffed chair there are two newspapers.

The costumes are considerably outdated.

Scene 1

Eve sits on the left stuffed chair. She wears a hat. She carries a purse and holds a newspaper in her hand. Oscar sits in a wheelchair very close to Eve. He wears a dark grey suit. Oscar is being charming.

OSCAR: What is your name?

EVE: . . . Eve.

OSCAR: And where do you come from?

EVE: From Franklyn.

OSCAR: Our Franklyn? (*Eve nods.*) Hm. You're one of our little maidens then?—And what do the girls in Franklyn look like? (*Eve looks at Oscar in disbelief. He goes closer to her and speaks in her ear.*) What do the girls in Franklyn look like? (*Pinching her breast.*) Do the girls in Franklyn have a pretty little tit. Like a bird. That goes pip pip. (*Pinching her other breast.*) Do they have another little bird who wants to go pip pip. (*Pinching at each breast with each word.*) Pip pip pip pip. (*He laughs with delight and spins on his wheelchair.*) What do the girls in Franklyn talk about? Do they go, (*Using both hands to move her lips and imitating a young child.*) "The little girl is in the garden drinking tea with her daddy and her mommy? (*Wheeling himself around.*) The little girl is in the garden. Mommy's in the garden. Daddy's in the garden." (*He wheels himself to her with a fiendish look. She goes left. He goes after her. She runs right. She stands against a wall. He goes after her. He puts his head under her skirt.*) Pow!

(*He moves his head up and down making slurping sounds. She gets away. He makes a move towards her. She takes a step back. He makes another move. She takes another step back.*)

EVE: Stop.

(*Oscar looks at her arms.*)

OSCAR: Hairy.

EVE: What.

OSCAR: Hairy legs. And your arms? Are they hairy? (*She hides her arms behind her.*) Let's see.

EVE: Don't.

(*He wheels himself to her, breathing heavily. She hits him with the newspaper repeatedly. His head drops down gradually while making orgasmic sounds. Bertha enters from the corridor. She wears a dark blue suit. She and Oscar speak almost simultaneously.*)

BERTHA: What did you to do to her?

OSCAR: I did what I wanted to. What I wanted to. That's what I did.

BERTHA: And did you ask her what she wanted? (*Getting closer to Eve.*) What do you want, honey? (*To Oscar.*) And you treat her like that? (*Reaching for Eve's newspaper.*) Give me that!

(*Bertha hits Oscar with the newspaper. He takes the newspaper from the table and hits her back. They hit each other for a while. He stops hitting her.*)

OSCAR: Were you looking through the keyhole?

BERTHA: No. I wasn't!

OSCAR: Did you see me do it?

BERTHA: No.

OSCAR: Were you listening? — With your ear against the door.

BERTHA: No.

OSCAR: You were. I know you were. You heard it all. Did you see me go under her skirt? Did you see me bite her thigh? (*He reenacts his going under her skirt.*) Did you see me like this . . . ? Like this . . . ? And like this . . . ?

BERTHA: No, I didn't.

OSCAR: You saw it all.

BERTHA: No, I didn't.

OSCAR: Liar, won't admit it.

BERTHA: No. I won't.

OSCAR: (*To Eve.*) Can't stand her. (*Bertha spits. Oscar spits. He speaks to Eve.*) My sister!

BERTHA: Did you come in answer to the ad?

EVE: Yes.

BERTHA: Come here, honey.

OSCAR: Don't touch her! We did it! She and I! So get out!

BERTHA: You did nothing! That's what you did! Nothing!

OSCAR: What do you mean . . .

BERTHA: You did nothing.

OSCAR: . . . Oh . . . What I did . . . What I did . . . Oh . . . If you knew . . .

BERTHA: You did nothing. I saw you through the keyhole.

OSCAR: Peeping tom!

BERTHA: (*Going to Eve.*) Come here, honey.

OSCAR: (*Hitting Bertha with the newspaper.*) Peeping tom!

(*Bertha hits him with the newspaper. Eve hits them both. They hit her. Oscar falls off the chair. He speaks from the floor.*)

OSCAR: And you! Do you get pussy! Do you get cock! Do you get anything! Go tell them I do! Me in a wheelchair! Never out on the street! And yet me! I get pussy! (*Eve helps Oscar on the chair.*) Pussy! And what do you get! You get nothing! I get pussy! And you get nothing! Like it or not!

BERTHA: You're ridiculous!

OSCAR: I'm mean and I'm nasty. Mean and evil. I'm a cad! A cad! So! Now you know!

BERTHA: Know what!

OSCAR: What I do.

BERTHA: Nothing!

OSCAR: You can tell everyone what I am.

BERTHA: You're disgusting!

OSCAR: A cad.

BERTHA: Disgusting.

OSCAR: A cad.

BERTHA: Disgusting.

OSCAR: Shut up! She liked it!

EVE: I didn't like it.

BERTHA: Disgusting!

OSCAR: A cad.

BERTHA: Disgusting.

OSCAR: I liked it. She liked it! Why disgusting!

BERTHA: Disgusting!

OSCAR: (*Mocking refinement.*) You want tea! Honey!

BERTHA: Did you wash your hands?

OSCAR: It's my nose I should wash! (*He makes slurping sounds.*) Not my hands! My nose! Smell my nose! She loved it!

BERTHA: (*Walking seductively towards Eve.*) How come she says nothing. (*Putting her arm around Eve's waist. She speaks to Oscar while looking at Eve.*) You keep saying she loved it but she says nothing. (*To Eve.*) Why don't you say something, honey? (*To Oscar.*) You're a pig.

(*Bertha looks at Eve intensely during Oscar's speech.*)

OSCAR: You're a pig! Busybody! Looking behind doors! I'm sexy and you're not! I'm sexy! I'm so sexy! So sexy! She loved it! She loved it! She loved it! Didn't she! She loved it! You saw it! You saw her! She loved it! And don't tell me she didn't. Go tell the world! Tell the world! Tell the world that you saw it!

BERTHA: (*Still looking at Eve.*) I'll tell them that you're lousy.

OSCAR: I'm mean!

BERTHA: You're lousy!

OSCAR: Jealous of me!

(*Bertha brings Eve close to herself.*)

BERTHA: Had it been me . . .

EVE: Oh! God!

BERTHA: Why do you say that. You can work for me, honey. A girl like that from a small town. Alone in the city. All you want is to get your lapping and have her tell the whole world. I hope she tells no one!

(*Bertha brings Eve closer to herself.*)

BERTHA: So you're looking for work!

EVE: That's right.

BERTHA: (*Holding her closer.*) Well . . . (*Eve pushes her off. Bertha loses her balance and steps backwards until she hits a piece of furniture and falls to the floor.*) I knew it!

EVE: What.

BERTHA: (*From the floor.*) Rotten luck. Always had rotten luck. He's got all the luck! Rotten luck! You let him do it! Him yes! Him yes! But me no! To me it's no!

OSCAR: That's right!

BERTHA: Can you cook?

EVE: Not too good.

BERTHA: Good. Cook for him. Lousy food. Poison him.

(*Oscar spits. Bertha spits. There is a shift of light. Eve exits left. Oscar pivots on the wheelchair. Bertha grabs him by the collar.*)

BERTHA: Where did she go?

OSCAR: (*Choking.*) She left.

BERTHA: 'She didn't leave. Where is she?

OSCAR: (*Choking.*) In the kitchen.

(*Bertha exits left. Bertha and Eve are heard arguing offstage. There is the sound of pots and pans falling. Oscar laughs fiendishly. Bertha enters tumbling backwards. Her hair is disheveled. She flies around the room bumping on furniture and falls to the floor at Oscar's feet.*)

OSCAR: What happened?

BERTHA: Oh, buzz off!

OSCAR: Did she slap you in the face! Did she push you against the wall! Did she throw hot water at your face? Did she say I hate you? I'm sure she did all that.

(*There is a shift of light. Eve enters. She looks slightly paler and begins to show dark circles around her eyes. Through the rest of the play Eve gradually looks more sickly and haggard. She wears an apron. She carries a serving dish and a cloth. She goes to the dining-room. Oscar wheels himself to left of the table. Bertha sits to the right. Eve wipes the table and places the dish in the center.*)

BERTHA: Sit down. Sit with us. You can eat at the table. You pay for the food, don't you? So you can sit with us.

OSCAR: She pays?

BERTHA: It's a loan. (*To Eve.*) You shouldn't eat standing up.

(*Eve sits. She looks at Bertha, then at Oscar, then down. Oscar and Bertha look at each other and smile. There is a shift of light. Eve takes the serving dish to the sideboard. Oscar exits. As Bertha goes to the up side of the sideboard, she gets as close to Eve as possible. Eve takes the cup from the sideboard. She lifts the up-right corner of the tablecloth, pours water on the table, and wipes the table. Bertha watches Eve's buttocks move. Bertha walks to Eve. Her pelvis touches her. Eve thrusts her buttocks against Bertha. Bertha goes flying around the room bumping on furniture. She falls on the floor. She speaks fiercely.*)

BERTHA: You're wasting water! (*She moves on the floor towards Eve.*) You're wasting water! You're wasting water! You liked it. (*She moves closer.*) . . . You liked it. (*She moves closer. Pleadingly.*) . . . You liked it?

(*Oscar enters. Eve puts the tablecloth over the table and puts the cup on the sideboard.*)

OSCAR: (*Chasing Eve around the table and up the hallway.*) A cad! A cad!

(*There is a shift of light. Eve exits left. Oscar follows her. Eve crosses the corridor from left to right as Bertha sits at the down side of the table. Eve re-enters. She walks to the living room.*)

BERTHA: You came back, Eve. For me?

(*Eve looks under the cushion of the left stuffed chair.*)

BERTHA: (*Starting to go to Eve.*) I thought maybe you came for me.

(*Eve goes to look under the table.*)

BERTHA: Don't tell him.

EVE: What!

BERTHA: Tell him you came for me. (*Oscar enters.*) She came for me, Oscar. She came for me!

(*Oscar chases Eve around the table and into his bedroom. Eve trips and falls on the bed. Oscar jumps on the bed as Eve rolls off the bed. Oscar bounces up and down. Eve stands and watches him in disbelief.*)

OSCAR: For me! For me! For me! For me! She came for meeeee!!! (*Eve exits right. Oscar jumps out of bed. He goes to the hallway. He speaks to Bertha.*) I did it.

(*He exits left. Eve crosses left on the corridor.*)

BERTHA: You're back.

EVE: (*Without stopping.*) I forgot something. (*Eve screams offstage. She crosses right on the corridor.*)

BERTHA: I was remembering when we were sexual.

EVE: (*Re-entering.*) When was that?

BERTHA: Just remembering.

EVE: (*Exiting right.*) We never were.

BERTHA: We were.

EVE: (*Offstage.*) Never were.

BERTHA: We were!

EVE: (*Offstage.*) Never were!

BERTHA: Ah—buzz off!

EVE: (*Offstage.*) Ah—buzz off!—You buzz off!

(*Pike and Eve are heard speaking offstage. Bertha listens.*)

BERTHA: Who's that! (*They continue speaking offstage.*) Who's that! Who's that! Who's that!!!

(*There is a shift of light. Bertha goes to the living room. She sits on the left stuffed chair and reads a newspaper. Oscar enters.*)

OSCAR: (*Going to her, petulant.*) What are you looking at—what are you reading?

BERTHA: Nothing!

OSCAR: Let me see!

(*Bertha puts the newspaper behind her. She whispers.*)

BERTHA: There's something I have to tell you.

OSCAR: What.

BERTHA: Something I heard.

OSCAR: What.

BERTHA: Eve.

OSCAR: What about Eve?

BERTHA: Talking to a man.

OSCAR: What man?

(*Eve's and Pike's mumbling is heard throughout the following speech. Bertha listens for a moment.*)

BERTHA: Something sexual. (*Hitting her own forehead and falling on the floor.*) Like being hit in the head with a big stone or a blunt instrument. (*As her whole body shakes.*) Or being burnt with a high voltage electric charge which is powerful like electricity but it doesn't hurt. Or feeling the ground sink under your feet— (*Standing.*) When she's not touched she feels a longing that weakens her. But when she's touched she burns with desire powerful like a rocket taking off the ground. (*Lifting a leg.*) And tearing her entrails. Either way it's strong. That's what she said to him—when she spoke. (*Eve starts to cross left. She stops to look at them. They look at her.*) Is that what you said?

(*Eve exits left. Oscar exits right. He re-enters.*)

OSCAR: (*Accusingly.*) There's no one there. (*Grabbing the newspaper from Bertha.*) What's that you're reading!

BERTHA: (*Grabbing the newspaper back.*) A murder!

(*They pull the newspaper back and forth during the following lines.*)

OSCAR: What murder!

BERTHA: Man kills wife! Let go!

OSCAR: Let me see!

BERTHA: What for?

OSCAR: Let me see!

BERTHA: What for?

OSCAR: Let me see.

BERTHA: What for.

OSCAR: (*Pulling harder.*) Let me see.

BERTHA: What for.

OSCAR: Let me see.

BERTHA: Man kills wife.

(*Oscar gets the paper. She bites his arm. His face contorts. His foot hits the floor repeatedly. He reads the newspaper.*)

OSCAR: *Brother* kills sister! Ha ha ha.

BERTHA: (*Taking the paper.*) *Sister* kills brother! *She* kills him! *Sister* kills brother! *She* kills him! She *kills* him!

OSCAR: *He* kills her! *He* kills her. *He* kills her. *Brother* kills sister! (*Grabbing the paper.*) You read garbage!

BERTHA: (*Grabbing the paper.*) Give me that!

OSCAR: It makes you more stupid and hateful. (*Grabbing the paper.*) Give me that. (*As he exits left.*) At your age.

BERTHA: At your age Oscar!

OSCAR: (*Offstage.*) At your age!

(*Bertha goes to the down side of the table and sits. There is a shift of light. Eve crosses the corridor from left to right. She wears her hat and carries her purse.*)

EVE: (*Without stopping.*) I'm going now.

BERTHA: Go ahead. I hope you come back.

EVE: (*Re-entering.*) Why do you say hope?

BERTHA: Why not? I can hope, can't I? Anyone can hope. Take care of your feet.

EVE: What's wrong with my feet?

BERTHA: Nothing. Can't I tell you to take care of your feet? Where are you going?

EVE: To the store.

BERTHA: What for?

EVE: Food.

BERTHA: Take money from the drawer.

EVE: (*Walking down.*) What money?

BERTHA: The money in the drawer.

EVE: There's no money in the drawer.

BERTHA: Who took the money?

EVE: The money was spent.

BERTHA: Oscar!

OSCAR: (*Offstage.*) What!

BERTHA: Who took the money! (*Oscar does not answer.*) Oscar, who took the money!—Someone took the money, now we're broke! (*Short pause.*) Did you hear that Oscar?

OSCAR: (*Offstage.*) I heard.

BERTHA: (*To Eve.*) So how are we going to pay?

EVE: The same as always. Credit.

BERTHA: Oscar, you have to look for work.

OSCAR: (*Offstage.*) Who says.

BERTHA: Eve.

OSCAR: (*Offstage.*) What does she know.

BERTHA: You have to work. There's no money in the drawer.

OSCAR: (*Offstage.*) Oh no?

BERTHA: No. We can't live on credit.

OSCAR: (*Offstage.*) So, if we can't we won't.

BERTHA: That doesn't help, Oscar.

(*Bertha burps. Eve sits.*)

EVE: What do you want for dinner?

BERTHA: Same as always I guess.

EVE: Turnips.

BERTHA: Yeah, turnips will do.

EVE: What else?

BERTHA: I don't know what else. Bread I guess.

EVE: How about him?

BERTHA: Oscar!

OSCAR: (*Offstage.*) What.

BERTHA: What do you want for dinner?

OSCAR: (*Offstage.*) Let me think.

BERTHA: Same I guess.

EVE: Sure what else. Day old bread and turnips. Not too good. Shit is what you eat.

BERTHA: That's because you cook like shit. If you cooked good it wouldn't taste like shit.

EVE: I get blamed for everything.

BERTHA: Not everything. There's a lot more you could get blamed for.

EVE: And you? Is anything ever your fault?

BERTHA: What do you mean?

EVE: Whose fault is it that there is no money?

BERTHA: Not mine.

EVE: Whose fault is it?

BERTHA: Oscar.

EVE: When is Oscar getting work?

BERTHA: Oscar?

EVE: Someone has to work.

BERTHA: (*Calling out to Oscar.*) Oscar!

OSCAR: (*Offstage.*) What!

BERTHA: Eve says you have to get out and work.

OSCAR: (*Offstage.*) She says what!

BERTHA: She says you have to get a job. Oscar, did you hear that! (*Silence.*) Good! Luck!

EVE: A job that pays.

BERTHA: You hear that, Oscar. A job that pays.

(*Eve starts to go.*)

EVE: Good! Luck!

BERTHA: Sure.

EVE: Bring some money in.

BERTHA: Sure.

EVE: (*As she exits.*) I'll get some garlic. You can put garlic on the bread.

BERTHA: What for.

EVE: (*Offstage.*) For taste.

BERTHA: (*Disdainfully.*) Peelease ...

(*There is a shift of light.*)

BERTHA: Eve, what happened? (*Eve stares front and doesn't answer.*)

What happened!

(*Oscar enters. He goes to Eve.*)

OSCAR: What happened? Did you get the garlic. Did they take it from you?

(*Oscar exits. Eve walks to the living room and sits. Bertha follows Eve. She is in a state of romantic dispair.*)

BERTHA: Eve, people can have children even when they haven't been married. If a person does certain things with another—a child may be conceived. If they do certain things . . . the things that persons do when they marry. (*Bertha goes on her knee.*) You know what I mean, Eve. If people do those things they can have babies even if they are not married. Did you know that? Eve, don't you know that persons do certain things when they marry?

EVE: Yes.

BERTHA: What, Eve? What do they do? (*Pause.*) Eve. (*Pause.*) We can do those things! Eve!

EVE: What.!

BERTHA: I asked you a question. (*Pause. Pleading.*) We can do those things. The things that people do.

EVE: (*Annoyed.*) What!

(*Bertha sits on the left stuffed chair.*)

BERTHA: Have you ever? (*Suspiciously.*) I know you have—Who did you do it with! —Don't tell me you haven't. (*Pause.*) Did you do it with him? (*Pause.*) I wish I'd never met you. (*Eve starts to stand.*) I wish I'd never met you! (*As she speaks the following lines, Bertha straddles the arm of the chair and moves her pelvis against it.*) I wish I'd never met you! (*Eve exits right.*) I wish I'd never met you!

(*Oscar enters.*)

BERTHA: (*Still moving her pelvis against the arm of the chair.*) This is private! Get out! This is between Eve and me! (*Oscar looks around the room. Bertha falls off the chair. Pike and Eve are heard speaking offstage.*) Who's that? (*Oscar starts taking off his jacket.*) Who's that? (*Pause.*) Who's that? (*To Oscar.*) Listen to that. Why are you taking off your jacket?

OSCAR: To show you my tit. (*Lifting his shirt. There is a lipstick mark on his breast.*) Lipstick marks. I have lipstick on my tit.

BERTHA: How did it get there?

OSCAR: ... Eve.

(*She looks closely at his chest.*)

BERTHA: Those are dog lips. You put lipstick on a dog, then put his snout to your tit so it would leave an imprint. I know you. What dog did it? What dog? What dog?

OSCAR: Eve! Eve! Eve did it! (*He becomes saddened.*) She's with child.— My child.— I'm the father.

BERTHA: You're crazy!

OSCAR: She's pregnant with my child.

BERTHA: Well, that's not so.

OSCAR: It is.

BERTHA: I put it in her.

OSCAR: Put what?

BERTHA: The baby!

OSCAR: Don't be ridiculous. I put it in her. (*Hitting his fist against the palm of his hand.*) Fireworks! That's how it was! Passion! Out of my ears—and hers too.

BERTHA: (*Suspiciously.*) What was out of her ears.

OSCAR: The cum.

BERTHA: The baby's not yours.

OSCAR: Oh no?

BERTHA: No.

OSCAR: You think it's yours?

BERTHA: I wouldn't say it wasn't.

OSCAR: You'd say it was.

BERTHA: I'd say that.

OSCAR: In your head!

BERTHA: (*Proudly.*) Well . . .

(*Eve enters.*)

OSCAR & BERTHA: Whose is it!

EVE: What?

OSCAR: Out with it!

EVE: There's someone at the door.—I've had it!

OSCAR: Who!

EVE: A man.

OSCAR: What man?

EVE: The man from the bank.

OSCAR: What bank?

EVE: He has a briefcase.

OSCAR: Tell him I'm not in. (*Eve exits right. Pike and Eve are heard speaking offstage. Oscar goes to the entrance way.*) What does he want? (*Pause.*) Move aside. (*Eve crosses left.*) What does he want?

(*Oscar exits right. Bertha sits on the down right side of the table. Oscar speaks offstage.*)

OSCAR: What do you want! What are you staring at! (*There is the sound of the door slamming. Oscar enters.*) Got rid of him! You thought I couldn't handle him? One two three. That's how it is and there is nothing you can do about it. Who was that! Who was that at the door! (*To Bertha.*) You have to stop acting like that. Jealous of me!

(*Oscar goes to his bedroom.*)

BERTHA: Jealous!

OSCAR: Of me! (*He lies down.*) Because I can do things. Get right down and do them.

(*Eve enters. She goes to Bertha and whispers in her ear. Bertha goes to center. Eve follows. Bertha whispers in Eve's ear. Eve whispers in Bertha's ear.*)

BERTHA: (*Suspiciously.*) You say you know him.

EVE: I met him.

BERTHA: And you ate his pecker!

EVE: I did not.

BERTHA: Go on.

EVE: He said he wanted to meet you.

BERTHA: What for?

EVE: He didn't say.

BERTHA: Where is he now?

EVE: Downstairs. He said he would stand on the corner. He said if you wanted to see him you could look out the window and see him standing on the corner.

BERTHA: Did he say for what?

EVE: He didn't.

BERTHA: Is he from the bank?

EVE: Yes.

BERTHA: Did he have a bulge in his pocket? A sack, a bump on the side or on his back or on his chest, to the side, a big lump, a lot of money?

EVE: I didn't notice.

BERTHA: You didn't notice? You lapped his pecker and you say you didn't notice.

EVE: I didn't lap his pecker!

BERTHA: Where is he?

(*They walk to the downstage edge and look down.*)

EVE: That's him! That one! With the hat, the brown hat. See—he's smiling. Wave. (*Bertha looks at Eve.*) Wave! (*Bertha does.*) Wave again. (*Bertha does.*)

BERTHA: Tell him to come up. Who is he? If he likes me,—leave. He may like me.

EVE: Where should I go?

BERTHA: Go to Oscar's room.

EVE: Oscar's room?

BERTHA: Yes, go to his room.—Is he coming?

(*Eve looks.*)

EVE: Yes.

BERTHA: Go lock yourself in Oscar's room. Don't come out till I tell you. I don't care what you do with him. Go. Don't come out till I say so.

(*There is a shift of light. Eve exits right. Oscar is still lying on his bed.*)

OSCAR: I wanted to get married and I never did!

BERTHA: (*Sitting on the downstage side of the table.*) That wasn't my fault.

OSCAR: Yes it was.

BERTHA: How was it my fault?

OSCAR: You chased all my girlfriends away.

BERTHA: You never had any.

OSCAR: I had girlfriends. Many girlfriends. Cute, pretty. Lips like
strawberries when you cut strawberries and the flesh is fresh and
smooth and it sweats drops of juice.—That's what they were like,
fresh like juice. Their bodies were like the hind legs of a dog, tight
and warm and quivering. Did you ever put your hands on the inside
of the thigh of one of my girlfriends.

BERTHA: Yes, I did!

OSCAR: Hm.

BERTHA: In my mind, same as you!

OSCAR: I did it for real.

BERTHA: Only once.

OSCAR: Once is enough. You never did it.

BERTHA: I did so. More than once.

OSCAR: With Babette!

BERTHA: Sure.

OSCAR: You call that doing it. You never did it!

BERTHA: Well, it was something.

OSCAR: Not enough!

BERTHA: I did it with someone else.

OSCAR: Who?

BERTHA: Pike.

OSCAR: Pike? (*Pause.*) Who's that?

BERTHA: He delivered the money.

OSCAR: What money.

BERTHA: For the house.

OSCAR: From the bank.

BERTHA: Yes. He had a bulge. I thought it was the money. I touched it and it wasn't.

OSCAR: What was it? (*Pause.*) You say that because of mother.

BERTHA: What about mother?

OSCAR: (*Sitting on the wheelchair.*) I slept with her!

BERTHA: Ah buzz off.

OSCAR: (*Going to the living room.*) I slept with her. In the same bed!

BERTHA: So what!

OSCAR: She nursed me!

BERTHA: So what!

OSCAR: She was my woman. I owned her. I was her baby love—she never nursed you.

BERTHA: She didn't?

OSCAR: Did you ever put your lips to her breast?

BERTHA: No.

OSCAR: I did. I drank the milk that was intended for you. I have your milk inside me. You never went near her. I lay in bed with her as she fed me. And we climaxed. Both of us. My baby penis was erect like a torpedo and I climaxed and so did she.

BERTHA: Ah buzz off!

OSCAR: You think she enjoyed herself with Daddy? Ha! His cock was big but dull. My little penis was cheerful. She came so deeply and so beautifully. And me. I turned to her and when my little penis touched her belly I came. She put her hand on my fat little butt and felt it pulsate with the throes of orgasm. She held me and she climaxed. We never kissed. Our love was pure.

BERTHA: (*Looking around nervously for an imaginary dog.*) Here! Doggy, doggy, doggy! I never heard that. (*Going to the corridor.*) Here! Doggy, doggy, doggy. (*Walking left and right on the corridor.*) Here! Doggy, doggy, doggy.

OSCAR: Who are you calling?

BERTHA: I'm calling the dog. (*Walking to the living room.*) You'll have to leave. There is no room here for you.

OSCAR: Who says.

BERTHA: I say. This house is mine.

OSCAR: It's mine!

BERTHA: You're not wanted here.

OSCAR: Who doesn't want me.

BERTHA: A great many people don't want you.

(*Eve enters.*)

OSCAR: Eve ... (*Eve turns to look at him. He is speechless. He throws himself at her feet. He kisses her feet. Bertha goes to her bedroom and sits on her bed.*) ... Eve ... Eve ...

(*He grabs Eve's wrists and makes her go down on the floor.*)

EVE: Let go off me.

OSCAR: Shhh! (*In a whisper.*) Did you ever ask for advice?

EVE: Why?

OSCAR: Did you ever!

EVE: Maybe I did.

OSCAR: You think you may have?

EVE: Yes, maybe.

OSCAR: You look like a person who would be sinking in quicksand, drowning in a well, sliding off a cliff and never say, "Help me—what should I do?"

EVE: Why?

OSCAR: Would you ask for advice?

EVE: I would if I thought someone cared.

OSCAR: I care. Ask me for advice.

EVE: About what.

OSCAR: About a problem you have.

EVE: What problem.

OSCAR: How to get rid of someone.

EVE: Who.

OSCAR: Bertha!—Maybe you want to ask for advice about how to kill her.

EVE: Kill Bertha?

OSCAR: Yes, kill her.

(*Eve walks to the doorway to Bertha's bedroom.*)

EVE: Oscar wants me to get rid of you.

BERTHA: Oh yes?

EVE: He said you were a problem in my life. He said I could poison you or strangle you. He said he would help.

BERTHA: Did he say you could drown me in the tub?

EVE: Yes.

BERTHA: (*Suspiciously.*) And why didn't you mention that?

EVE: He said you could fight me and overpower me, and pull me in the tub with you which is what you always wanted.

(*Bertha writes on a piece of paper and gives it to Eve.*)

BERTHA: Give him this.

(*Eve goes to the living room.*)

EVE: (*Giving Oscar the piece of paper.*) Bertha sends you this.

(*He takes the paper and tears it in shreds.*)

OSCAR: Come here.

EVE: Where?

OSCAR: Close to me.—

(*She picks up the pieces of paper and reads from them.*)

EVE: "I would gladly see the liquid of your eyeballs drip down your face. I would gladly see a hole in your belly and see your innards fall out. I would gladly see poles go in your rectum. I would gladly see piss thrown on your face. I would gladly see your face destroyed. I would gladly see a foot step into your lower half and slush in it. You kill me and all that will happen to you." That's what she wrote.

OSCAR: (*Downcast.*) She wrote that?

(*He goes on the floor and sobs. Eve exits left. Oscar babbles. Bertha enters.*)

BERTHA: Who are you talking to?

OSCAR: I was talking to myself.

BERTHA: What about?

OSCAR: Nothing. (*He blows his nose.*)

BERTHA: You were talking to yourself?

OSCAR: (*Going to his room.*) So what.

(*Oscar lies in bed. Bertha goes to Oscar's room.*)

BERTHA: Why are you crying?

OSCAR: I'm in pain.

BERTHA: Why?

OSCAR: Men too have to cry.

BERTHA: What for?

OSCAR: Do you see how it's raining out? Drizzling. Do you see how gray the sky is? Do you see the birds taking shelter under the branches of the trees? That's how I feel.

BERTHA: You?

OSCAR: Yes, me!

BERTHA: Such a delicate sentiment.

OSCAR: So? Why can't I have a delicate sentiment! I'm human! Can't I think of suicide?

BERTHA: Oh, you always do.

OSCAR: I have reasons to say it!

BERTHA: Do it! Kill yourself! Why don't you! (*He puts his hand inside his jacket. She grabs his hand.*) What are you doing? What do you have there? (*She tries to feel an object in his pocket. They struggle.*)

OSCAR: Let go of my hand!

(*They struggle.*)

BERTHA: What are you trying to do?

OSCAR: I thought I may find something to eat.

BERTHA: (*Letting go of him.*) In your pocket! (*Pause.*) . . . Something to eat in your pocket . . . What about the shutters? Should I close them?

OSCAR: Close them.

BERTHA: Are you hungry?

OSCAR: Hungry enough to eat if I'm fed.

BERTHA: Didn't Eve feed you?

OSCAR: I don't know.

BERTHA: You should know if she fed you.

OSCAR: I should, but I don't. I don't eat what she feeds me.

BERTHA: Why not.

OSCAR: She puts poison in my food.

BERTHA: (*She opens the drawer on the side table.*) Here's food. I'll warm it up for you.

OSCAR: Why? To eat warm poison?

BERTHA: Eve doesn't put poison in your food.

OSCAR: There's poison in it.

BERTHA: Should I get you something else?

OSCAR: Everything else is poisoned.

BERTHA: Well then, I'm poisoned.

OSCAR: You are. (*Lifting the front of his shirt and exposing his breast.*) Look! Look at this. Look. (*She looks.*) It's your mother's tit. (*She goes to the living room. He follows her.*) It's your mother's tit.

BERTHA: Why is it her tit?

OSCAR: It looks like her tit. (*She looks again.*) Look closely.

BERTHA: Why is it hers!

OSCAR: Look at it! It's hers! It's pretty! It's pretty! Isn't it pretty! It's pretty!

BERTHA: Who says her tit was pretty.

OSCAR: I say.

BERTHA: Oh, what do you know.

OSCAR: (*Covering his chest.*) I saw it. You don't know and you'll

never know. Mother's tit was pretty and mine looks just like hers.
It was pretty. And I saw it.

BERTHA: When?

OSCAR: When! You want to know when! In the lake.

BERTHA: You never saw it.

OSCAR: Yes I did! She was swimming in the lake! And her tit floated
in the lake! I saw her naked in the lake! More than once! Naked!
Nothing on!

BERTHA: Oh, buzz off!

(*Eve enters.*)

OSCAR: (*To Bertha in a low voice.*) Don't say anything in front of her!
Don't tell her what I said. She's not one of us.—Not one of the
family.

EVE: There's someone at the door.

BERTHA: You and your lies.

EVE: What lies?

OSCAR: (*In a low voice.*) Don't tell her what I said. Shh. Don't tell her.

(*Eve exits right.*)

BERTHA: I won't!

(*Pike enters. Bertha walks to him. They walk down together. Bertha walks
to the living room, takes the album, and sits on the left stuffed chair. Pike
stands next to Oscar. Oscar sobs. Pike picks Oscar up, carries him to the
right stuffed chair, sits down cradling Oscar, hums Brahms' "Lullaby."
Oscar falls asleep. Pike stops humming.*)

BERTHA: You hear the canary?

PIKE: You never told me you had a canary.

BERTHA: I have a canary and I also have a gerbil. Would you like to
see the pictures now? (*He nods. She sits on the arm of Pike's chair and
opens the album. She points to a picture.*) This is my dog.

PIKE: A dog.

BERTHA: He died. And this is me.

PIKE: And this?

BERTHA: That's him.

PIKE: Who?

BERTHA: Oscar! I wish he were dead. (*Pointing.*) This is my mother.

(*She squints and moves the album close to her face.*)

PIKE: What.

(*She looks at another picture.*)

BERTHA: I'm looking.

(*Bertha's head moves slowly up. Pike's head moves to the picture and back.*)

PIKE: What.

(*She pushes Oscar off Pike's lap.*)

BERTHA: Her tit is different! You don't have her tit, Oscar! —

(*Oscar sits back on Pike's lap. Bertha pushes him off. They hit each other with newspapers. He retreats up the hallway and exits left. She returns to the chair, sits on the arm, picks up the album, and looks closely at the picture.*)

BERTHA: He doesn't.

(*She turns the page. She looks very closely at one of the pictures.*)

PIKE: Who's that?

BERTHA: That's my Dad.

(*She looks at the picture again. Stephen Heller's "Tarantella in E minor op 53" is heard. Oscar enters. He wears a long dress over his clothes and a veil and tiara on his head. He dances around the table in an expressionistic dance of nightmarish horror. Neither Pike nor Bertha look at him. At the end, Oscar collapses on the floor. He is out of breath and sobbing. Bertha and*

Pike start to exit right, arm in arm. As they pass, Oscar grabs Pike's leg. Pike drags Oscar as he walks. As they pass Oscar's bedroom, Oscar crawls into it. Eve enters. Oscar grabs her by the ankle and pulls her in. Pike and Bertha are heard offstage.)

OSCAR: Now's the time.

EVE: For what?

OSCAR: To kill her.

BERTHA: (*Offstage.*) Oscar, if you don't get work you're out and I'll get Pike here to take you to a home for the mentally inept. Isn't that so, Pike?

(Pike mumbles. There is the sound of the door closing. Oscar starts to have a heart attack. Eve helps him to the dining room table. He takes the newspaper from the drawer and looks for the want-ads.)

OSCAR: Handy person. Must be well organized, clean, personable.— God! (*He looks at another ad.*) Grocery. Seeking long-term employees for stocking shelves and deliveries. High school graduate. Oh god! (*He looks at another ad.*) Bookkeeper. For nursing home. Ugh. Must be kind to the elderly. Ugh. (*He looks elsewhere in the newspaper.*) Beautician. Haircuts and permanents. Also manicures. Must be talented. (*He grabs Eve.*) Eve, is there a job for me? Is there a place in the world for me? Can you get me a job? Help me.

(Bertha enters. She goes to the down side of the table. Eve puts on Oscar's jacket and goes to the hallway.)

EVE: I'm going to look for work.

BERTHA: You look just like him.

EVE: I'm wearing his jacket.

BERTHA: Well, you look ridiculous.

EVE: (*Starting to go.*) I'm getting a job.

BERTHA: (*Goes to the entrance way.*) Take off that jacket!

(Eve throws the jacket in Bertha's face. Bertha is knocked down on the floor.)

EVE: (*Offstage.*) I'll find work for him.

(*There is a shift of light. Bertha stands. Eve re-enters. She has dark circles around her eyes.*)

BERTHA: Don't tell me you got a job?

EVE: I did.

BERTHA: I'm going to have to ask you for money.

EVE: What for?

BERTHA: You live here so I'm going to ask you for money.

EVE: It's hell out there.

BERTHA: Worse than here?

EVE: Worse. Where's Oscar?

BERTHA: In bed. Reading comics. (*Eve starts to go to Oscar's bedroom.*) Where are you going?

EVE: To see him.

BERTHA: Why him? Always him!

EVE: Yes him!

BERTHA: I missed you! (*Eve goes into Oscar's bedroom. Oscar is reading a comic book.*) Don't go in there! He's a mess!

OSCAR: How did it go?

EVE: Fine.

OSCAR: You don't look well.

EVE: I don't feel well.

OSCAR: Lie down, Eve. (*Eve lies down next to Oscar.*) Eve . . . You feel warm. (*Eve gasps. Oscar puts his arm around her.*) Are you sick, Eve?

EVE: I don't feel well.

OSCAR: I hope nothing happens to you.

(There is a shift of light. Oscar goes to the dining room.)

OSCAR: Eve's sick.

BERTHA: Now Eve's sick.

OSCAR: She needs money. Take money from the box and give it to her.

BERTHA: What box? There's no money in the box.

OSCAR: Take some money from my sock then.

(He throws a sock on the table.)

BERTHA: *(Taking the sock.)* You keep money in a sock?

OSCAR: Eve gave it to me.

BERTHA: Where is she?

OSCAR: She may be in the hospital and she may be in her room.—Last night she said she was going to the hospital.

BERTHA: *(Taking money from the sock.)* How much should I give her?

OSCAR: How much is there?

BERTHA: Three fifty. Three fifty is not enough. I'm not going to give her three fifty.

OSCAR: Why not?

BERTHA: Three fifty?

OSCAR: Why not?

BERTHA: That's not enough.

OSCAR: For what?

BERTHA: Were you thinking you were going to pay for the hospital? — with that?

OSCAR: I thought it'd help.

BERTHA: To pay for what?

OSCAR: Maybe to buy food while she was there.

BERTHA: How long is she going to be there?

OSCAR: Three days.

BERTHA: Why do you think that?

OSCAR: That's a long time.

BERTHA: Maybe she'll be in the hospital three years. (*Pause.*) You're silent? Well, that may happen. Some people are in the hospital for years.—What was wrong with her?

OSCAR: She had a pain.

BERTHA: Where?

(*He points to his abdomen.*)

OSCAR: She worked too hard.—For you!

(*Oscar and Bertha go to Oscar's bedroom. Eve is lying on his bed. Bertha stands against the back wall. Oscar sits on his wheelchair at the foot of the bed.*)

OSCAR: (*To Eve.*) What were you going to say? (*Oscar's arm begins to move towards Eve.*) What did you say? (*He leans towards her.*) What?

(*Bertha grabs Oscar by the collar and pulls him out of the chair. She pushes him against the wall by the collar.*)

BERTHA: You were always closer to her. You just did. You got closer to her because you just did. She didn't ask you to. She never said you could. You just got closer to her. You never wondered if you could. (*Pushing him under the bed.*) You never wondered if she wanted you to. You just did. I never thought she wanted me. You never questioned it. It never occurred to you to question it. You wanted to be near her and you were. (*She puts her cheek next to Eve's. She whispers.*) . . . Eve . . . (*Eve's body vibrates.*)

OSCAR: (*Pushing Bertha off the bed.*) Get off her!

(*He crawls in bed.*)

BERTHA: Oh, buzz off!

OSCAR: You buzz off!

(*There is a shift of light. Pike enters and sits on the down side of the table. Bertha sits on the right of the table. Eve sits on the left. She wears a sheet around her shoulders. Oscar sits up center. They play euchre. Bertha shuffles the cards and deals three to each, then two to each. She places the cards center, then takes the top card and places it to the left. They play one round. Oscar looks at Eve adoringly. Pike mumbles.*)

BERTHA: You haven't had her yet. Have you?

OSCAR: Many times.

BERTHA: In your mind.

OSCAR: It doesn't matter where.

BERTHA: That is just not the way you do it.

OSCAR: Don't tell me how to do it.

(*They play.*)

PIKE: How's work?

OSCAR: It's not bad.

BERTHA: They haven't paid him yet.

OSCAR: I'm an apprentice.

BERTHA: Eve got paid.

OSCAR: She knew how to do it.

BERTHA: Why don't you learn.

OSCAR: I'm just getting the knack of it.

PIKE: That's good Oscar.

OSCAR: (*Playing.*) . . . yes . . .

EVE: . . . It takes time.

(*The lights begin to fade.*)

OSCAR: . . . Yes. It takes time. It's not all that easy.

END

Almost

Asleep

by

Julie

Hebert

Almost Asleep originated in a Re.Cher.Chez workshop headed by Ruth Maleczech in association with L.A.C.E. and the Otis Parsons Gallery in Los Angeles.

Cast	Priscilla Cohen, Tyra Ferrell, Patricia Mattick, Tina Preston, Deborah Slater

Collaborators:

Sculptor	John Mayne
Choreographer	Deborah Slater
Stage Manager	Liebe Gray
Taped Sound	Don Preston

Almost Asleep was presented at Intersection for the Arts, San Francisco, Paul Codiga, producer, in January 1989.

Cast	Mary Forcade, Gina Leishman, Lynn Odell, Esther Scott, Deborah Slater

Collaborators:

Composer	Gina Leishman
Sculptor	John Mayne
Choreographer	Deborah Slater

Designers:

Telephonics	J.A. Deane
Costumes	Laura Hazlett
Lighting	Novella T. Smith
Stage Manager	Robin Veder
Assistant to the Director	Elisabeth Dumont

Almost Asleep was further developed at the 1989 Padua Hills Playwrights Festival headed by Murray Mednick.

The 1989 Padua Hills ensemble was as follows:

Cast	Mary Forcade, Patricia Mattick, Tina Preston
Assistant to the Director	Kenn Norman
Lighting Design	Jason Berliner

All productions were directed by the author.

NOTES ON THE PRODUCTION OF *ALMOST ASLEEP*:

What follows is the text of a collaborative theatrical performance. Other elements that must have an equally strong presence are gestural choreography, a sculptural environment, and sound composition. The text should be dealt with rhythmically, musically, as well as literally. There are overlapping arguments, obsessive repetitions, dreamy melodic avoidances, irrational associations, suspended moments of no thought . . . all working to create a contrapuntal, psychic fugue structure. The movement stems from a precise, shared gestural vocabulary. The word "loop" in the stage directions designates repeated lines and/or gestures in random order.

The five performances represent different aspects of one woman's mind as she falls asleep one night after a confusing, humiliating encounter earlier in the day. The encounter triggers the release of long-repressed emotion.

The DREAMER is of the unconscious mind and propels the action.

The SLEEPER is of the body; she thinks and remembers through her body.

The WARRIOR and the CHATTERER are of the conscious mind; they protect against attack and silence, respectively.

And the FOOL is the intuitive child. She moves through the environment on ropes, suspended in air. She speaks in a high voice.

The first day's night had come—
And grateful that a thing
So terrible—had been endured—
I told my Soul to sing—

She said her strings were snapt—
Her Bow—to Atoms blown—
And so to mend her—gave me work
Until another morn—

And then a Day as huge
As Yesterdays in pairs
Unrolled its horror in my face—
Until it blocked my eyes—

My Brain—begun to laugh—
I mumbled— like a fool—
And tho' 'tis Years ago—that Day—
My Brain keeps giggling—still.

And something's odd—within—
That person I was—
And this one—do not feel the same—
Could it be Madness—this?

#410 Emily Dickinson

Scene 1

Five women in surreal dream-beds, sleeping in peculiar positions. They roll over in unison. Pause. They fluff pillows, then lie down in unison. Pause. They sit up, wipe noses, pull noses, lie down in unison. Pause. WARRIOR sits up sharply, quick turn to the left. She fluffs her pillow, then the others follow in unison. They all lie down except CHATTERER, who sits up, quick turn to the left, and speaks. The others, except the DREAMER, immediately begin their physical loops, and then with staggered entries, add in their verbal loops. Their verbal loops consist of their first lines plus echoes of some of the CHATTERER's lines. The DREAMER thrashes in her sleep.

CHATTERER: AGAIN APOLOGIZING FOR MY BEHAVIOR. Okay, maybe I was wrong not to be more "Positive!" Excuse me. I thought we were all adults. There was a problem. I commented. He was STUNG, poor man. They laugh when I am STUNG, they make me pay when they are STUNG. There was a problem. I commented. I'm not a bitch. I'M NOT A BITCH. There was a problem. I commented. I'm not a bitch. Okay, okay, I criticized, I criticized, I CRITICIZED. I'm shocked. It's a serious flaw. I'm shocked. A woman without grace. Harsh. Not gentle. I have gall, not good manners. I FAILED. I FAILED to surround him with warmth and acceptance. I FAILED to be his MAMA! I was unforgivably DIRECT. ONCE AGAIN I BLUNDER. ONCE AGAIN I BLUNDER. And he made me pay. He made me pay. He know the secret rules. ONCE AGAIN I BLUNDER.

WARRIOR: Fuck it. I don't have to hold his wanger when he feels bad. Fuck it. I'm not his mama.

FOOL: Me no say nothing. Nothing.

SLEEPER: Embarrassed. He grabbed me I forgive him.

(The loop is broken by the DREAMER, who wakes up and coughs. Her voice is amplified, preferably with a slight delay. The others respond to the cough, like an electric shock. They freeze then move slowly.)

CHATTERER: He grabbed my head under his arm and ruffed my hair . . . in front of my colleagues.

DREAMER: A foggy night in May dragged under another man's arm.

SLEEPER: Sweatstink.

WARRIOR: In front of everyone.

SLEEPER: Not my brother.

FOOL: He not my brother.

CHATTERER: He's my boss.

WARRIOR: I'm his boss!

CHATTERER: Boss. Boss. Nobody ever says boss anymore. Except to say there is no boss. Liars. Another secret rule. Who's the boss? Spit it out. Who's the boss?

WARRIOR: (*Matter of factly.*) I'm the boss. And that guy's gonna pay for making me look like a fool. He's got an ego like a Mack truck.

CHATTERER: Unlike you, of course.

DREAMER: A foggy night in May, headlines of my death . . .

FOOL: Nothing, nothing, nothing. Me no say nothing. Nothing at all.

CHATTERER: AGAIN APOLOGIZING FOR MY BEHAVIOR. Okay, maybe I lost control. A bit. A bit. Hyperventilation in a leader is loss of control in some books. Okay, I criticized. He was wrong. I criticized. He was wrong, and I criticized. So hold a knife to my throat and make me pay.

WARRIOR: (*Pulls out an invisible knife.*) Who's gonna pay?

CHATTERER: Why was I born a girl with a mouth and a mind like mine? I'm shocked. It's a serious flaw. I'm shocked.

SLEEPER: Bent over pressed under his arm, I see sweet cakes on the table, half-eaten, and dirty coffee cups. I feel every other person in the room, staring . . . (*Breaks.*) He wants near my body. My body.

CHATTERER: Oh he likes my body all right. He'd like to have it in a harness.

WARRIOR: Power play. He'll pay.

FOOL: I'm hungry.

SLEEPER: He likes me, it was nothing, I shook and lost my breath and couldn't speak.

CHATTERER: Overreaction. It won't happen again.

DREAMER: My secret my secret is eating me.

SLEEPER: It's nothing.

DREAMER: A foggy night in May, no breath, no voice.

CHATTERER: Why do I feel so sad? He needed a good slap and I gave it to him.

WARRIOR: And then you hyperventilated.

CHATTERER: Once again I blunder. Once again I blunder.

WARRIOR: Fuck it.

SLEEPER: He forgives me.

DREAMER: Men love to forgive women.

WARRIOR: I don't really like holding limp wangers.

CHATTERER: Maybe that's why I can't get a job.

SLEEPER: My mouth. My mouth is numb. I feel my face, aaahhhh, I look in the mirror, Who is that?

CHATTERER: There's just no escaping it, wherever I go, there I am. Different clothes, same face. Different people, same blunders.

SLEEPER: She's so worried in the mirror.

DREAMER: I should be worried.

SLEEPER: Don't look! I feel so much better. (*She feels her torso.*)

DREAMER: Look! My hair yanked from behind.

SLEEPER: I like short hair.

FOOL: I'm really hungry. I would like one of those half-eaten cakes right now.

DREAMER: Quiet.

CHATTERER: Quiet? Is something going on? I have no cake.

SLEEPER: He yanked my hair. Stinking smell. Of his armpit. I, I, I. . . (*She begins to vaguely remember something.*)

CHATTERER: Quiet. Quiet. I have to pay attention. There's something going on and we all have to be awake and alert and look it in the eye. Where is it? What's going on? I'm ready, really I am. No question. Bravery is not an issue.

WARRIOR: (*Menacingly.*) What's going on? (*CHATTERER & WARRIOR stare at the SLEEPER.*)

DREAMER: I remember . . . my hair . . .

SLEEPER: I, I, I, I . . .

ALL: (*Very softly, staggered.*) I, I, I, I . . .

SLEEPER: I forget. (*She becomes groggy and falls to her bed.*)

WARRIOR: Good. You'll sleep better.

CHATTERER: I was prepared. I was open. I was ready. I've done nothing wrong. I handled that well.

DREAMER: The foggy night in May won't go away. (*Begins to search through newspapers.*)

FOOL: Sirloin petite, please. Can I have a Sir Loin Petite? Hello, hello, come in, Sirloin Petite?

WARRIOR: (*To CHATTERER.*) You look beautiful.

CHATTERER: I do? That's funny. I've been sick.

WARRIOR: Sometimes between sickness and health, people look more beautiful.

DREAMER: Lovely, lovely suffering.

CHATTERER: I do?

WARRIOR: Yeah.

CHATTERER: I've been sick.

WARRIOR: You look beautiful.

CHATTERER & SLEEPER: Thank you.

FOOL: Garcon!

DREAMER: (*She rocks in her chair, smokes and searches the newspapers.*) No one hears me. The pictures are choking me, my throat is filled with pictures. No food, no air, no voice. I'm choking.

CHATTERER: I'm afraid to talk.

WARRIOR: Bull Shit.

CHATTERER: I conquer my fear over again every time I speak. Every time. And in the process of conquering fear I'm not paying attention to what I'm saying, so I blunder and stumble and offend people . . . which makes me afraid to speak all over again. I'm a danger to myself and others. I shouldn't be allowed to speak.

WARRIOR: I like to be alone and then I don't have to speak so I don't have to speak and then I don't have to worry.

CHATTERER: Strangers are the worst. I feel like Atlas holding up the conversation that at any moment could crush me.

(*FOOL & SLEEPER begin to sing "You Talk Too Much" very quietly and do tandem gestures.*)

CHATTERER: Acquaintances are almost as bad. Friends are okay some of the time. Family, now families vie with strangers for being the worst. Families are fragile and dangerous. I can never remember what they know about me. I don't care if they know, but they told me not to tell them certain things, so I'm always guessing what they don't want to know. For safety's sake I have a rule to strictly avoid talking about anything important.

SLEEPER: I saw a pretty dress today. I'm too grown-up for flowers.

FOOL: I like flowers, I like food. I want food.

CHATTERER: I try to keep my lover from becoming my family, but that's tricky. I'm so used to hiding that I don't trust he means what he says. But he uses the right words. He knows Names. Names of Things. So I have to do what he says, because I don't know what to call it. So, I think it helps when you know the name of something. Gives you an edge.

FOOL: (*Snaps her fingers, she's got it.*) Sirloin petite! No, that's not right, is it? Sirloin petite?

WARRIOR: It never helps to talk about anything.

CHATTERER: Maybe. Maybe not. But I think so. You have to talk. So you have to call it something so you can talk about it. But what worries me is calling it the wrong thing. Then you're in trouble. I think calling things by their right name is crucial, but it's really hard.

WARRIOR: Yeah, it's really hard.

CHATTERER: Yeah. That's what's frightening about talking.

WARRIOR: Yeah. Talking . . . (*She spits.*)

CHATTERER: Yeah.

WARRIOR: Yeah.

FOOL: What color were the flowers?

SLEEPER: Periwinkle . . .

ALL: (*Daydreaming, staggered delivery.*) Periwinkle . . .

SLEEPER: . . . with apple green leaves on a dark blue background. White raindrops fell on them. It was the prettiest dress I've ever seen.

CHATTERER: (*Pause, begins speaking slowly, still daydreaming a bit.*) Many times I realize I'm not calling something by its right name, but I keep talking anyway.

WARRIOR: Why?

DREAMER: Fear.

CHATTERER: Maybe I'll stumble into the right words if I just keep talking.

WARRIOR: Maybe you won't.

DREAMER: Fear.

CHATTERER: What an attitude! What am I supposed to do, stop talking until I have the thought exactly right? Heavens, that could take a while. I could die before I get out one good sentence. (*Song ends here.*) I can't think when I'm silent.

DREAMER: I'm afraid of silence.

CHATTERER: You with me?

WARRIOR: No.

CHATTERER: I mean, do you follow what I'm saying?

WARRIOR: No.

CHATTERER: Oh. (*Silence.*) Would you like to talk about something else?

WARRIOR: No.

CHATTERER: Okay. (*Nervous gesture.*)

DREAMER: (*Gesturing with the newspaper.*) Years Ago! Years Ago! This says, "By this time Weeks Ago!"

(*CHATTERER loops "Oh. Okay." and plays her instrument. As FOOL performs a solo on her suspended ladder. A peaceful moment of no thought.*)

DREAMER: (*To the FOOL.*) Come here. (*She does.*) Read this. (*FOOL begins to read silently.*) Out loud.

FOOL: "Last night a young woman was robbed, assaulted and raped repeatedly by two men on 24th Street between Church and Noe. Her assailants yanked her hair as she ascended the steps to her home, causing her to fall backwards and split her head open on the concrete sidewalk. One man stated repeatedly, 'I am a rapist. I am going to rape you.' Fearing discovery the men forced the woman to an isolated area behind tall grass and held her there for three hours before abandoning her. The men threatened her with a pocketknife found in her purse. The woman reported being able to see police cars cruise the street while she was being raped."

(*They all stop their movements and tasks and slowly face outward.*)

SLEEPER: Yanked.

WARRIOR: Split.

CHATTERER: Abandoned.

DREAMER: One foggy night in May.

FOOL: I didn't know that.

SLEEPER: I know this.

CHATTERER: I know this.

WARRIOR: I know this. So what?

SLEEPER: This is no secret.

DREAMER: This is not my secret.

SLEEPER: Yanked into an armpit. I remember.

WARRIOR: That's why I overreacted today.

CHATTERER: (*Correcting her.*) Hyperventilated. It's natural. A natural response. I'm forgiven. It's all right. A small slip. It's all right.

WARRIOR: Why didn't I scream?

CHATTERER: I did. I did. They covered my mouth.

WARRIOR: Why didn't I fight?

CHATTERER: I did. I did. I was bleeding. I was in shock. I fought and I was hit harder. I was unprepared. I thought it was a joke. I thought my friends were playing a joke on me and it would all go away soon.

WARRIOR: I'll never let it happen again. I'd rather die.

DREAMER: NO! I choose not to die.

ALL: (*Overlapping, not simultaneous.*) What!?

DREAMER: Floating above my body, I looked into the eyes of the rapist who feared killing. I saved my life with that look. I will not be killed now.

(*DREAMER makes a sound that scares them, perhaps a creaking door. They respond in unison.*)

SLEEPER: Sound shook me awake . . . afraid and confused . . . listening. Turn quickly . . . listen hard . . . someone walking in the hallway . . . just Loretta, right?

WARRIOR: (*A major distraction, repressing the fear with aggression. The capital letters designate a different voice. With one voice she invokes the Ratwoman for power, with the other she recounts a cartoon fantasy of her prowess.*)

Ratwomen unite. Gather round the ancient pussy rodents. We have a tale to tell, only we don't know what it is. (*Laugh.*) I KNOW WHAT NO ONE KNOW TILL IT'S TOO LATE. I FLIP BACKWARD OUT OF MY SEAT OVER THE HEADS OF SEVEN PEASANTS LANDING SQUARELY IN BACK OF THE BUS. AS THE DOOR OPENS.

Visit me, Ratwoman. Was that you scratching my neck, running blood through the mask? ONE OF THE MEN REACHES FOR A PENCIL IN MY POCKET. I SAY, "NO YOU DON'T BUDDY." Your face doesn't scare me, I haven't seen it. (*Laugh.*) I GRAB THE TWO PENCILS AND STICK HIM IN THE EYES. HE REELS BACKWARD SCREAMING IN PAIN. Who are you, Ancient Cunt?

HIS BUDDY, the pretty, CLIMBS OVER HIM AND TRIES TO GET ME, the insignificant. THINKING I'M ONLY A FRAIL WOMAN, scrabbling up the mountain alone, HE'LL LEARN NOT TO UNDERESTIMATE SHORT, DARK WOMEN. Big Butt, Skinny Fingers, Darting Eyes. I GRAB THE LUGGAGE RACK AND SWING MY POWERFUL LEGS OUT, KICKING HIM IN THE CHEST. Ugly, ugly, she don't care. ANOTHER MAN HULKS TOWARD ME, I HANDSPRING BOUNCE LANDING ON HIS

HEAD AND SQUASHING HIM.

Ratwoman don't care 'bout nothin' but eating and avoiding danger.

DREAMER: Run and hide at the mere suggestion of danger.

WARRIOR: Corner the Ratwoman, she'll bite a hole through your face to get out. A hole through your face. She don't care.

DREAMER: She doesn't think well either. She could be misreading the situation entirely and still bite a hole through your face. She's a wild rat, difficult to train.

SLEEPER, CHATTERER, FOOL: We don't care. We like her. We use her. We need her.

WARRIOR: I warn you. No joke. This Ratwoman recognizes sarcasm . . .

WARRIOR, CHATTERER, SLEEPER, FOOL (*To DREAMER.*): Bitch.

(*WARRIOR leads CHATTERER, SLEEPER and FOOL in a slow attack of the DREAMER. They echo some of WARRIOR's lines.*)

WARRIOR: You want to see skin baby? You want to see tits? You want to see holes? All the holes? Drown in them, suffocate in them. No, you can't come up for air. Yes, I will pull out all your teeth. You want me to be mama? Then we'll pull out all your hair. To start.

DREAMER: (*Overlaps previous speech.*) Approaching me bow-legged, approaching me cross-eyed. Staring. Scared. Strained. Tight smiling when I don't know what to do. Fake snarling when I don't know what to do.

(*DREAMER laughs and gestures. She makes the same sound as before. The others respond to her in unison. They hear a frightening sound in a quiet house late at night.*)

SLEEPER: Just Loretta, right . . . jiggle on the front door . . . wind blowing, wind. Listen hard, don't move. Eyes ache from being so open, ache trying to see through walls. Clammy sweat behind my knees, under my arms, in the crook of my elbows. Wishing I wasn't alone. Wishing I was alone. Wishing I wasn't alone.

Wishing I was someone else, staring at the clear, dark sky.

DREAMER: (*To SLEEPER.*) I am not afraid.

FOOL: (*Delivering the message to the SLEEPER.*) I look beautiful.

SLEEPER: Stars twinkling in the night sky. Singing by moonlight. Wading and bathing, bathing and wading in lavender moonlight. Wading and bathing in moonlit waters . . . I'm not even here anymore.

DREAMER: (*To WARRIOR.*) I am not afraid.

FOOL: (*Delivering message to WARRIOR.*) I look beautiful.

WARRIOR: I've been sick. I don't have my strength back. I don't have my strength back yet. I'll get it. Or I'll be stabbed. On the street. Late at night. I'll scream and no one will hear me. The police will arrive too late, just to take the story.

CHATTERER: (*Possibly nervous laughter.*) I'm terrified of making a false move, doing something wrong. If I'm careful no one will notice me.

DREAMER: (*To CHATTERER.*) I am not afraid.

FOOL: (*Delivering message to CHATTERER.*) I look beautiful.

CHATTERER: I'm frozen. If I'm frozen, no one can hurt me. I won't feel a thing.

(*Brief loop of the following lines.*)

SLEEPER: I'm not even here. Not even here anymore . . .

WARRIOR: I don't have my strength. I don't have my strength back yet. No one will hear me . . .

CHATTERER: If I'm frozen, no one can hurt me. I won't feel a thing.

DREAMER: (*This speech, amplified, could be said on top of the previous loop.*) I damn myself. I am weak in everything save damning myself. I learned it I learned it I learned it well. My lessons in fear choke me silent. Silence has protected me, now silence is choking me. The throat must be opened. (*She sings non-verbally and quiets the others, who become still, breathing audibly. Strange, haunting single notes, sung with conviction. Finally, the CHATTERER breaks this by moving chaotically through the room. The others make gestural loops. All loops intersect. The following three speeches overlap.*)

CHATTERER: Panic! Panic! PANIC! Bad bed, dark corridors, no shades, dirty beat up room, strange people, recurrent mentions of "girls alone . . .", recurrent warnings to always keep doors locked, complicated explanation for the double and triple locks, bad bed, dark corridor, dimly lit parking lot, broken windows covered by cardboard, cardboard, cardboard, bad bed, dirty beat up room, strange magazines, bad records, complicated explanation for the single, weak lock on the door to the street.

SLEEPER: Quick turn to the left. No one. Choking me from the past. He's forgotten me. I'll never forget him. Ever. The smell. His cheap cologne freezes my muscles. Quick turn to the left. No one. I'm sleeping in circles, circles, all different sizes. All different kinds of circles. I'm sleeping in circles and he's sleeping in lines.

WARRIOR: I'm volatile. I'm afraid of myself. I'm looking for trouble and I know it. I don't think I'm dangerous to anyone here. I'm afraid of myself, but I can probably control it. I could killl with my bare hands. As long as he doesn't bring a gun.

FOOL: (*Reading through DREAMER's newspaper clippings and throwing them on the floor.*) Where does all this sadness come from?

DREAMER: (*Sounds like an announcement in an airport.*) In case I forget, everybody dies. Many times a day. Very few people die a graceful death in their sleep when they're 95 after a three day literary illness.

FOOL: Right. (*FOOL leaps on her rope into the air, the others drop their loops and focus on her solo.*)

ALL: Right.

FOOL: If I am dying alive and please and if I am flying—Oh Dear I am falling out of the plane. (*The others laugh.*) It's not funny.

SLEEPER, WARRIOR & CHATTERER: You will still be the cutest little girl in the world.

FOOL: So if you are flying around with your wings little girl, you will be ready for the show if you die.

DREAMER: If you die . . .

(*This triggers the WARRIOR to act out a memory.*)

WARRIOR: (*Staring straight ahead. The SLEEPER responds to the WARRIOR's moves, even though the two performers are far apart.*) Tell me you love me.

DREAMER: Tell me you love me.

SLEEPER: I love you.

WARRIOR: You don't mean it.

SLEEPER: I love you.

WARRIOR: No you don't.

SLEEPER: Yes I do. I really do.

WARRIOR: You better tell me the truth.

DREAMER: You better tell me the truth.

SLEEPER: I don't love you.

WARRIOR: (*WARRIOR motions, SLEEPER responds, DREAMER actually slaps.*) Tell me you love me.

SLEEPER: (*Turns to face WARRIOR for first and only time in this sequence.*) Don't hurt me.

WARRIOR: (*Turns to face SLEEPER for first and only time in this sequence.*) I can't even hear your voice when your lips move.

SLEEPER: (*Both turn to face front again.*) I love you.

WARRIOR: You don't mean it.

SLEEPER: I love you.

WARRIOR: No you don't.

SLEEPER: Yes I do. I really do.

WARRIOR: You better tell me the truth.

DREAMER: You better tell me the truth.

SLEEPER: I don't love you.

WARRIOR: (*Slap.*) Tell me you love me.

SLEEPER: No.

WARRIOR: Use your mouth. (*Gesture of grabbing her hair.*) If you use your teeth, I'll break your neck.

DREAMER: I'll break your neck.

WARRIOR: No teeth.

SLEEPER: I wouldn't do that.

WARRIOR: You better not bitch. You better not use your teeth. You better not. (*Gesture of pulling SLEEPER's head to crotch.*)

SLEEPER: Such fat thighs—hairy all the way up—and stuck together. Fat but solid because he's young.

WARRIOR: Be careful, baby. You better make me come, baby. If I don't come, I'm gonna kill you.

DREAMER: If I don't come, I'm gonna kill you.

SLEEPER: His dick's not even hard.

DREAMER: His dick's not even hard.

SLEEPER: It doesn't even fill up my mouth. I'll grab his balls.

WARRIOR: Whatcha doin'? No way. (*Gesture of pulling her head away.*) Stick your finger up my ass.

SLEEPER: No.

WARRIOR: What? You don't like my ass? (*Laughs.*) Look what I found. Your little pocket knife. Too bad, baby. (*Repeats.*) Too bad, baby. Too bad, baby . . .

DREAMER: (*Repeats.*) Your little pocket knife. Your little pocket knife . . .

SLEEPER: (*Singing.*) Fly me to the moon and let me play among the stars, let me see what spring is like on Jupiter and Mars. In other words, hold my hand. In other words, darling, kiss me. Fill my heart with song and let me sing forever more, you are all I long for, all I worship and adore. In other words, hold my hand. In other words, darling, kiss me. (*Humming.*)

FOOL: (*Starts in middle of SLEEPER's song. She doesn't work well under pressure.*) If someone attacks you . . . if someone attacks you . . . with your own weapon . . . if someone attacks you with your own weapon . . . if someone . . . oh hell! I can't remember it. (*She writes as much as she remembers on the wall.*)

DREAMER: (*As she continues to gesture.*) There are no maps, no street signs. There are no maps, no street signs. There are no maps. There are no maps . . .

FOOL: He raped me.

DREAMER: Yes he did.

FOOL: I hate him.

DREAMER: Yes.

SLEEPER: (*Standing on her bed.*) I love men. Touching my body. Looking at me. Different from me. My body fits his body like a puzzle.

FOOL: I hate him.

SLEEPER: It was unfortunate.

FOOL: I hate him.

SLEEPER: It was a lesson.

FOOL: I hate him.

SLEEPER: I hate what happened.

FOOL: I hate him.

SLEEPER: I hate him, but I love the others.

FOOL: I hate him.

SLEEPER: I, I love the moonlight.

DREAMER: Secret Poison.

SLEEPER: I have no secrets.

CHATTERER: I can't keep secrets. I'm terrible at keeping secrets. Secrets jump right out of my mouth . . .

FOOL: (*To CHATTERER.*) Shhhhhhhh!!!!

DREAMER: I am choking.

SLEEPER: I have no secret.

DREAMER: I am choking on poison.

SLEEPER: I don't know any secrets.

DREAMER: I hate.

SLEEPER: I can't.

FOOL: I hate him.

WARRIOR: I hate them all. (*All heads turn to the WARRIOR.*) I hate men. (*She is ashamed to discover this in herself.*)

DREAMER: Down to the marrow of their bones.

WARRIOR: Down to thir bones—their bone marrow. What is it that makes them so stupid and vicious—their pricks dicks sticks—coming at us sweaty and naked with eyes rolling—floppy dick in hand—fondling heavy hairy balls. Writhing and laughing, fucking children and unwilling women—hitting and bombing and scarring and stabbing—I hate them down to my bones. Down to my bone marrow.

(*The SLEEPER is in pain. She rejects hearing this. For a while.*)

CHATTERER: (*Overlapping the end of previous speech.*) Down to my bones. Down to my bone marrow. They want to kill me and my children—they want to stab me and fuck my dead body in the stinking dark of a hallway while my babies watch and scream—and have their brains burned with, seared with the vision—branded by a man. And he has many excuses, many reasons for his insanity, his violence, his violations—

CHATTERER & FOOL: I hate him—down to the marrow of his bones—I hate him—

CHATTERER: So deeply it excites the cells of my body to remember it—

SLEEPER: (*Simultaneously with above.*) The cells of my body remember it.

CHATTERER: I tingle with the hatred of men—Bigger and Fatter and Stupider and Louder and Hairier and Stupider and Stupider and Stupider—Why? You fucking idiots—WHY DO YOU DO THE THINGS YOU DO?

FOOL: WHY DO YOU DO THE THINGS YOU DO? I hate you.

CHATTERER: Why do you kill the children and maim the women?

(*WARRIOR & CHATTERER overlap.*)

WARRIOR: I want to smash the birth head of all men beneath the heel of my boot.

CHATTERER: I want no male children sloppy brats that they are idiot drooling fumblers that they are—

SLEEPER: No touches no glances no words from men.

WARRIOR: (*Overlapping again with CHATTERER.*) I don't want to eat them and devour their poison—vile bile rising from the very marrow of their bones.

CHATTERER: —horrifying set of cells that they are—AWAY FROM ME.

SLEEPER: Not from my body.

WARRIOR: Smash the birth head to death.

(*They all breathe audibly.*)

DREAMER: More, before the throat closes.

CHATTERER: (*She complies almost unwillingly.*) Stupid thick men—you never got it and you'll never get it—one stick or another one dick or another gun or another—

WARRIOR: (*Whispered.*) Die idiot Mother fuckers!

FOOL: I hate you all.

CHATTERER: Each one—down to the marrow of your bones—

ALL: (*Overlapping very quietly through the next speech.*) Down to the marrow of your bones.

CHATTERER: Deeply sinister and wrong you are—Killers and Violators—unknowing and unseeing dick holders and pushers—sticky dicky mouth fags—suck your own vomit and come and bile and shit—suck it and die—suffocate in yourself as you try to suffocate us in you—you bombers—you flailing idiots in time—mouth and asshole wide open and spewing—you pitiful fucked up creatures—Die and Die and Die many painful deaths—All torture return to you—

ALL: (*Overlapping, not simultaneous.*) All torture return to you . . .

CHATTERER: Who owns it. I hate your mind your body and your soul—Down to the marrow of your . . .

ALL: (*Not in unison, CHATTERER leading, others quiet.*) Bones. Down to the marrow. Down, Down, Down. To the marrow. Of your bones.

(*All breathing audibly.*)

DREAMER: Ah. (*She begins to breathe and feel her throat, something has been dislodged, released. Eventually, CHATTERER and WARRIOR speak, overlapping in whispers.*)

CHATTERER: What was that? Careful. Harsh. Gonna pay. Gonna pay.

WARRIOR: I'm an asshole, a stupid asshole. Gonna have to pay for that.

SLEEPER: I didn't mean it. (*All stop.*) I didn't mean it. Don't hurt me. (*C & W resume their loop above and SLEEPER joins them with hers.*)

DREAMER: Ssshhhhhhhh. Calm. It's all right. It's all right.

(*CHATTERER and WARRIOR join the SLEEPER, sitting at the foot of her bed, three in a row. They have a gestural conversation through the next lines, crossing their legs, turning their heads like birds, wiping their noses, etc.*)

SLEEPER: I like men. Many, many, many men I like very, very, very much.

WARRIOR: I can't say I really like them.

CHATTERER: I'll, uh, I'll go with the majority on this one. Somebody speak up and tell me what to think about what just happened. I'm, uh, I'm kind of at a loss as to what to say here.

WARRIOR: I don't really like them, but that was harsh.

SLEEPER: Harsh, mean, ugly lies. . .

CHATTERER: Harsh, unnecessary, not true. . .

WARRIOR: A little bit true. . .

SLEEPER & CHATTERER: I don't know what you mean.

WARRIOR: No, right. Too harsh. I'll find another way. . .

CHATTERER: Something more acceptable. . . more polite. . .

SLEEPER: More like that beautiful dress. . .

DREAMER: Stop! Don't choke me.

WARRIOR: I'll be punished.

CHATTERER: I'll be punished.

SLEEPER: I'll be punished.

DREAMER: Look at my face. Look at my rage. (*Repeats*)

(*The WARRIOR turns to look at the DREAMER.*)

CHATTERER: And yet, you know, uh, there was an unmistakable ring of truth to it, uh, . . .

SLEEPER: To what?

CHATTERER: The feeling.

SLEEPER: To what?

CHATTERER: You're right. It's not practical. You can't just walk down the street feeling something like that. You know, you know, I, I, I, I, I, I, I just don't, I, I, I, I just don't, uh, actually think, I just don't actually think something like that is healthy.

DREAMER: Wrong, wrong. Can anyone hear me? (*Whispered.*) Don't run away. Don't shut me up.

FOOL: What's going on? I thought we hated them.

SLEEPER: I like men. Mark, Luke, John, and Matt. Paul, Michael, Andrew, Mitchell, Brad. Earl, Percy, Nelson, Oscar. Jose, Jamie, Lloyd, Ellis. Gregory, Ray, Curly, Joe. Ian, Demo, and Jesse.

DREAMER: (*Interrupting.*) This is not about them. This is about me. I prefer fear to anger. I prefer fear and silence. Say it.

FOOL: I prefer rear sand filence.

WARRIOR: Sorry. I shot my mouth off.

FOOL: I refer rear.

WARRIOR: I'm an asshole. I'm as bad as I say they are. Why pay any attention to me? I'm a fucking asshole with a big mouth.

DREAMER: I hate myself.

FOOL: I ferear fear.

WARRIOR: Once again I blunder.

WARRIOR & CHATTERER: Once again I blunder.

FOOL: I prefear fear.

SLEEPER: Have I blundered?

WARRIOR: Have I blundered?

CHATTERER: Have I blundered?

DREAMER: I have scared myself too much.

FOOL: (*To the DREAMER.*) I prefer fear. And silence.

DREAMER: Many ways to open the throat. No blame. (*She retreats.*)

FOOL: Skull pain? Skull pain? Skull ache? Skull ache? Skull head . . . Skull head . . . Skull head pain . . . Head pain . . . Head pain . . . Headache! Headache, I have a headache!

CHATTERER: (*Very softly, these words make a soft sound bed.*) What's the matter with these fingernails—they're completely terrible—I mean they used to be—well they always were paper thin—but not—this flaking—off in strips—painfully thin in hot water—you know this has gone on for months—there was a short hiatus for a few weeks—god only knows what I accidentally did right—then they started again with this horrible affliction—what—gelatin pills—is that it—vitamins—where is the lovely crescent moon at the base of the nail—that delicate female crescent—attacked by slight ill health—slight lack of attention—slight lack of information—can beauty be found in a cookbook—is there a recipe or more—yes—but it's a secret—to be bought bought bought— sought sought sought—fought fought fought. Ah me. My head aches.

SLEEPER: (*Singing, overlapping the above speech.*)
Do I dare tell you why
I cried
Yesterday for hours

I could not sleep
I had no dreams

WARRIOR: (*Joining SLEEPER.*)
There was a blackness that settled
And blinded by mind's eye

I could not see

I felt the blades in my brain

In and out
   In and out
      In and out

WARRIOR: Where does all this fucking sadness come from?

DREAMER: A pool of tears, dark blue and very still, fathomless human water.

WARRIOR: I don't like it.

DREAMER: I will not drown. I will not choke. I will not be stabbed to death.

WARRIOR: I don't know that. I don't know what's going to happen.

DREAMER: I never will.

WARRIOR: I was attacked.

DREAMER: It's true.

FOOL: If you're attacked . . . if you're attacked with your own weapon . . . and you survive . . . good! that's the next part . . . and you survive . . . very important that you survive . . .

WARRIOR: I was attacked.

FOOL: And I survived! Very important to know.

WARRIOR: I was attacked. And I survived. I was attacked. And I survived. . .

(*All characters participate in a gestural, vocal loop. The SLEEPER continues her singing.*)

CHATTERER: I've been sick. I didn't sleep well last night. I'm on medication. The signs are *tres* terrible. I don't know where I am. I can't find the damned road.

DREAMER: It's true. It's all true. Truth is more than I can hold in my mind in one moment. It's true. It's all true . . .

(They are interrupted by a loud ringing. At first it sounds like an air raid, then it gradually melts into the sound of a telephone ringing. During the ringing and the DREAMER's dream, the others run around the room very quickly, circle their beds several times, then dive onto their mattresses into a sleeping position.)

DREAMER: *(Very fast.)* There were four people each at a single bed, packing four suitcases with deheaded gutted fish with scales, layer after layer. I almost finished when I realized my last fish had not been cleaned. I slit its belly and gutted it. There was blood, but it was not messy. I took a large razor sharp spoon and scooped the head off. I realized I had left part of the head on, and had to finish the job.

(They sit up in unison, phone stops ringing, and they gesture chorally.)

ALL *(Simultaneously.)*: Hello. Oh, hi. No, I wasn't sleeping. Just lying here doing nothing. I'm glad you called. How are you? Good. Oh, I'm fine, fine. Are you coming over? Oh. That's okay. It's just as well. Actually, I'm feeling kind of sick. I think it's that medicine I took for my sinuses. I wouldn't be much fun tonight. *(She laughs at something he says.)* Oh. Okay. You're sweet. I'll talk to you tomorrow. Okay. Bye.

CHATTERER: *(Pause.)* I'm depressing. No wonder he doesn't want to come over. Who would want to talk to a melancholy, paranoid female? Oh-ohhhhh, she's too moody, oh-ohhhhh, ten-foot pole time.

WARRIOR: Shut up.

CHATTERER: Thank you, I needed that. I'll see him tomorrow. Everything's fine. Nobody knows.

WARRIOR: Everything's fine. Nobody knows.

CHATTERER: He didn't see me humiliated this afternoon with my head under my boss's armpit.

SLEEPER: Just kidding around.

WARRIOR: Making me pay.

DREAMER: Waking me up.

CHATTERER: He doesn't know my secrets.

WARRIOR: He doesn't know.

DREAMER: Unless I tell him.

CHATTERER: Can't do that. He'll leave.

WARRIOR: Or laugh.

DREAMER: He won't leave. . .

CHATTERER: He's got his own secrets to protect.

DREAMER: . . . but I might.

CHATTERER: Everybody's so busy worrying about themselves, they hardly notice anyone else.

SLEEPER and FOOL: I notice him.

DREAMER: Sometimes.

CHATTERER: (*Pause.*) It's lonely at my house.

WARRIOR: It's better that way.

CHATTERER: Doesn't feel good.

WARRIOR: If I'm alone then I'm alone then I don't have to speak then I don't have to worry.

CHATTERER: If I could speak, what would I say?

WARRIOR: (*Thinks it over for a second.*) I know I can be attacked. At any moment. I have reason to protect myself. I have reason. I know the truth and nobody wants to hear it. But I don't care, I'm on guard.

CHATTERER: I probably won't get attacked tonight.

WARRIOR: You never know.

CHATTERER: I haven't been attacked in many years.

WARRIOR: So?

CHATTERER: The windows are locked. The doors are locked. It's a safe neighborhood. The bad guys are hurting somebody else tonight.

DREAMER: No. They're still hurting me after all this time.

FOOL: I'm feeling better.

WARRIOR: I gonna doze for awhile, so I'll be sharp in the dead of night.

CHATTERER: I'll sit here.

WARRIOR: Good. (*WARRIOR arranges her weapons of protection for the night.*) Stay awake.

CHATTERER: I will.

WARRIOR: Don't leave.

CHATTERER: I won't.

WARRIOR: Play a lullabye.

CHATTERER: I will. (*CHATTERER plays her instrument. WARRIOR falls asleep holding her weapon. CHATTERER sings a wordless lullabye.*)

FOOL: Aaahhhh. (*Enjoying the peacefulness.*)

DREAMER: There is a dog in my throat. A Golden Retriever.

FOOL: (*Softly.*) Aaaaaarrrrooooooooooo.

SLEEPER: Sleeping.

DREAMER: No, not sleeping. Silent. I want to speak to the dog.

SLEEPER: Mute.

DREAMER: What do you say, Dog?

SLEEPER: Can't speak.

DREAMER: Yes he can. Dog, speak.

SLEEPER: (*She makes a rusty, scratchy sound coming from a long unused throat.*) Aaaaaaaaaaarrrrrrrrrrrrr.

DREAMER: (*Joining her.*) Aaaaarrrrrrr.

FOOL: (*Joining them.*) Aaaarrrrooooo.

DREAMER: What do you say?

SLEEPER: Nothing.

DREAMER: Why do you say nothing?

SLEEPER: Debris. In my throat.

DREAMER: Cough it up.

SLEEPER: Stuck.

DREAMER: Just a little. Speak a little of it.

SLEEPER: Makes no sense.

FOOL: So what?

DREAMER: Of course not. It's only debris.

SLEEPER: Too much. It's all too much.

DREAMER: Yes.

SLEEPER: Many collisions.

DREAMER: Yes. What is the worst thing that makes no sense

SLEEPER: (*Self-mocking tone.*) "I hate sexz . . . and I looooove it."

DREAMER: Last night he touched my thigh.

SLEEPER: Sweetness. Feeling good. Feeling good. Then sticking
things into me. Freezing. Freezing up. Freezing inside. My
vagina is a mine field. Careful. Hold on tight. Don't let him in. . .
to touch . . . me. Hold my body tense, fantasy in mind, and no one
is home to kiss my lover. From a distance, the ocean approaches.
Oh I want it. To come to me. The obliteration. I want it. I see
ivory lace and swollen sex and a wall of water above me. I lunge
and rock. Ah. Then. The sea surges in me again.

I open my eyes to the mysterious face of a man staring at me. Who is he? Where have I been? I feel caught, like I've cheated. I cry and say, "Do I have something to be sorry for, do I, do I?" And he says, "No, nothing, everything's fine." And it isn't. And we both know it. It's sad. It's so sad.

DREAMER: Why is no one home in my body?

SLEEPER: Horrible pictures tucked into my vagina must not be touched. On my knees, a stinking penis in my mouth, my face forced into the crotch of a vile man. Staring into space, a fat, greasy rapist grunting on top of me, calling me baby. "If I don't come, I'm gonna kill you, baby."

DREAMER: "If I don't come, I'm gonna kill you, baby."

SLEEPER: His penis, so soft. I hate penises in my mouth, I hate pubic hair in my mouth, I hate semen in my mouth, I hate the smell of assholes. I don't want anybody to touch me. Ever. Ever again. Ever. Who bludgeoned me? My mouth hurts. My jaw hurts. My back hurts. My head is bloody and aching. No one helps me. My face sliced open with a hatchet, and no one notices. And I pretend I'm fine, so as not to disturb them. Nice people don't talk about rape, and terror, and dying, and forcing stinking dirty penises into the mouths of stunned young girls.

DREAMER: Help me. I want my body back.

SLEEPER: No one to help. No one to trust. No point in telling. All to fear from soft and open. All to fear from talking.

WARRIOR: (Wakes up.) Only the truly uninformed believe the world is a good place, but it is all we've got, so I toughen up and move along. I'm nothing special.

SLEEPER: I'm nothing special.

WARRIOR: So I was raped. So what. A boy's uncle beat him with a hose everyday because he tried to eat. A girls's father fucked her twice a week, and her mother knew about it. My pain is nothing special.

SLEEPER: My pain is nothing special.

WARRIOR: So I was fucked by two strange guys on the street. So what. Didn't I fuck strangers before that. The rapists left no scars, nobody cut me, nobody shot me, nobody strangled me. Too bad, I got fucked one night. We're talking about one night, hell, about three hours! Poor me, I don't like sex! You think it matters? (*Laugh.*) No. (*She goes back to sleep.*)

SLEEPER: I hate myself.

DREAMER: Yes.

FOOL: I love you.

SLEEPER: I want to wear a flowered dress and sing in the moonlight. And forget.

DREAMER: Let the dog sing and talk and tell and talk and talk and remember.

SLEEPER: No one to tell.

FOOL: Tell me.

DREAMER: The dog will talk and I will show my true face.

SLEEPER: Hatchet slice and all?

DREAMER: Hatchet slice and all.

SLEEPER: Who to?

DREAMER: Who to?

FOOL: Who to?

SLEEPER: (*A sigh.*) Ohhhh.

FOOL: I go slowly. Hello. Hello?

SLEEPER: So tired.

DREAMER: Sleep deeply.

SLEEPER: My thigh is my earth, most flesh of all my flesh. What does she hear when I'm dreaming?

DREAMER: Dogs on gravel roads, old three-story houses, delta and oak trees and too much heat and picking pole beans in the garden at twilight, a nameless faceless infant, notebooks and sculptures and funky libraries and old pianos and singing and dancing old women in dirty dresses working real hard. Sweaty days and powdery nights. (*Repeats last line as SLEEPER goes to sleep.*)

FOOL: I've got it! Filet mignon, filet mignon, not sirloin petite! Hello, come in, I want filet mignon, filet mignon!

DREAMER: Too late.

FOOL: I'm hungry.

DREAMER: What's that saying? If you're attacked with your own weapon. . .

FOOL: . . . and you survive. . .

DREAMER: . . .you are foolish,

DREAMER & FOOL: but you will live forever!

FOOL: That's it. I live forever, me live forever! (*In her exuberance, she runs into the wall and hits the deck.*)

DREAMER: I am foolish. And I will live forever.

FOOL: Me no know nothing. (*DREAMER finishes writing the axiom on the wall.*)

FOOL: Me wanna be

Good.
Just okay
Okay.
Selfish Little Girl
Want pretty things
Want people
Go oooooooh
Pretty little girl
Oooooooh.
Me want Pretty Little Girl go away.
Leave me alone.

Who me is?
No Pretty Little Girl.
Just me.

You see me. . .

Who me is?
Me hiding
Behind
Pretty Little Girl

Who me is,
Sad Linda?

Everybody big busy
For me
Big parade
Going on.

But me
Still here.
Mystery me
Still
Here
Still.

Tired.
No perky.
Where gone
Me?
Where gone?
Oh you
Linda
Linda

Oh you
Linda
No need
Carry so much.
Things they is
Much easy
Much easy
Much easier

Than you think.

Ah Linda
My Linda

How to walk like this?
Clear and soft
No effort.
Here is Linda

Linda is not sad.

(*As the FOOL climbs into her sleeping position, the DREAMER walks to each of the other beds and gathers a thin cord from each. She then proceeds on her way out into the Dreamworld, singing her strange, haunting notes.*)

CHATTERER: (*Having resumed playing her lullabye.*) The Dreamer doesn't know the way out, though she walks it every night. She wades into the Stream of Forgetfulness and remembers what she has forgotten a thousand times. The dream river licks her feet. Tears from the bottomless pool wash the souls that wade.

(*Pause.*)

SLEEPER: (*Sits up abruptly.*) You know what I . . .

(*All heads turn to her, then she slips back to sleep without completing her thought. The DREAMER exits the theatre as lights fade.*)

END

KINDLING

BY

LEON

MARTELL

Kindling was first performed at the 1990 Padua Hills Playwrights Festival with the following cast:

Lucille	Molly Cleator
Roger	Rick Dean
Barry	Leonard Donato
George	Jim Haynie
Director	Leon Martell
Assistant Director	Susan Hayden
Lighting Design	Jason Berliner

NOTES:

Though the play seems "realistic," there are abstract elements. The language, costumes and set elements are "realistic," but the short scenes are broken by a "Mooing" tape, which should be a loud "sound effect," not an attempt to convince the audience there are cows off stage. The "work" the characters do is abstract. The gesture of work. They build things with real boards and hammers, but no nails, so everything they build immediately falls apart. All their labor should have this futility which they don't overtly recognize. When they shovel manure, it's glued to the fork — they shovel the same forkfull over and over. Also, whenever the rural characters stand at the fence down stage, they are able to speak their mind *to* the audience in a fearless manner impossible in their real lives.

SET:

The play happens on and around George's farm. The set is a general purpose "barn yard." The play is very episodic and the space should function as a fluid playing area. Upstage, a shed or barn area, from which tools can be retrieved. Up center, down from the shed, a large deciduous tree (or suggestion of such). Stage right, center, a pile of brush/small-fire wood. Center, a hole with a crude wooden cover over it — a dry well. Down center, a stump/small-log. Down, right center, a small piece of an aged white fence. There are old boards scattered about.

"Barry's property" is somewhere, not far, off left. References to his place are directed off left. On one occasion he is trimming a bush — represented by an obviously dead branch stood up against the wall, upstage left.

CHARACTERS:

ROGER (In his mid thirties, large, strong and very shy. He stutters
   very badly, varying from mildly when talking to George to virtually
   unable to speak when talking with Barry.)

GEORGE (Late sixties. Due to advanced emphysema, he coughs and
   spits constantly. He stutters when particularly excited.)

LUCILLE (Mid to late twenties. Sexy and alluring in an offbeat way.
   She is in advanced stages of pregnancy.)

BARRY (Mid thirties. Handsome, very urban in appearance. He's a
   middle weight T.V. star.)

The play happens over roughly a month in "real time."

Scene 1

"I Can Tell By the Way You Smell," by Ry Cooder, plays. As it fades out, Roger, in worn work clothes, enters, carrying a chain saw. He moves to downstage center. He gives the audience a serious look. He yanks the starter cord on the chain saw. Nothing happens. He yanks it a couple more times. Nothing. He becomes immersed in starting the chain saw. He steps back to the downstage fence and rests on it, lowering his head. When he lifts his head he directly addresses the audience. Whenever anyone goes to the fence, they are empowered to address the audience.

ROGER: A f-f-f-farmer and his boys were out hayin'—when a flat lander come up to 'em.

(FLAT LANDER): Certainly is a lovely farm you and your sons have here.

(FARMER): Eyat.

(FLAT LANDER): Of course the frost comes so early here and the top-soil is particularly thin and rocky—what do you grow up here?

(FARMER): Men.

(Roger spits and returns to the chain saw. He tries a couple more pulls then takes it up center to work on it.)

(George emerges from hiding. He's an older man in bib overalls. He stutters. He's oblivious to the audience. He throws twigs at Roger playfully. He keeps it up as Roger tries to ignore him, concentrating on the saw. Eventually Roger just can't stand it anymore, picks up a rock and heaves it at him.)

ROGER: Jesus Christ, Pa!

(George ducks into cover and laughs. Roger returns to fixing the saw. The game is over, George emerges. During this conversation Roger stutters moderately and on occasion, so does George.)

GEORGE: If I was an Indian, you'd be scalped.

ROGER: If yyyyou was an Indian, IIII'd be an Indian ya stupid shit.

GEORGE: Hey! Don't call me that kind a' shit! (*George hawks up and spits.*)

ROGER: And yyyyou'd be dead—from that shit in your lungs. If din't have noooo doctor, noooo medicint—you'd been dead last winter.

GEORGE: Nah—they used to be able to take a plant right outta the woods 'n fix theirselves up. You laugh, but that's what they did. All this doctors 'n high price medicint is just a racket.

ROGER: Then you'd be dead from some Iiiindian disease.

GEORGE: No—people didn't used to get the kinda shit I got. It's all the chemicals they put in the food. (*Watching Roger work.*) You ain't never gonna start that piece of shit. If you'd go on that wood with the buck saw you'd had it all done by now.

ROGER: Bull shit too.

GEORGE: Christ, when I was young I could cut almost as much wood as that chain saw when it's working—you gotta spend so much time to fuck around with it you don't ever ggggget to use the fucking thing.

ROGER: You ccccould cut as much wood as this chain saw?

GEORGE: Pret' near.

ROGER: Well why don't you do it then?

GEORGE: When I was young I said!

ROGER: Well, I wish to fuck I'd been around then to stack it for you.

(*Roger goes to smash the chain saw.*)

GEORGE: DON'T BREAK THAT!!!!!

ROGER: You said it's piece a' sh-sh-sh-, no good.

GEORGE: Well, we paid for the son of a bitch—you shoon't break it— maybe you can get it fixed—

ROGER: Last time I took it in, Ol' Whitney said it was pppplayed out, not worth fiiiixing anymore.

(*George takes the saw into the shed and tinkers with it.*)

GEORGE: He's just tryin' to sell you a new saw.

(Roger gathers up boards around the yard, stacking them with a vengeance.)

ROGER: He said we ccccan't be cuttin' logs all 'a time with that dinky saw. I gotta do my chores.

(Roger begins to exit.)

GEORGE: You be sure to close the gate down there, those cows get on that De-tec-ative's lawn he'll holler like hell!

ROGER: *(Stopping.)* What are you tellin' me? You the one forgets it alla time.

GEORGE: You seen him?

ROGER: Yeah I seen him.

GEORGE: He looks different than he does on the T.V., don't he?

ROGER: Ain't all of us can stay up all hours to watch that shit.

GEORGE: You never bitched when I was up all night workin' at the fuckin' tannery, breathin' lime and chemicals so we could afford to keep this place goin'. I got so's I don't need no sleep.

ROGER: Yeah. You're just sleep walkin' alla time.

GEORGE: Prob'ly a good thing too. If you're just gonna stand there, fix the cover on that well.

(Roger takes a bucket with hammer and nails in the bottom. He hammers on the well cover but doesn't use the nails.)

GEORGE: If I ever woked up an' seen the shitty mess the world's in, I'd prob'ly have a heart attack an' croak on the spot. I'm fuckin' retired. If I want to sit up an' watch T.V. with Lucille, by the Jesus I'm goin' to.

ROGER: It's all just a buuuunch a bullshit —' bout people in California. That fellah, he's supposed to come up here to get away. Whaaat's he gonna get away from, he's onna T.V. He'll just bring all that up here with him. They'll say he's up here in the Eeeenquirer or some shit an we'll have every old aunt in the world up here.

GEORGE: You talk to him?

ROGER: No, he told Lucille . . . She talked to him.

GEORGE: WOW. She recognize him right off. She said right out, "He's that guy onna T.V. He's that detec-a-tive." (*Laughs.*) He drives like hell (*Laughs.*)

ROGER: That's all fffake, it's somebody else drivin'. They just make it look like him . . . that 's what he tole Lucille.

GEORGE': Boy she's gettin' an earful from that guy hunh?

ROGER: Well what's he gonna do to her? She's already knocked up!

(*George hands Roger the saw.*)

GEORGE: Try dat.

(*Roger goes to the brush pile, sets up a limb for cutting. Pulls the starter cord—nothing.*)

ROGER: I'm goin' to do my chores.

(*Roger exits up right. George calls after him.*)

GEORGE: Careful you don't get scalped.

(*George steps up to the fence, sings.*)

> Elle et morte
> la vach a Marriot
> elle et morte
> et don terre'.

GEORGE: You don't speak French? Hell, I don't anymore neither — there ain't been nobody to talk to for so long. My wife Mary use' to speak real good, but she's gone. She's dead. (*Sings to tune of "Tipperary".*)

> It's a long way
> to tickle Mary—
> it's a long way
> to go—

(He coughs and spits up.) Oh—son of a bitch.

(He exits up right. We hear tape of cows mooing loudly. Lights shift to inform us we're in another place.)

Scene 2

Lucille and Barry enter from up left. They've been talking for a while. Lucille wears a house dress. She's aglow with pregnancy and the excitement of a fan meeting a star. She's pretty and girlish here. Barry wears a Hawaiian shirt, shades on top of his head. He's comfortably trendy/rural.

LUCILLE:—I got two other kids, two-and-a-half and 1.

BARRY: You must like children.

LUCILLE: I love my babies.

BARRY: How long you been married?

LUCILLE: Three years, but we went out together, off an' on, for three years before that. *(She points off.)* That big tree there, that's your property line. *(They start to wander back the way they came.)*

BARRY: *(Pointing to an imagined bush in audience.)* These bushes flower?—In season?

LUCILLE: Bleedin' hearts. You know those bleedin' hearts, I think that's what these were—there's no blossoms now, but there will be in the spring—'less you gonna put somethin' else in?

BARRY: I don't know . . . I like this Queen Anne's lace.

LUCILLE: You do? That's a weed.

BARRY: It's pretty.

LUCILLE: Well, we got too much of it around here, and it's no good for nothin'. Cows won't eat it, and it makes some people sneeze. Not me. I'm healthy as a horse. Good breedin' stock. *(Pause.)* Your wife sure is pretty. She a model?

BARRY: She was. We're not married, but we've been together for a long time. Longer than you and Roger.

LUCILLE: Oh! Roger's not my husband. My husband is in town. I just come and stay up here sometimes. It's not good for me to be around my husband when I'm pregnant, so I come up here. He . . . plays too rough, an' could hurt the baby, so I get out of his way. But I love him, and he loves his girls, me an' the two little ones . . . an' whatever this (*Touches her belly.*) is. (*She continues.*) You gonna build a fence?

BARRY: For what?

LUCILLE: To keep your fans out.

BARRY: Fuck me, I hope not.

(*She's taken aback.*)

BARRY: Oh, I'm sorry. Did I offend you?

LUCILLE: Oh, no I'm—I mean—fuck me! I'm just surprised. I never heard that come outta your mouth before.

BARRY: Yeah—you disappointed?

LUCILLE: No. Why should I be? I hear that kinda thing from Roger and his dad all the time. I guess it's just, you been to college, right? (*He nods.*) and you live in Hollywood and everything—I just figured you'd have something better to say.

BARRY: You are disappointed.

LUCILLE: No. It's kinda special. How many people get to hear you swearin'. Sayin' what you think, not words from some T.V. show. It's excitin'. (*Pause.*) Fuck me!

(*We hear the mooing. They exit up left, abruptly. Lights shift.*)

Scene 3

Roger and George enter from up right, hauling a pile of old boards.

GEORGE:—pigs feet, head cheese, wild leeks, wild blueberries we'd get from under the power lines, where they cut the brush. You need sower ground for blueberries—

(They lay out the lumber to build a box, Roger gets the nail bucket and they nail corners, using the hammer but no nails. Roger raises each corner and holds it for George to nail it. When the "nailing" is complete, Roger lets go and the corner disintegrates. They don't notice. They nail each corner in turn, working around and around, actually accomplishing nothing, throughout the scene.)

ROGER: Don't pppick those no more, Pa! They spray that weed killer, that Aaaarmy Orange, on the brush now stead a' cuttin' it. The blueberries ain't no good no more . . .

GEORGE: That's just a racket . . . to make you buy 'em at the store. I even eeeet blackbirds with that ol' Ay-talian lived in that huntin' camp on the Dome. The thing is, you can live off the land here.

ROGER: How'm I sposed to gggget my milk cans down to the co-op if I ain't got no gas money?

GEORGE: You gotta cut some more a' them logs—we still got a couple a' them big oaks left. Or maybe they'll put in a Democrat again. Nobody helped the farmer since Roosevelt—Kennedy was gonna do somethin'—so they shot him.

(Roger looks off left.)

ROGER: Sssshit, what the hell is ssshe bbbringing in here?

(George and Roger focus hard on their work.)

(Lucille and Barry enter from up left. George and Roger ignore them, moving from corner to corner until they're practically running before them.)

LUCILLE: Hey! Roger, Pa—this is Barry. "Nick Slade—Private Investigator".

BARRY: How you doing?

(He extends his hand. George takes his hand and looks him in the eye.)

GEORGE: What you come up here for?

BARRY: Whoa. Well—uh—you mean over here to your place—or up here to live?

GEORGE: Yeah, why you want to come up here?

BARRY: Well, if you must know. The air's fresh, it's so green here — it's beautiful here. Don't you think it's beautiful?

GEORGE: I spose so—(*Cough. Spit.*) Wait till it gets cold.

BARRY: It gets kind of chilly even now. It amazes me how it can be so cold in the morning till the sun gets up. In fact I was wondering, Lucille said Roger could give me some advice on our fireplace? (*Barry moves toward Roger.*) It's not making enough heat. Like I said, the mornings get kind of brisk so I just tested it out and— something seems to be wrong. It's not warming the room. Am I burning the wrong kind of wood or what?

(*When Roger answers he stutters terribly.*)

ROGER: SSSSS'nnnnno gggggood.

BARRY: I beg your pardon.

ROGER: Fffffor he-he- he-heat.

BARRY: For heat? The fireplace?

ROGER: Yyyyy—(*he nods.*)

BARRY: Isn't that what Mr. Montgomery used when he lived there? Isn't it?

ROGER: Nnnnnn—

GEORGE: Nope. He had a wood stove. His son took it away before he sold the place to you.

BARRY: But, could I use the fireplace? It's one of the reasons I bought the house. It's the original authentic fireplace. I mean, people used to heat with fireplaces.

GEORGE: Froze their asses off too. Heat goes up the chimney and it pulls in the cold air from outside.

BARRY: Well, I guess that leaves me out in the cold. (*Laughs—alone.*) so what should I do, get a wood stove? I'm asking you.

ROGER: (*Stuttering badly.*) oi-oi-oi oil fur-fur-fur—.

(Roger gives up. Barry guesses.)

BARRY: Oil furnace?

GEORGE: Nah, get a wood stove. Cook on it, heat your water—an' you can burn wood right off the lot. Then you don't have to deal with the oil truck tryin' to get up this hill in the winter.

LUCILLE: That's right. Just when it's the coldest and you need oil the most, the road's too bad for that fat old tanker to come up here.

GEORGE: You burn wood you don't have to pay attention to none a' that shit. They say there ain't no coal and oil left—that's just a racket to drive the price up. If there ain't no coal what the fuck's burnin' down in the earth then. Makin' all that fire in them volcanoes an' 'at? Hunh?

BARRY: Uh—I don't know. *(He does but won't confront the argument.)* So, a wood stove seems to be the answer. I like the smell of a wood stove. Probably because I quit smoking—the stove does it for me. *(Laughs. Lucille tries to be supportive.)* I'll order one from the dealer in town. Thanks a lot for the advice, nice to meet you—finally. George. *(Shakes hands.)* *(Talking as if Roger is deaf and stupid.)* Nice to meet you, Roger. *(Shakes.)* I'll be seeing you.

(He starts to exit left.)

LUCILLE: *(Whispers to Roger and George.)* He's so nice!

(She follows Barry off. Roger follows a little way staring after them.)

GEORGE: When we come up here, everybody said, "Dey won't last one winter and they'll be off that mountain . . . 38 years we're still up here.

ROGER: Well every asshole in the wwworld ca-ca-can come up here now. Cccchrist all you need is a fffour-wheel drive and you can live anywhere. Eeeverybody's got 'em. Down street. I seen women in dreeesses an' hi-hi-high heels with four-wheel drives could climb right up this road in the winter—and we-e-e-e're the only son-of-a-bitches still don't have one.

GEORGE: What the hell you so pissed off about? You got everything. What's to bitch about.

ROGER: I got nooothing. I got what you ggggot and but now it's all leeess—now I got it, aaaan'—it doesn't make any sense.

GEORGE: It's the Republicans!

(The mooing cuts the scene. George exits into the shed and Barry enters as lights shift.)

Scene 4

Roger works on the box while Barry tries to yank one limb out the bottom of the pile. Roger is trying to move the box more centerstage. It falls apart. He tries to deal with it, moving it a piece at a time and reassembling it.

ROGER: Yyyyou ought to wwwwear gloves if you're going to handle wood like that—with your hands.

BARRY: Actually I was hoping this would give my hands a little character. *(He rests.)* When I was a kid I used to look at my grandfather's hands and think mine would be like that when I grew up. He had cracks in his skin as big as my fingers. He used to let me help him in his garden, he had one of those little alley gardens in Brooklyn—and when we'd get cleaned up we'd each get on the opposite end of the towel and dry off—his big dark hands rolling the white towel—I always wanted hands like that— character.

ROGER: Yyyou'll get bliiisters.

BARRY: That'll do for now.

(Mooing cuts the scene. Lights shift. Barry travels to far left and waits.)

Scene 5

George enters from the shed carrying two manure forks with fake manure attached. As they work they shovel the same manure endlessly into the box, which now acts as manure spreader. As the mooing stops, Barry enters.

BARRY: Afternoon George, Roger. *(They nod.)* you know—shit—I'm sorry to bug you about this—but, I promised Michelle I'd bring it up—it's the manure pile. I know you've had it here forever but, here's the problem. I'm sure Mr. Montgomery was totally used to the smell of it, but my girl friend is made of weaker stuff than Mr. Montgomery—she's never really lived out of the city her entire life— she's used to a controlled environment and—she gets sick when the wind from your manure pile blows our way. It's just when the wind shifts—but it's enough to upset her. In fact she went back to New York for awhile, but I promised her I'd talk to you about it.

GEORGE: What do you want to know?

BARRY: Could you move it, maybe to the other side of the barn? I'd be happy to pay for the cost of moving it—to keep peace in my home. So—(*Pause.*) is that possible?

(*Roger stutters horrifically.*)

ROGER: We're sp-sp-sp-sp-reeeeeadin' it.

BARRY: Yeah, I've seen this old wagon that flings it up in the air and all over—yeah.

GEORGE: In another week, we won't have no manure pile left. It'll all be spread out on the field—it gets built up in the winter. You're smellin' it now cause we're stirrin' it up.

BARRY: Great. (*As he exits.*) Well—then maybe I can help you do something about it in the fall, so next spring we won't have a problem.

(*Barry has exited left.*)

GEORGE: (*After him.*) Don't worry, there'll always be some goddamn thing.

(*George steps up to the fence. Roger sits on the stump to listen to him.*)

GEORGE: I wish to Christ everybody would stay in the city. Everybody—(*He notices Roger.*) What the fuck you lookin' at?! Get back to work! (*Roger goes back to work.*) Eeeeverybody—made so much of livin' in the city then laughed at us for livin' up here. Called us hhhhhhicks, an' worse. An' now they get the city all shittied up they want to come up here . . . 'nd shitty up our place. I wish to hell they'd stay right to home and fix their own place up. What they come up here and criticize us for? They say the barn ain't right, the shit pile stink . . . they want us to move it . . . Why they—(*Realizing who the audience is.*) Why'd *you* have to come up here in the first place? The fuckin' city. Peeeeeople built it, peeeeeople should live in it.

(*George exits up right. Roger skips up to the fence.*)

ROGER: I got so's I llllove the smell of shit-cow manure—'cause it means feeeertility, po—-tential—it's fulla life—worms in it—stuff lives off it. I can stand in shit up to my knees and I'd just feel taller. I'm growin'. Give me enough cow shit and I could do anything—grow anything—feed everybody—it's good for flower boxes too. Why'd shit get such a bad name? They put stuff in hamburgers would make you run to the toilet, an' you eat it, but you won't look fertilizer straight in the face—

(*The mooing cuts the scene. Lights shift.*)

Scene 6

Roger puts his fork against the shed and brings his saw just down left of the tree and begins working on it. Lucille slips up on him and blows a grass whistle, startling him. They laugh and he chases her gently around the tree.

ROGER: Wwwhat the hell are you doin'?

LUCILLE: Callin' in the ducks. (*She blows it again.*)

ROGER: Wwwe'll never see them again.

(*He starts to return to his work. She grabs his hand and playfully tries to pull him up right.*)

LUCILLE: Dinner's ready. I made them green beans with the salt pork like you like.

ROGER: (*Gently pulling free.*) I'll be—gggonna try one more thing.

(*He returns to the saw. She follows and stands over him.*)

LUCILLE: Oh! (*She pulls a paper from her pocket.*) The artificial insemination man came by while you were out in the field.

(*She routinely gives Roger the paper. He's obviously uncomfortable with it.*

She catches her mistake and bends to read it to him, pointing at the words.)

LUCILLE: He bred . . . two . . . Holstein . . . cows . . . Jersey. Like you said.

ROGER: *(Trying to read and speak.)* Hol-hol-holstein, cccccc—- *(Returning to his saw.)* good.

LUCILLE: He's got a funny truck. Funny sayin's on it.

ROGER: I ddidn't knnnow that.

LUCILLE: "The Cow's Best Friend!"

(They laugh. She lights a cigarette and leans against the tree. When Roger notices there's a flash of disappointment.)

LUCILLE: You don't like me smokin' do you?

ROGER: Oh nnno. It ain't that. You do whaaaat you wwwwant. It's just—the baaaaaby—they say smo-smo-smo-kin' ain't no good when you're pregnant. *(He digs for this.)* They said when my Ma was carryin' me, it was so cold she ran out of wood. She went out with the axe an' chopped up some kiiiindlin' for the stove. She musta huuuurt somethin' inside a' her an' thaaat's why I'm like this.

LUCILLE: I don't think that's it. Stuttering is a medical thing— happens to a lot of people.

(She puts out her cigarette. She starts to leave but comes back and returns to the playful spirit with which she entered. She pushes Roger over.)

LUCILLE: Come on in before it gets cold.

(Roger puts out his hand. She helps him up. They are very close. Roger slips his hand in and caresses her pregnant belly. She exits up right. Roger hops over to the fence.)

ROGER: It's ssssomethin' about the soft part of her belly—where she makes babies—there's no fffear in it. You could hurt it—or fill it— iiit'll take you in. She knows how to mother—she grows baaabies in there and they suck her milk up. Every step she makes is like a slow easy fuck—hot—natural.

(Mooing cuts the scene. Lights shift. Roger exits up right.)

Scene 7

Lucille enters with a long stick and repeatedly scratches a line in the dirt, down center. Barry enters to up left and stand next to the dead branch leaning against the wall. He stares at it, then snaps at it savagely with a hedge trimmer. He doesn't touch it. He notices Lucille nearby and calls to her.

BARRY: Hi Lucille.

LUCILLE: *(She doesn't want to be bothered.)* Hi Barry.

BARRY: Did you see the show last night?

LUCILLE: It's all reruns now, ain't it?

BARRY: Yeah, but it was a good one — we had Helen Hayes as a guest star.

LUCILLE: Helen Hayes— she's really old right?

BARRY: First Lady of the American Theatre, worked with Harold Clurman and the Group Theatre—

LUCILLE: I like that Golden Girls, that makes me laugh—but I don't watch T.V. much, when it's nice out.

BARRY: Yeah—*(Looking toward her scratching.)* You know, you ought to put some Belgian endive in there.

LUCILLE: Michelle go back to New York again?

BARRY: Yeah, this is a very busy season for her. She's usually very busy. I'm usually very busy, but I've been actively trying not to be busy—does that make any sense?

LUCILLE: Sure—must be lonely with her gone.

BARRY: Yes and no.

LUCILLE: She seems so—serious. To tell the truth, I don't think she's said more than ten words to me with all the times I been over to your place.

BARRY: Her mind is elsewhere right now. But—isn't that the pot calling the stove bellied? (*He laughs.*)

LUCILLE: What?

BARRY: People who are quiet and serious, you can't tell me you're not used to that.

LUCILLE: Oh, Roger? Yeah but it's different somehow. Maybe cause I feel like he doesn't have a choice—but I don't know nothin' about Michelle, so I'm just gonna shut up.

BARRY: And I don't know anything about Roger—or—Jim is that you're husband's name?

LUCILLE: That's right—you don't know anything.

(*The lights shift. Mooing. Barry exits up left. Lucille goes to fence.*)

LUCILLE: I love to watch Roger milk the cows—up to each one with the bucket and the washrag—he washes off her bag with the warm water—and wipes each teat. 'Specially the ends of the teats 'cause that's where she's the most sensitive—and then, he fits her with the milking harness, slips on the milking cups. "Shloop" "Shloop" "Shloop" "Shloop" and turns the pump on—"Kushtunk" "Kushtunk" "Kushtunk"—till she got no more to give. Then he undoes her harness—strips out the last in the end of the teat. An' then, he turns her loose and she goes out and gets a drink. When she comes in her bag's all hard and swollen, but after, it's all—wet 'n soft 'n limp. What's that sayin' the Carnation Dairy used to have? "Milk From Contented Cows". Well I can tell you, if they ain't contented, it ain't his fault.

GEORGE: (*From offstage.*) Lucille! it's your Old Man Jim on the phone. He's checkin' up, wants to talk to you.

(*Lucille looks visibly chilled. She lingers at the fence.*)

LUCILLE: Jim was fixing Roger's truck at the shop. He made a deal to help out for a cheaper rate. Jim was the one always talked about Roger's place, said how great the view was. Jim went up—comes up here to hunt, Deer Season. It sounded better and better—an' then

Roger brought me a mess of sweet corn—and finally I asked to go up to visit. Jim didn't want to go so I went up alone with Roger. Somethin' about the smell. I read where you fall in love with someone 'cause of their smell. I believe that. It's the smell up here that makes me come back. You think about fresh air—you don't think of a smell, but there is one. It's not a pretty smell, it's like—there's stuff—fermentin'—it's a strong smell, really goes right up your nose and makes you giggle. 'Course you can't giggle all the time—so after a while, I go home.

GEORGE: (*Fom off.*) Lucille! Jim wants ta talk to you. He says he's all outta them dinners you froze for him. You gotta come in an' cook some more—I don't give a fuck—you talk to him—

(*Mooing cuts the scene. Lights shift. Lucille begins to exit up right. Roger, with nail bucket, enters from up center. As they are crossing center, the mooing and light shift stops, as if they had been caught mid-cross. They stare at each other.*)

LUCILLE: (*Impatient.*) What do you want?

ROGER: N-N-N-N—What?

LUCILLE: What do you want!?

ROGER: Nothing.

(*Mooing and light shift resumes. Lucille exits up right. *)

Scene 8

George enters from up right, gets the chair and puts it down right and sits in it. Roger gives George the nail bucket and begins ripping the wooden box apart as if it had nails holding it together. He throws the boards to George, who removes the nails that aren't there and puts them in the bucket.

GEORGE: Your girlfriend's gettin' pret' near to foal—

ROGER: Yeah. So what. It ain't my kid.

GEORGE: Yeah, well, so the hell what, she's your girlfriend ain't she? Who the hell knows who's kid's what today anyway. What the hell diiiifference does it make.

ROGER: You wish I was yours, donncha?

GEORGE: I still raised you—I taught you everythin—we're still blood
—

ROGER: Uuuuncle George.

GEORGE: What the hell's the bug up your ass?

ROGER: You staaarted it, talking about the baby.

GEORGE: I said a gooood thing. She gonna have it. Iiiiii'm glad. I
love Lucille. We—love Lucille. (*Big pause.*) You know I loved your
mother, too. (*Roger collapses against the tree.*) When she died, a lot of
fellahs woulda took that insurance money and gone on big trips an'
'at. I didn't take nothin'. I spent every dollar on her. She had the
best coffin money can buy. Stainless steel, with big silver angels on it
—you seen it! That coffin is sealed too. Sealed. She safe in there.
That insurance was her money and I didn't take none of it. She took
every bit of it with her right into the ground.

(*Mooing cuts the scene. Lights shift. George exits up right.*)

Scene 9

Lucille stomps in from up right.

LUCILLE: Why'd you call him Uncle George?

ROGER: He's my Uncle.

LUCILLE: He's your father—

ROGER: Step-father. My real father got buried in a silo when I was a
litle kid.

LUCILLE: George loved your Ma, didn't he?

ROGER: (*Nods.*) George haaaad been livin' with us. After Pa died,
fellahs come around to see Ma . . . we didn't like none of 'em . . . but
she was lonely so we tol' her to marry Uncle George . . . we knew he
was in love with her. An' we knew—he loved us. He'd do anything
to protect us. When Joey died it all but kilt him.

LUCILLE: They didn't have any kids, hunh.

ROGER: I'm her yyyoungest.

LUCILLE: Did she love him?

ROGER: Nnnope—neeever—that's why he's nnnnuts.

LUCILLE: Roger—if you want me to leave—say so.

ROGER: No.

(Mooing cuts the scene. Lights shift. Lucille exits up right.)

Scene 10

Roger returns to working on his saw left center. Barry enters from up left and crosses to sit in the chair right center. He smokes a cigar.

BARRY: —So I was thinking, it's between the Homelite and the McCullough. The Homelite seems a little more more versatile but the McCullough is more heavy duty. What I'm wondering is, is that overkill for what I'll need it for? What do you have?

ROGER: *(After pulling frantically on the starter rope.)* I wwwwouldn't get one a' these, if i was you.

(Roger pulls the rope again. George enters. He carries papers. He's obviously pissed about something.)

BARRY: Hiya George.

(George grabs a board and threatens Barry with it.)

GEORGE: Just get the fuck outta here.

(Everybody stands startled.)

ROGER: Ppppa?

BARRY: What's the problem?

GEORGE: Taxes—from the clerk's office. Twice what it was last year.

ROGER: Jesus—

GEORGE: That ain't all. I got a government paper. Lucille read it to me. They're gonna having "Zonin'" laws up here. You know what that means—(*Roger shakes his head.*) Everything's got to be up to code—

ROGER: Jesus—

BARRY: Well, that'll probably make sure things are safe—

GEORGE: (*Brandishing his board.*) You'll have to get a licensed plumber to put pipe in! You won't be able to use old lumber, they'll make you buy new two-ba-fours for everything you put up, an' it's cause a' this asshole movin' in. All the property went up. We didn't do nothin' and the tax assessor doubled the price.

BARRY: Yeah, but now it's worth twice as much—

GEORGE: (*Ready to take a heavy swing at Barry.*) Go tell that to the fuckin' cows!

ROGER: (*Disarming George.*) Take it easy pa—

(*Lucille rushes in from up right.*)

LUCILLE: What's going on? Pa, I knew you was gonna do this!

(*Roger and Lucille work to keep George off Barry.*)

GEORGE: All this shit got stirred up 'cause of the bitch he lives with.

BARRY: Just a fucking minute. (*Roger has to keep Barry from attacking George.*) It's one thing to call me something—

GEORGE: Pussy whipped, that's why he's smellin' around Lucille alla time—he's afraid of his old lady.

(*Barry controls himself for the moment.*)

BARRY: This has nothing to do with the women.

GEORGE: Sure, change the subject—he's foolin' around Lucille half the time while we're workin'.

LUCILLE: Pa! We never did nothin'! He never touched me.

BARRY: What business is it of yours anyway. It's her business, Christ, if anybody ought to get pissed it's her husband.

(Tense pause. Then Roger starts for Barry but Lucille cuts him off.)

ROGER: Gggget ouuuut.

LUCILLE: Roger! He didn't mean it.

BARRY: I'm sorry, I —

(George takes this opportunity to get a new board and resume his attack.)

GEORGE: You got the balls to fuck up my property value and tell me I'm better off.

(Barry faces off George.)

BARRY: You are, you ignorant son of a bitch—you won't listen to anybody. That's your real problem—you lack desire—any real desire to improve anything. I don't know how you can work so hard and be so lazy. You've just got a boost in property value—you can parlay that into something—it's a gift.

(George makes a decision and drops his board.)

GEORGE: If this place is worth so much—why don't you buy it? Hunh? Hunh?

BARRY: Alright —if you're serious—how much do you want?

LUCILLE: Pa, this ain't the right time to talk about this—

GEORGE: The time to sell is when someone wants to buy. Says here it's worth $80,000, but I'm addin' ten percent—how much is that?

BARRY: $88,000.

BARRY AND GEORGE: Sold!

ROGER: Wwwait—

LUCILLE: George, it might be worth a lot more than that—

GEORGE: Not to me —

LUCILLE: You ought to think about it —

GEORGE: I've been thinking about it for 38 years. It took everythin' I got to keep this place goin' and now I got nothin' left. It's just gonna bleed Roger the same way.

BARRY: Shake on it George? (*Barry offers his hand.*) A gentlemen's agreement till we get the papers from my lawyer—but we're into it now—and once I call him, I start paying him—and once the money starts to move, it's very hard to stop.

ROGER: Pa, tell him nnnno—

GEORGE: He's givin' me a fair price. I'm sellin' it.

BARRY: Last chance to back out. (*Offers his hand again.*)

GEORGE: (*George shakes.*) I'm in.

(*Barry exits up left.*)

ROGER: What the hhhell are you doin'?

GEORGE: You always say how hard it is here, well, you finally got me convinced. I figured I could always provide for you as long as we had land and knew how to farm it. Well, I don't no more. I got through the big depression—the big wars. I taught you everything I know and it don't mean shit no more. What should I a' done? Made you go to school? I don't know no more. But I know, you gotta get outta here. I'm sellin' it to him. Maybe he can make a go of it.

ROGER: Well wwwhat am I gggonna do?

GEORGE: You're gonna have eighty thousand dollars. Take that money and—go live in town, go to Florida like your Aunt Mabel, I don't give a good goddamn, 'cause I'm gonna be dead. I'm goin'. (*As he leaves.*) I'm gonna stick a hambone up my ass and let the dogs drag me away for food.

(*George exits up right.*)

Scene 11

LUCILLE: (*Calling after him.*) George? (*Returning to Roger.*) Roger, is this sale really gonna happen? Can't you do anything?

ROGER: It's hiiis name on the dddeed, hiiis place, there's nothing I cccan do.

LUCILLE: Well, you're gonna have to do something—now, I have to do something—

ROGER: Mmmaybe I could get a place in town. Could I get a place in ttttown?

LUCILLE: Sure, for $80,000, you could buy a nice place—even have some money left to live on.

ROGER: Cccould you cccome there?—and ssstay?

LUCILLE: It wouldn't be the same Roger—Jim is in town—I tell him I come up here to get away from town—that's what he tells people—I couldn't be in town with you.

ROGER: Dddo I ever hhhit you? Wwwould I? I don't hhhit women. Maybe you'd lllike that.

LUCILLE: Now that's a bunch a shit! I've heard that before, "They like it". No! I don't like it!! But you know what I do like? Someone that can support me, not just the money neither. Someone who's there and strong—

ROGER: I dddddo tttthat —

LUCILLE: Someone who ain't gonna get scared and go live in their truck on a logging road when somethin' bad happens at home.

ROGER: You ai-ai-ai-ain't never had to lllive on nothin'—

LUCILLE: That's what you asked for. Nothin'. That's what you figure you deserve, and that's what you're gettin'. It's in your blood. That's why I don't want it in my baby's blood. 'Cause I got it too, and my babies gotta have somethin' strong in them, even if it's mean and bad, at least they won't have to hide all the time like I do.

(She starts to leave but Roger grabs her. She cringes, expecting a slap, but Roger pushes her to the tree, sits her down firmly, and steps back. He stutters

convulsively.)

ROGER: I want—somethin' that's mine—somethin' that nobody can take away from me. Anything . . . if it was a fuckin' stone. I want somethin' safe, anyplace, any fuckin' thing. I come up here 'cause I can't talk. I'm 12 years old in the second grade. I ain't gettin' anywhere. I don't go no more. The cop said they'd drag me into town to go to school . . . so kids could laugh at me. It's not for me. It's somethin' they want. So I said fuck 'em. They come up, an' I was on the roof of the barn. I was gonna jump right on the cop car, if they wouldn't leave me alone. So they did. And that's where I am— alone. And I don't want that no more. You didn't come out here just for the farm. You didn't go sleep in the barn at night. You come sleep with me—whose hand was that on your belly at night? That was me. I'm tired a' just raisin' calves. I want a baby of mine. My blood.

(There's a long pause as they both catch their breath.)

LUCILLE: You never said none a' this before.

ROGER: *(Knowing it's funny.)* It ain't easy to say. I feel like I ch-ch-choked up a bone.

LUCILLE: Roger—I didn't mean to say bad things about your blood.

ROGER: I know. 'S okay. If bbbbad talk'd kill me, I'd been dead when I was a kkkkid. Shit. *(Roger puts his hand on his chest.)* my heart's pppoundin' like a racehorse kickin' its stall in.

(Lucille feels Roger's chest.)

LUCILLE: Roger, the baby's kickin' too. Feel.

(Roger puts his hand on her belly.)

LUCILLE: This baby loves you, Roger.

ROGER: I lllove this bbbaby. I lllove you Lucille—we got some th-th-th-ings to tttalk about—

(There's a roar from up left. Barry enters with an electric chain saw. Barry wears safety goggles and gloves, and drags the cord. When he reaches the tree he sees Roger and Lucille, he shuts the saw off.)

BARRY: Oh Roger —I—hope there's no hard feelings—

ROGER: Nnnope—

BARRY: I saw all —

LUCILLE: Just a second. I love you too, Roger.

BARRY: Well, that's nice. Hey, what do you think? (*Showing the chain saw.*) I saw all the trouble you had, I decided to go electric. I was looking out my window and I was thinking that the view would really open up if I'd "lose the tree"—and I was dying to try this out —and I've only got enough cord to reach this tree.

ROGER: Wwwwatch your fffingers—an' iiif you hiiit old fence wire that grooowd into the tree—be caaareful when the saw kicks baaack toward your face.

BARRY: Could you explain that again—

LUCILLE: We gotta get going.

ROGER: We're gggoin' into town.

BARRY: Well. Good luck.

(*Roger shakes Barry's hand firmly.*)

ROGER: Yyyou too.

(*Roger crosses down and picks up his old chain saw. He crosses to the well and opens it.*)

ROGER: Ccccut logs in Hell.

(*He drops the saw in the well. Roger and Lucille exit up right. Barry starts the saw and moves toward the tree. Just short of the tree, it sputters out. Tries to get his saw started—it won't.*)

BARRY: Fuck me.

(*Barry exits, following the cord up left. "I Can Tell By The Way You Smell" plays. The lights fade to black.*)

END

SHATTER
'N
WADE

BY

MURRAY

MEDNICK

Shatter 'n Wade was first performed at the 1990 Padua Hills Playwrights Festival with the following cast:

Wade	David Officer
Sayer	William Dennis Hunt
Cross	Scott Paulin
Wally	Matthew Goulish
Shatter	Susannah Blinkoff
Bint	Mark Fite
Ann	Allison Studdiford
Martin	Nick Love
Ginnie	Laura Owens
Sally	Elizabeth Iannaci
Bruno	Bob Craft
Bill	Peter Schaaf
The Screamer	Joseph Goodrich
Director	Murray Mednick
Assistant Director	Kim Brown
Music	James Campbell
Lighting Design	Jason Berliner
Stage Manager	Nick Flynn

Shatter 'n Wade was subsequently produced in February, 1991, by Diantha Lebenzon and Wayne Long at the Matrix Theater in Los Angeles and was directed by the author. The cast was the same except as follows:

Wally	James Cox Chambers
The Screamer	Hank Bunker
Set Design	Kenton Jones
Stage Manager	Kathi O'Donohue

CHARACTERS:

SAYER (Middle-aged; wired; golden hair.)
MARTIN (Sharp; balding.)
WALLY (Early thirties; cowboy outfit.)
CROSS (Fifty; white hair.)
BINT (Thirty-one; blue hair.)
ANN (Late-thirties; sensitive, emotional; brown hair.)
GINNIE (Late-thirties; strong; black hair.)
SHATTER (Twenty-two; wired; red hair)
WADE (Nineteen; bandage on thumb; green hair; carries boom box.)
SALLY (Thirties; blonde.)
BRUNO (Corpulent.)
THE SCREAMER (Unseen.)
WALK-ONS

The Scene

In front of the entrance to a meeting hall. Night. Sayer, Martin, Wally, Bint and Cross hanging out; waiting. Cross and Martin stand off at opposite sides, the others stand with Sayer:

SAYER: When I was growin' up there were families! A man had a family! A person belonged to a family and a man had a job and supported the family!

CROSS: Did you know that tombs and mausoleums lined the Appian Way from Rome to Brundisium?

SAYER: No. Brundisium? Is that Brindisi?

MARTIN: So what?

CROSS: Different attitude toward the family dead is all. Visibility. That's all I meant.

SAYER: *(To Bint.)* Chairs set up?

BINT: Yes, sir. There's people.

SAYER: *(To Martin.)* Cross here is new.

MARTIN: I know he's new. We've met, we've talked. *(A man—Bruno —enters, approaches behind them. Of Cross:)* He says odd things at inappropriate moments.

SAYER: Goin' to the meeting, Bruno? *(Bruno ignores him, goes inside.)* Attaboy!

MARTIN: You know how people bob their heads?—here, like this— they bob their heads like ducks—guys—guys do it—they get up, they're on their way to the john—they do this—*(Demonstrates as the others laugh.)*

WALLY: That's it, Martin! *(Martin walks off a few steps—he likes privacy.)*

SAYER: *(Uneasily.)* Hey, anyone see my two mutants? One's got red hair, the other's got green. Ha!

BINT: Uh, uh, no.

SAYER: Kids these days, they do actions. (*To Cross.*) You know what an action is?

CROSS: Well, yeah.

SAYER: What? (*Cross doesn't know.*) Observe.

WALLY: Anger is a disease. (*Pause.*)

BINT: Anger is not a disease. (*The Screamer screams, off.*)

SAYER: (*To Cross.*) You don't know. Watch this.

WALLY: (*Formally.*) A woman who sleeps around—it's bad news. You have to guard against it, like the Muslims. It's a problem old as the rocks. A good body can get whatever it wants. Whomever, whenever. A wink and a smile, let's fuck around, have a good time. It's elemental. You want to stone such a woman, and destroy her power. Don't you? In a bed, a car, under the stairs, in an alley. . . .

BINT: Say no more!

CROSS: Wait a minute. Are those your thoughts? Do you think that?

WALLY: Me?

CROSS: No, I'm looking at the moon.

WALLY: That's not me.

CROSS: Because otherwise you have serious problems.

WALLY: I didn't think it. I regret it now, okay?

SAYER: Ha! (*A woman—Sally—arrives for the meeting.*)

CROSS: (*To himself.*) Wild.

SAYER: Welcome, Sally!

SALLY: Well, I can't believe I'm here, really. I don't know how anyone can arrive at a point of view. One second I'm thinking one thing and the next second I'm thinking the opposite. How can anyone make up their minds about an issue? (*Sigh.*) Well, I guess there's feelings.

SAYER: There you go, Sally! (*She goes inside.*)

MARTIN: She's so cute. She's so cute I can't stand it. What is that?

WALLY: Marry her, Martin!

MARTIN: You marry her, Wally! What you need—round off the edges.

SAYER: Ha!

CROSS: (*To Sayer.*) An action is oratory. It is speaking. (*To Martin.*) That's what I was talking about. I didn't think it was inappropriate. It is relevant. In the ancient city, in the days of old, that's how it worked. You spoke before the assembly—

MARTIN: (*Walking away.*) Yeah, yeah, rock and roll.

CROSS: What's with this guy?

WALLY: He never married. Independent fellow, Martin.

BINT: (*Awed.*) He's a lawyer.

WALLY: Got close to bein' pussy-whipped once and ran like a jackal.

CROSS: Who is he to judge?

BINT: He's a judge? (*Cross looks at him.*)

SAYER: (*To Cross.*) Whatsamatter? Everybody has to like you? (*To Bint.*) What's the worst thing that can happen?

BINT: You can get married?

SAYER: Come on!

BINT: You can die.

SAYER: You do die! Everybody dies! That's not the worst thing! Come on!

BINT: You can be sick.

SAYER: No. You can get better! Come on! (*Pause.*) YOU CAN LOSE! LOSERS DON'T WORK! LOSERS DON'T MAKE IT! LOSERS

CRAWL LIKE DOGS!

BINT: Okay. (*Walks off.*)

CROSS: The father was the priest of the household, and he knew the sacred formulas and rites—he knew what to SAY—in relation to the household gods and to the family dead. You know what I'm saying?

WALLY: I don't think so.

SAYER: (*Ruefully.*) Where are the families now? Look what happens! Guys make it and live in fortresses behind iron gates. Inside the fortress nobody's talking. They don't know who each other is. These are the ones on top. In the middle they are changing partners like rabbits. On the bottom there are no fathers. The fathers are on the street and there's no money for the women and children! The women are in there exchanging sex for crack! They're doin' it in what they call crack houses! So aids and syphilis are skyrocketing and the kids are gettin' born with it!

WALLY: "Skyrocketing." I love it.

SAYER: Wally, the students we got here are beastie boys and bums! They are a tribe of barbarians! They are a primitive-type people addicted to noise! It's awful! They are just beating our brains out with the bass and the drums!

WALLY: Fantastic!

SAYER: My ex says it's because they got pushed out of the womb, slapped around, and dumped into the school system! Yeah, yeah, rock and roll! Noise and dope! And they start fucking when they're twelve!

WALLY: Whoa!

SAYER: I heard Wade today, he's talking about these high school coke dealers, they're teenagers walking around with beepers so they're available day and night, they're driving thirty-thousand dollar cars and they're afraid of no one! They're too young to do time and they fit snugly into the fuck you, fuck me entrepreneurial—tradition! Who can fault them?

WALLY: Good, Dr. Sayer!

SAYER: They're loading up, these functional illiterates and know-nothings! They can do business—they are organized and armed! Wade, he's telling me how these kids get initiated into the business, into the gang. You stick a shotgun out the car window and blow somebody away, he says. It doesn't have to be a person you know. It could be anyone—you do a murder and that's how you make your bones.

WALLY: It's the fucking cars! You got teenagers shooting around in lethal weapons—they're always on the verge! (*Enter Ann.*)

SAYER: Ha!

ANN: Hi, honey!

(*Cross, startled, goes to her as Sayer and Wally watch.*)

CROSS: (*Trying not to be overheard.*) I feel crazed. I feel disassociated. I am not myself. I am appalled.

ANN: Let's take those one at a time.

CROSS: What am I? Somebody is acting like he's me, and he's not me, and he's outa control.

ANN: What do you mean?

CROSS: Crazed. I'm doing things and saying things and I don't feel like it's me and I'm appalled at what I'm doing and saying. (*Ann calls to Sayer and Wally:*)

ANN: What time is the meeting?

WALLY: Uh, it's now! (*Sayer opens the door, looks in.*)

SAYER: Meeting 's now! (*He goes inside, followed by Wally.*)

CROSS: There's a guy pretending to be me, and he's outa control. (*They watch Wade approach: he stops, stands shyly, walks away.*) I would call it the pain of manifesting, of having to be in this world.

ANN: Then do something about it.

CROSS: WHAT?

ANN: Well.

CROSS: WELL, WHAT? (*Pause.*) I don't want to stand here like I'm dumb and paralyzed.

ANN: I'm sorry.

CROSS: I feel like I'm seeing everything very clearly and guess what, Ann?

(*Wade re-enters behind them, goes to door, looks in, hesitates.*)

ANN: No laceration, Cross. At this stage in life, we might not get over it.

CROSS: That's what I feel. I definitely feel that. I couldn't agree with you more, Ann. I just don't know where that comment came from.

(*She sighs, looks around to Wade, who is leaving again.*)

ANN: (*To Wade.*) Are there many people in the meeting? (*He walks away. To Cross.*) Odd. (*Off, the Screamer screams.*) God, who is that?

CROSS: Do you pray for the dead?

ANN: What are you getting at?

CROSS: Do you pray for the dead?

ANN: No, do you?

CROSS: No. I don't pray at all. I don't know how.

ANN: Maybe you should learn how.

CROSS: A prayer for my ancestors. In the old days, they worshipped the dead. That's how they found meaning.

ANN: Why don't you ever talk to me about what you're doing?

CROSS: We were just talking about what I was doing with reference to the meaning of what I was doing, which is research into the ancient world.

ANN: Never mind, we should go in. (*Bint reappears, lights up a smoke.*)

CROSS: You go on in.

ANN: What are you doing?

CROSS: I am going to continue to stand here.

ANN: Gimme a kiss. (*He hesitates, relents.*) Come in soon.

CROSS: Yeah, sure. (*She goes inside. He mutters fiercely to himself.*) Goddamn it! I hate that! I hate that shit! What am I! Am I a slug! Am I an actor! Am I a toad! What is that! Damn it! (*Regards Bint smoking.*) Looks good and smells good.

BINT: Want one?

CROSS: No, thanks. I quit.

BINT: Hey, that's awesome. (*Pause.*) That's a wonderful present you've given to yourself.

(*Pause.*)

CROSS: Thank you.

BINT: You should feel good about yourself. (*Pause.*) Do you?

CROSS: (*Sardonic.*) I feel great about myself.

BINT: How long you been not smoking?

CROSS: Three months.

BINT: Congratulations. (*Offering his hand.*) That's a real statement, a positive affirmation on your part.

CROSS: I'd rather smoke.

BINT: Why'd you do it?

CROSS: I turned fifty.

BINT: Fifty. Whoa.

CROSS: Yeah.

BINT: I'm gonna put it out now, go to the meeting.

CROSS: Okay. (*Ann steps out.*)

ANN: Cross!

CROSS: What?

ANN: Excuse me. Are you coming in?

CROSS: No! Not yet!

ANN: All right. (*Goes back. Bint starts to cough.*)

CROSS: What's the matter?

BINT: (*Gulping.*) I can't breathe!

CROSS: Take it easy.

BINT: It's my heart!

CROSS: You wanna glass of water?

BINT: What a shock! I can't believe it! Cindy! Jesus Christ, that was Cindy! Was that Cindy?

CROSS: You know each other?

BINT: Hell, yeah—I know her! She still looks good, too! Unfuckinbelievable! (*Gasping.*) She looks great.

CROSS: Pull yourself together.

BINT: I'm impressed is all, I'm totally impressed. Cindy! She looks fuckin' great . . .

CROSS: Cynthia.

BINT: Cynthia?

CROSS: That's her name.

BINT: Oh, wow.

CROSS: How do you know . . . Cindy?

BINT: Hey, are you kidding? This is a charge, man. This is intense. We're talkin' twelve or thirteen years here.

CROSS: Really?

BINT: Yeah, I dunno if I can go in there now.

CROSS: You can do it. What's your name?

BINT: Bint.

CROSS: You can make it, Bint.

BINT: (*Nodding.*) Thank you. I appreciate that.   I'll wait a minute. Where are you from?

CROSS: New York.

BINT: Yeah, I can hear that. You're not from here. (*Martin re-enters, stops at door.*)

MARTIN: Hey, Bint!

BINT: Yes, Sir! (*Bint doesn't move, so Martin goes to them.*)

MARTIN: Sayer. He's a fantastic guy. But he's hysterical, ya know? We love him, ya know, but what are we gonna do with him?

BINT: It's not for me to say, Sir. (*Cross shrugs.*)

MARTIN: Yeah, yeah, rock and roll. (*Hunches himself, starts for the door, stops.*) Bint! Don't let anybody slam the door!

BINT: I'll try, Sir! (*Martin goes inside.*)

CROSS: What happened twelve years ago?

BINT: Cindy?

CROSS: Yeah, yeah.

BINT: Nothin' happened. I just knew her. Hey, she was great. Cindy.

MARTIN: (*Inside.*) The world is abusive! Life is abusive! Who is looking to feather someone else's nest? You don't have to go far—if you walk on your ass you'll end up with a sore ass!

SAYER: (*Inside.*) Don't interrupt others when they are speaking, Counselor!

(*Someone closes the door. Off, the Screamer screams.*)

BINT: Weird neighbor.

CROSS: (*To Bint.*) How 'd you know her? Cindy?

BINT: Actually, my brother knew her. I met her through my older brother, Brian. (*Pause.*) You okay? (*Pause.*) Yeah, Brian knew her first.

CROSS: And then you knew her.

BINT: What a knockout! Beautiful! Still is. And friendly? Boy! (*Pause.*) I mean, she was such a beautiful woman, ya know? (*Starts heaving.*)

CROSS: Are you having convulsions, or what?

BINT: No, I'm all right. I'm all right. I'm goin' to my brother's house. Tonight. After the meeting. Maybe now, actually. Maybe tomorrow. Clean up. He's a neat guy.

CROSS: Sounds like a good idea.

BINT: Yeah, I need a rest. It's harsh out there, harsh. No mercy. You must know, right? New York City.

CROSS: New York City. Tell me about Cynthia.

BINT: I was just a kid, an' here's this beautiful woman, gorgeous, and she's just real friendly. It makes an impression. You know what I'm saying?

CROSS: I think so.

BINT: Cindy. She was the hottest thing in the Valley, man. (*Silence.*)

CROSS: Meaning?

BINT: I'm sure she 's changed. Ya know, older.

CROSS: I'm sure.

BINT: I was still in high school, man. It was like a dream, like a dream come true, like a movie. A kid would go a long way for that ya know, a long way.

CROSS: Times have changed.

BINT: I hear ya there. Kids are goin' at it now. No holding back now. Ha! (*Pause.*) A beauty, man. A total beauty. And she really got around, I'll tell ya. I guess I was too young to be jealous.

(*Pause. Young guy walks on: Bill.*)

BILL: Meeting happening, Bint?

BINT: You bet! It's a happening, Bill!

BILL: Listen to this. There's gonna be a whole new breed of people comin' through: they're called Brazilians. Once they got all the forests down, once they've cut all the trees, then they're comin' over the border! They're gonna invade America! A new species! Brazilians! Okay?

CROSS: Thank you.

BILL: Brazil! They got death squads now, knockin' off the street kids!

(*Goes inside.*)

BINT: (*To Bill.*) I hear ya!

CROSS: Let me ask you something.

BINT: Go for it.

CROSS: Why do you talk like that all the time?

BINT: (*Pause.*) Is that an insult?

CROSS: And why do you love noise so much?

BINT: Who?

CROSS: You people. You love noise.

BINT: What people?

CROSS: You—the young Californian. The dudes. You like noise. Why is that?

BINT: You mean like loud music?

CROSS: Yeah. Loud music. Loud cars. Loud bikes. Loud talk. Empty noise.

BINT: You hostile, man?

CROSS: Just answer me the question.

BINT: It's comforting, Pal. Comforting.

CROSS: Comforting. Thank you.

BINT: You're hostile. I don't need nobody being hostile. It's like the last thing I need, man.

CROSS: Take a hike, asshole.

(*Tense pause.*)

BINT: I get it. You guys together?

CROSS: She's my wife.

BINT: Hey, it's not my fault. How do I know? (*Stepping away.*) I'll bet you're a fucking Arab. Arabs can't handle it, man. They like their women closed. (*Makes gesture of turning a key.*) Click. (*Laughs. Enter Sayer from inside.*) Hello, Dr. Sayer.

SAYER: Hello, Bint. (*Sarcastic.*) Comin' to the meeting?

BINT: Yes, Sir.

SAYER: You gentlemen know each other?

BINT: No, Sir.

CROSS: (*To Bint.*) Get outa here before I piss on you.

BINT: I don't like that.

SAYER: Go on in, Bint.

BINT: Right, Dr. Sayer! (*Goes inside.*)

MARTIN: (*Inside.*) Don't slam the door! (*Bint slams door. Sayer laughs.*)

SAYER: What an assembly, Mr. Cross. (*Takes out a large cigar. Enter Wally from inside, leaving the door slightly open.*) Here comes another one. Can't take the heat.

WALLY: Hello, Mr. Cross!

CROSS: Hello, how are ya.

WALLY: (*Half to himself.*) Fuckin' Bill's talking.

BILL: (*Inside.*) . . . I think tension grows on the planet ya know?, and it's got to be expressed by like, war. It's like, ya know, a boil, it's like lanced by fighting, like on the street, right? You know what I'm saying?

WALLY: NO, Bill!

BILL: (*Inside.*) . . . The stuff gets kicked off into space, maybe even to the moon. It's not just the asshole in front of you on the freeway fucking up your day, or the crazed sharks biting around in the culture for money and power: it's death squads and invasions and massacres and epidemics! And I'll tell ya something else here: you can't sit on the downtrodden too long—it's starts to stink—that's my opinion, that's my point of view on it! (*Boos and applause.*) One more thing: they're trying to buy into Africa now, for a dumping ground, a place to bury the garbage! Africa!

SAYER: Who was that?

WALLY: Sounds like Bill.

SAYER: Close the door, will ya? (*Wally closes it.*)

CROSS: (*To Sayer.*) Are you gonna light that thing?

SAYER: (*Not lighting up.*) They were talking about the dead in there.

CROSS: What dead?

SAYER: Children . . .

CROSS: There are no dead, Sayer. People vanish and that's the end of it. No problem about the ancestry, the bloodline, the family name. But in the old days the dead were around, they were in the house or in the tomb or in the field. The dead were near.

WALLY: They're in graveyards, Mr. Cross.

CROSS: Yeah, but you don't see 'em.

WALLY: So what? Who wants to see 'em?

CROSS: You don't know anything. And you're a sycophant on top of everything else. (*To Sayer.*) The dead are important.

WALLY: Why?

CROSS: Because once they were alive, Sir, like you and me. Like Tacitus, who breathed air and shit and had opinions. Walkin' about with ears and smells and hungers and strategies. (*Pause.*) He had a Roman education and he worshipped the dead. (*Wally partly opens the door.*)

BILL: (*Inside.*) YOU WANNA TALK ABOUT CENTRAL AMERICA? YOU WANNA TALK ABOUT THE RIGHT WING? DEATH SQUADS AND TORTURE? YOU WANNA MENTION BRAZIL?

BRUNO: (*Inside.*) BRAZIL IS NOT IN CENTRAL AMERICA.

BILL: (*Inside.*) THEY KILL THEIR WIVES IN BRAZIL! THEY KILL THEIR WIVES WITH IMPUNITY!

SAYER: (*To Wally.*) Shut the door. (*Wally does so.*) Kids don't wanna real education. Don't wanna learn nothin'.

WALLY: This is a good subject for a meeting. Talk about dollars and sense. The economy. Values. (*Bint is on his way back out.*)

BILL: (*Inside.*) THEY GOT PACKS OF WILD KIDS ROAMING THE COUNTRY!

SAYER: Don't slam the door. (*Bint carefully shuts the door.*) Christ, can't anybody stay in the meeting?

BINT: (*To Cross.*) I looked at her. I coulda been wrong.

CROSS: I'm gonna kick your fuckin' head in.

SAYER: Stand clear, Bint. (*Bint steps back. Martin comes out the door. To Cross.*) Reproduction's the most important thing, anyway. That's all that's goin' on. Reproduction. Planet Earth don't care 'bout nothin' else. Get 'em all reproducin', vibing into the stratosphere.

MARTIN: What kind of an idea is that, Sayer?

SAYER: What kind of idea?

MARTIN: What kind of idea.

SAYER: A big idea. What I've been trying to tell you, Martin. An observable phenomenon, Martin. (*As Martin goes back in.*) Why you look at the girls and the girls look back, Martin.

WALLY: I love that! (*Pause.*) Electricity is what it is. Ever seen it?

BINT: In the air?

WALLY: Everywhere. Right, Dr. Sayer?

SAYER: Ha! Right on, Wally!

WALLY: Seen the grid from the sky? Satellite Point Of View? Come on!

SAYER: I got two kids to talk about, myself. That's Shatter and Wade. Shatter's the girl. They're totally dysfunctional.

WALLY: For example, forty years ago we beat the Japanese and the Germans and now they're both trying to slap us around. (*To Cross.*) That's an historical truth. (*Bint starts to go back in.*)

SAYER: (*Stopping him.*) Bint! Ha! Kids don't wanna work, neither one of 'em. Wanna live for free. You take my daughter, Shatter—

WALLY: Shatter, I love it!

SAYER: Yeah, that's my wife's idea, "Shatter." Ex. Shatter, she's been living off me. I told her, get out, find a job. You can stay with me a month or two, the minute I find any booze or drugs, you gotta leave. I go to empty the trash, there's empty whiskey bottles and beer bottles. I told her, no partying in my house. I threw her out. She goes to live with this woman on welfare, the old man is screwing the kids!

BINT: Sonofabitch!

SAYER: Wade, he ploughs right under the axle of a tractor/trailer! Engine's in the back seat, they had to slice him outa there. Kid lives! He's got cuts and bruises and a broken thumb. Third time in a year he's totaled a car. You think he's trying to tell somebody something? Nineteen years old, he's going eighty, ninety miles an hour into a load a timber, he's leveled by the axle of the truck! Broken thumb and he lives! He's banged up, though. This time it's his mother's car, my ex-wife's. I told him, you're not driving my car! He did his, then he did his girlfriend's, now he's smashed his mother's!

CROSS: I have no opinions, Sayer, and no preferences. As far as I'm concerned, you can sell both your kids for meat.

SAYER: Yikes, Cross. (*Lights his cigar. Martin comes out, quickly shuts the door.*)

MARTIN: (*Frustrated.*) It's a free for all in there.

CROSS: (*Stepping away.*) That's how we get into trouble, Sayer. With our beliefs and requirements.

SAYER: (*To Martin.*) Trouble, Counselor?

MARTIN: They don't understand the rules of order! They don't understand the goddamn law! The law is clear—you do wrong—wham, bam, into the slammer!

CROSS: Our expectations and delusions.

MARTIN: Oh, that's just your fuckin' attitude of the day, Cross.

CROSS: (*Stunned.*) What?

SAYER: (*To Bint.*) You don't work, you don't eat! You can't read, you're illiterate! Hey, Martin! What's a virus?

MARTIN: Don't do that shit with me, Sayer.

SAYER: A virus is a formula! It is neither dead nor alive! It's in between! It is numbers, Martin, actin' like parasites! And they mutate! (*Goes abruptly inside.*)

CROSS: (*To no one.*) "The first bringer of unwelcome news hath but a losing office."

MARTIN: What is that referring to?

CROSS: I wasn't talking to you.

MARTIN: That's how people do!—They come around with an attitude —this week they got one attitude, next week they got another one! And don't start talkin' about the fuckin' Romans! They were choppin' people's heads off and throwin' 'em off cliffs and sewin' 'em up into sacks with chickens and dumpin' 'em into the fuckin' river! Fuckin' animals!

CROSS: (*Quietly.*) It was to deprive them of burial, of the sacred rites.

MARTIN: (*Going to the door.*) Rights! (*Bint opens the door slightly, listens.*)

SAYER: (*Inside.*) There will always be torture! Because torture is interesting! And I will tell you why! It is a way of playing with the energy of a man! It is a way of saying No to life! It is rebellion! It is a poking, a tweaking of the invisible, a provocation to God, a denial! It is a stripping away of conscience! It is a form of sexual activity! For some, it is a method of preparing the will for the spirit world! For this life is only pain, pain is its product, its substance, which can be transformed, through endurance, into Power! (*Martin shuts the door.*)

MARTIN: (*To no one.*) He's a fuckin' maniac. (*To Wally.*) You got people in there—they're so fuckin' nervous—they squeak—

WALLY: I know it!

MARTIN: You got people in there—they feel your eyes on 'em—they shrink—their heads turn like fuckin' snails, man!

WALLY: I know it!

MARTIN: You take pills?—I take pills—I take aspirin—I drink coffee — I used to guzzle booze—

BINT: Whoa! (*They watch as someone else arrives for the meeting.*)

MARTIN: Don't slam the door! (*Door slams.*) Christ!

CROSS: (*Uncomfortable.*) I guess the real meeting's inside. (*Turns to go, hesitates.*)

MARTIN: They don't know! Nobody knows! Electromagnetic fields! Who can talk about that? We've got power stations and cables all over the country fer chrissakes! What are we gonna do, tear 'em down? There's no evidence magnetic fields are causing cancer in kids! You wanna live in society, you got exposure to electric and magnetic fields! You hear what I'm saying? This is a world that uses electricity!

BINT: Whoa! Say no more! (*Screamer screams, off.*)

CROSS: Man was meant to walk through Earth's direct current, steady-state magnetic field. Man-made alternating currents will cause anything magnetic in their path, including the human brain, to vibrate sixty times a second.

BINT: Whoa!

CROSS: (*To Wally.*) That's a scientific fact. (*Screamer screams.*)

MARTIN: (*Of the Screamer.*) Someone should shoot that guy. They're all kindsa diseases fer chrissakes—we just got over polio!— Remember?

BINT: No.

MARTIN: That's right—before your time—buy lands—way things are goin'—the Japanese'll beat us to it—be so many fuckin' people there won't be room to piss—buy lands!

WALLY: People don't have jobs, you can forget about it. You gotta build. (*They watch as Shatter goes by.*) Pacific Rim, Martin. Pacific Rim . . .

MARTIN: (*Watching her.*) Pacific Rim, Wally. (*Of Shatter.*) Cute. I can't get over this thing—what drives us?—she's so cute.

BINT: You mean . . . ?

MARTIN: I mean—she looks at me, I look at her, she looks at me, I look at her—she gets in her fuckin' car!—What is that?

BINT: I get it!

MARTIN: She seems like she's a real honey—I think I'm gonna have a good time—like she's gonna worship my dick and what have you— and what?—She starts sayin' things!

WALLY: (Sly.) Scares ya, eh Martin? Scared they'll leave ya, scared a betrayal.

MARTIN: Forget about it, Wally.

WALLY: You know what it takes? Get on TV? Make a commercial?

BINT: You gotta be gorgeous, right?

WALLY: Big lips. That's what it takes, big sexy lips. I know, 'cause I buy ads.

MARTIN: First they're Daddy's little girl—Daddy's girl. Then calamity falls—(To Cross.) That's GREEK—

WALLY: You almost got married, didn't ya Martin?

MARTIN: Don't get cute, Wally.

WALLY: That's right. Better see what's goin' on. (Opens door, listens.)

SALLY: (Inside.) I just don't know if you can walk the streets anymore! I can't cross the street near my house! I can't get across because of the cars and the trucks! I just want to say that! Because you can get run over! You can get smashed! They don't stop and they don't slow down! The whole neighborhood is shaking and rocking with the noise! When I was a girl right here a person could cross the street! Hasn't anybody noticed what's going on anymore? I just wanted to say that!

BILL: (Inside.) Thank you, Sally!

BRUNO: (Inside.) Can I add to that? I'd like to mention the homeless who are on our streets, the vagrants and panhandlers and poor people who are on our streets, who are living in the park and in the alleys and who can be quite aggressive!

ANN: (*Inside.*) I think that's a good point! But I don't agree with this man's attitude! What kind of a society is this? What kind of a culture is this? What kind of a neighborhood is this?! Where families don't have a decent place to live?! And people have to threaten and beg for their lives?!

WALLY: (*Shouting in.*) Next time someone asks me for money, I'm gonna crush his face!

FOLKS INSIDE : BOO! SHUT THE DOOR!

MARTIN: Shut the door. (*Wally, laughing, shuts the door.*) I'll tell ya— I'll tell ya what I think—

CROSS: What's that?

MARTIN: I think we should protect the rich—I'll tell ya—I go to the opera—and I see all these white-haired gentlemen in the audience with their ladies—and I'm comforted—I'll tell ya—these guys are holding the whole thing up.

CROSS: I see what you're saying.

MARTIN: If you're gonna take care of people, who should you take care of? The ones who have a stake in everything or the ones who wanna bring it down? Who? Think about it.

CROSS: I do.

MARTIN: It's the upper classes—we wanna make sure they survive— that they take an interest—I'm telling ya the truth, I see all those guys in the audience with their ladies, and I'm reassured—I feel better about the future.

WALLY: Yeah, yeah, and they listen to the music.

MARTIN: Well, not only that—they hold it up—they hold the damn thing up—you gotta be stupid not to see that the ones with the most investment are the ones most needing the protection! (*Sayer steps out, annoyed.*)

SAYER: Jesus, can't anyone stay in the meeting? This is serious! Say what you got to say in the meeting!

WALLY: (*To himself.*) Yeah, yeah, rock and roll.

MARTIN: Come on! (*He and Wally start in—a confusion at the door—Sayer stays out and Cross starts off.*)

SAYER: (*To Cross.*) Where you goin'?

CROSS: I'm goin' to the bathroom. (*Exits. Bint snickers.*)

SAYER: What?

BINT: I'll bet he's an Arab.

SAYER: He's not. He's a Jew.

BINT: Cross?

SAYER: Russian. (*Enter Ginnie.*) Ginnie! (*Bint sneaks off.*)

GINNIE: What's up, Sayer?

SAYER: You came to the meeting!

GINNIE: So?

SAYER: You don't come to public meetings.

GINNIE: This isn't going to the meeting. This is standing outside.

SAYER: (*Showing cigar.*) This is the real meeting, Ginnie.

GINNIE: Okay. (*Pause. Wade's boom-box music can be heard, off.*) What's this about power stations and cancer?

SAYER: Transformers and cables, Ginnie, adjacent to the school. Makes waves. (*They look around.*)

GINNIE: God. (*Facetious.*) Is there reason for hope, Sayer?

SAYER: Certainly. Anything can happen, Ginnie. Science. We'll unlock the secrets of nature. Who knows what's possible? We can get energy from sand, from sea water. We'll have skylabs. We'll monitor the planet from space. We'll have factories on Mars. We can solve everything. We just don't know now. It's in the future. There is a future, and it is endless, like the sand, the sea.

GINNIE: What do we need?

SAYER: We need more faith, faith in knowledge, in the future. Think of the future. Think of a hundred, a thousand years. Think of it!

GINNIE: That's good, Sayer. You're good. (*Pause.*) All these people in the Government know how to say is everything's all right. Don't predict anything bad happening at all, ever. Be a reflection on them. Don't predict anything good happening, either. No change at all, Sayer, good or bad.

SAYER: Status Quo. You have your reproductive processes and the eternal menace of the Left. Ha! You got that?

GINNIE: Conglomeration of timid assholes. It's not all right, Sayer.

SAYER: I'm not interested in making this a better world, Ginnie. Everything is just right and the way it ought to be and couldn't be otherwise. Let's legalize it and leave it alone. Come on, I'll escort you in.

GINNIE: Better leave the cigar, Sayer.

(*Cross reappears as Ginnie goes in, Sayer hangs back to put out his cigar. Ann passes him, looking for Cross. Sayer bows and tips his hat.*)

SAYER: That was Ginnie. Ol' Ginnie just wants to make sure the Real Estate keeps goin' up. Ha!

ANN: (*Distracted.*) Oh.

SAYER: (*Pointing.*) There he is, Mrs. Cross.

ANN: Thank you.

SAYER: (*Taking her arm.*) I just wanted to say, Mrs. Cross, since you're leaving the meeting—

ANN: I'm not leaving the meeting.

SAYER: It seems to me that certain people are harnessing the power of the universe in order to transform it into noise! They are doing it in all ignorance. I saw a program on television, the talking heads had figured out chaos! They could see chaos, there on the screen, the very design of chaos! They didn't know anything. (*Indignant.*) They thought they were important! (*Pause.*) And you could see the dying there that were plugged into the machines, into the sockets, into the walls! It had to do with the heartbeat, with heart attacks! The silent, intimidated anguish of chaos! That is, without sense or order or meaning!, not to the dying nor to the lives that had gone before!, all the moments to this moment plugged into the wall!

ANN: I'm sorry. I'm sorry you saw that.

SAYER: No problem, Ma'am. Excuse me. (*Sayer goes back inside. Ann approaches Cross.*)

CROSS: You didn't have anything to do with it.

ANN: I know I didn't.

CROSS: So why are you sorry? He's pulling your chain. (*Bint re-enters, pretending to be a man of hurried purpose; checks them out; goes to door.*) You know him?

ANN: No. Who is he?

CROSS: One of Sayer's boys. A subject. A pal. (*Snickers. Bint goes inside, leaving the door ajar.*)

GINNIE: (*Inside.*) So what the hell do you propose, Martin? What's your proposition?

MARTIN: (*Inside.*) MUTUAL PROTECTION! WE LIVE IN A DANGEROUS WORLD! SHUT THE DOOR BUT DON'T SLAM IT! (*Bint slams the door. Cross snickers.*)

ANN: (*To Cross.*) Why are you treating me this way?

CROSS: Did I ever tell you about the Greeks? Did we ever talk about that? (*She turns and walks away from him. Pause.*) Shit! (*Enter Shatter, smoking; Cross watches her, fascinated. Ann goes inside. Shatter approaches:*)

SHATTER: Do you despise weakness? (*Pause.*)

CROSS: Yes. (*Pause.*) Don't you?

SHATTER: Yes, it makes me sick, and I see a lot of it.

CROSS: (*Facetious.*) Just say, "no."

SHATTER: Feels like food poisoning. (*Pause.*) Nauseating.

CROSS: Do you always talk to strangers?

SHATTER: Always. And you?

CROSS: Ah. I take your point.

SHATTER: This is a good time and place for an action, a discussion.

CROSS: An action?

SHATTER: It's a protest. We're protesting.

CROSS: What?

SHATTER: The murder of the Universe.

CROSS: I see.

SHATTER: By Man. (*Pause.*) By poison and fire. (*Pause.*) By noise and anger. (*Pause.*) By wind. (*Pause.*) What will you do?

CROSS: Uh, I'll play a teacher.

SHATTER: Okay. (*Pause, formally.*) I have to destroy his power. I'll get into a trance and I'll stab him a thousand times.

CROSS: Who is he?

SHATTER: He has to be cut up, dismembered. I'll destroy his power. If I don't cut him up in a hundred parts, he'll still have his power.

CROSS: Did he come to this meeting?

SHATTER: He'll keep his power. I have to cut him up and throw his parts into the ocean. Then he's dead. Then he's in the spirit world, without his power.

CROSS: Do I know him?

SHATTER: Later, maybe I can forgive his spirit. I can evoke his spirit, and offer him forgiveness. Later. Now I must dismember him. First things first.

CROSS: Let's talk about it. Let's take it easy.

SHATTER: You're full of shit. You're not doing it.

CROSS: Are you Shatter?

SHATTER: What a bogus disappointing drag you turned out to be. (*Starts to leave.*)

CROSS: Wait! Listen! (*She stops.*) The set for the Greeks, the Ancient Greeks, was a giant door. This has to do with the old religion. Wait!

SHATTER: (*Stopping again.*) Go.

CROSS: For the Greeks there was a door, a big upstage door, the door to the household, to the palace. All the action was in front of the door or behind the door, and the chorus moved around like a wave and the messengers and visitors came and went. The action—(*He stops, considers.*)—was in motion, in progress, and the murder was behind the door. Wait. Not necessarily the murder. Behind the door was the hearth, and the household Gods, and images of the ancestors. Next to the house or in back of the house was the tomb of the ancestors. The Father and his father and his father's father!

SHATTER: Was what?

CROSS: Was the worship, the religion. (*Sayer steps outside, door open.*)

GINNIE: (*Inside.*) Society is not organized for cultural reasons! Society is not organized for justice! Society is organized for survival! Every other consideration is a pain and a joke and a waste of time!

CROSS: Survival . . .

BILL: (*Inside.*) May you be loved and liked and may you die immediately!

GINNIE: (*Inside.*) That means competition! You stupid clown! That means an economy!

SHATTER: I can't stand it.

FOLKS INSIDE: Shut the door!

SAYER: Come into the meeting, Cross! Ol' Ginnie is holding forth for the Real Estate! Ha!

CROSS: No!

SAYER: (*Closing the door.*) Why not?

CROSS: Too much smoke!

SAYER: There's no smoking anymore! (*Seeing Shatter.*) Talking to someone? Trying an action?

CROSS: I was saying how the dead were more with us in the old days, Sayer; they had a real place among the living, and watched, and waited, and were fed.

SAYER: As if alive?

CROSS: Yes, by virtue of the inheritance, the patrimony. The dead fathers were served by the sons. Burnt offerings, Sayer, sacrificed to the dead.

SAYER: Goddamned kids think everything just appeared, for their use. Forget it all got to be worked for and maintained. Want to live like bloodsucking parasites. (*To Shatter.*) This is Mr. Cross.

SHATTER: (*To Cross.*) How are you?

CROSS: Devastated.

SAYER: Don't let me interrupt the event, the action, the occasion.

SHATTER: We're talkin' power.

CROSS: Look up to him and admire him but stay out of his life.

SHATTER: Power plays with equal or more power.

CROSS: That's the law of power.

SHATTER: In obedience to the law of power, women are dishonored. Wives, daughters, secretaries, sisters—dishonored! (*Slaps hands with Cross.*)

CROSS: (*To Shatter.*) Very good. (*Pause.*)

SAYER: (*To Shatter.*) Where's Wade? Come on!

SHATTER: He's around.

SAYER: What's he doing? Come on!

SHATTER: He is skulking.

SAYER: How 'd he get here? You bring him here? Come on!

SHATTER: No.

SAYER: DID HE DRIVE HERE? DID HE DRIVE HERE IN A CAR? COME ON!

SHATTER: Yes, Dad.

SAYER: WHERE'D HE GET THE GODDAMN CAR? WHOSE CAR? (*Shatter doesn't answer.*) FUCKIN' IDIOT!

CROSS: (*To Sayer.*) Who? (*Sayer goes back into the meeting.*)

SHATTER: Wade. That's my brother. He stays down in the City of Commerce. He lives in rooms.

(*Ann re-enters from inside. She and Shatter size each other up. Shatter moves off.*)

ANN: Who is she?

CROSS: That is Shatter. Her brother's name is Wade. They're Sayer's kids.

ANN: I feel sorry for them. The man is out of his mind.

CROSS: He's ecstatic.

ANN: Oh, come on.

ROSS: Did people call you Cynthia?

ANN: When?

CROSS: Whenever.

ANN: Very few. (*Pause.*) Why?

CROSS: Do you know a guy named Bint and a brother, Brian?

ANN: I know neither a Bint nor a Brian. (*Pause.*) What kind of a name is Bint?

CROSS: Maybe the family name.

ANN: No.

CROSS: As in Cynthia Ann?

ANN: What's the matter with you?

CROSS: Sorry. You never bargained for this . . .

ANN: For what?

CROSS: For presiding over this decline of powers, this moral diminution.

ANN: Oh, stop it!

CROSS: Please don't talk that way!

ANN: How?

CROSS: With the OH prefix.

ANN: (*Choking him.*) I'll stop it if you stop it!

CROSS: Go ahead! Finish it! End the terrible slide!

ANN: My God! I thought I was marrying an intellectual, a historian.

CROSS: And instead?

ANN: Instead I got Bozo the Clown. Wait here.

CROSS: Where are you going?

ANN: To the ladies room. Which way?

CROSS: The other one. (*She goes off. Shatter reappears.*)

SHATTER: They're lying! They don't know what's real!

CROSS: How do you know? (*Wally sneaks out, singing to himself.*)

WALLY: Why not stay on her good side
And be on your own side too
A man has got a lotta strong
So what have you got to lose

A man knows how to play it
An actor knows how to choose
Dummies can't find . . . to say it
And smart guys get along . . .

SHATTER: (*To Wally.*) Shut up, you fucking male chauvinist putz.

WALLY: (*Staring at her.*) What?

SHATTER: You heard me. You're a male chauvinist putz and a liar. (*To Cross.*) Excuse me.

CROSS: Sure thing. (*She goes. To Wally.*) You two know each other? (*Wally doesn't answer.*) How's the meeting . . . ?

WALLY: (*Lighting a cigarette.*) Wally.

CROSS: How's the meeting, Wally?

WALLY: Oh, it's just fine. Peoples expressing their views. You ought to participate, it's the American Way.

CROSS: I brought my wife.

WALLY: There you go.

CROSS: Can I stand next to you and breathe your air?

WALLY: (*Alarmed.*) What's that?

CROSS: The smoke.

WALLY: Sure thing.

CROSS: What are you into, Wally? I mean in life.

WALLY: Cattle.

CROSS: Oh?

WALLY: There are four levels to the cattle business. First you got the ones who make the calves, the cow and calf operation. There's about a million of those in this country. They're marginal. Their place in this business is hard to see. They go to the bank—the bank's got the calves as security—and get a loan to produce the calves and then they sell the calves to the larger ranches where they pasture. There's maybe a hundred thousand of those. They get the calves up to three hundred pounds and then they're finished off at the feed lots with another coupla hundred pounds. And then they go to the packers. There's only three or four of those. And that's the structure of the cattle business.

CROSS: Thank you.

WALLY: You're welcome.

CROSS: H2-0, Wally.

WALLY: What's that?

CROSS: That's water, Pal.

WALLY: I know what water is. Are you saying something?

CROSS: Once the earth was a fireball, Wally. (*Pause.*) And then it rained. (*Walks away.*)

WALLY: I hear ya. (*Enter Wade.*)

WADE: I thought I'd come to the meeting.

WALLY: So?

WADE: Okay.

WALLY: What makes you think I'm interested in that? (*Pause.*) You don't know me. We've never been introduced. We've never talked. We have no idea who each other is, do we?

WADE: No. I just thought maybe I'd come to the meeting. I thought it might help me to talk about myself.

WALLY: It might.

WADE: I don't know, though.

WALLY: (*Referring to the bandages.*) What happened to you? Run into a truck?

WADE: Yeah. I don't go out much at all. You can't trust anyone. My sister wants to do an action. I don't know how things work. I can do refrigeration, I guess.

WALLY: Do you go out with girls?

WADE: Ha! (*Shyly.*) No. Do you think I should?

WALLY: Come on! What's your name?

WADE: Wade.

WALLY: Come on, Wade! Good for your health!

WADE: Do you do that?

WALLY: What?

WADE: You know. I don't think I could do that. You know, like talk to a girl.

WALLY: Pull yourself together! (*Starts away.*)

WADE: Do you think all women are the same? I mean, do you think there are any differences at all?

WALLY: Yes and no.

WADE: Of course.

WALLY: There's no free lunch, I can tell you that. Fuck 'em and watch the spin! Ha!

WADE: Ha!

WALLY: Humans!

WADE: Yeah.

WALLY: It's like we gotta do it!

WADE: That's what I mean! I mean, the family. . . . Actually, what I mean is, what if this is just a moment? Where it's here and it's gone, you know, where it'll be something else, some other kind of creature?

(*Pause.*)

WALLY: Nah! If I get your meaning, can't be.

WADE: No?

WALLY: Why? Because we got all the electronics now. That's why I see it that way. Sure. We've broken through into the electronic world. We've got all KINDS of electronics. Never go back, never flash off forever. Sure, that's why I feel that way. Can you feel that?

WADE: Oh yes, I do.

WALLY: Okay?

WADE: Thanks a lot. Thanks a lot for talking to me. (*Wally starts off, enter Ann. To Ann.*) Are you hungry?

ANN: I beg your pardon?

WADE: I'm sorry. I just think about food all the time. I don't know why. I. . . .

ANN: You have an eating disorder.

WADE: Are you . . . ?

ANN: Well, yes.

WADE: Is that all right?

ANN: Well, yeah, if you face up to it. (*Pause.*) I don't mean that in a violent sense. I just meant, you can see it for what it is and work on it, one day at a time.

WADE: I guess I don't understand.

ANN: That's okay. (*Pause.*)

WADE: Are you waiting for someone?

ANN: My husband was just here a moment ago . . .

WADE: Is he an older person?

ANN: Well . . .

WADE: People don't intend to look old.

ANN: He's got white hair. But he's not old.

WADE: Okay. (*Silence.*) I have poor communication skills. I saw you go into the meeting. I guess you didn't like it.

ANN: I like the meeting.

WADE: You like the meeting?

ANN: Sure.

WADE: You do? My father is in there.

ANN: Which one?

WADE: Dr. Sayer.

ANN: Why don't you come in?

WADE: I can't do that.

ANN: Why not? Don't you have views?

WADE: Views?

ANN: An opinion. You can speak up in the meeting.

WADE: (*Sincere.*) Do you think it would do any good? Do you think anybody is doing any good in the world?

ANN: (*Touched.*) Yes, I do. Teachers can help. Workers can help. Children can help. It's the children who are dying.

WADE: You don't ever see 'em.

ANN: They're dying of electricity. From the cables, the power stations. Near the schools, and the. . . And poison. It can be slow. It's in the air and in the water and in the food.

WADE: I'm hungry all the time.

ANN: Me too.

WADE: Are you?

ANN: Yes, I am.

WADE: For awhile, I didn't eat at all. I was starving myself, I guess. Now I eat everything.

ANN: You have to eat—(*Wally comes over: he's very interested in Ann.*)

WALLY: I just wanted to tell this kid—you think the Japanese would be into what they're into if, uhm, you know? Electronics?

WADE: I don't know.

WALLY: Electronics! The Japanese! Remember? It's forever!

WADE: Okay!

ANN: (*To Wade.*) You have to look at it. When you're hungry, is it a feeling?, or do you really need food?

WALLY: Oh, you guys talking about eating?

ANN: Well . . .

WALLY: (*Keeping her there.*) It's like bugs or something what people eat. They'll eat anything if it's got like a crust and it's soft and sweet inside. You got chemists, you got biological engineers all over the globe coming up with substances that the human organism will pay money for. Substances, stuff. They'll eat. They wanna eat, they gotta eat. They eat when they're hungry, they eat when they're not. They eat for reasons, any fucking reason. They eat because they're afraid, they eat for sex, they eat for entertainment. They like it, they'll buy more, they don't just eat once. They eat until they're sick, they eat until they die. They don't know what they're eating—it's in a package, it's called food, they'll eat it. So you got these professional junk food manufacturers—I saw a program on this—they make a study of what you like to chomp down on, what kind of texture you like, they plug you right into a computer and they figure out what the human brain will go for in the way of eating shit. Then the chemists go to work and they make it. Say it's like blue cheese, they wanna make a blue cheese deal to go in the middle of something with just the right texture on the outside, they take a molecule of blue cheese and they break it down and analyze its structure and they build up a molecule which tastes like cheese and smells like cheese but it ain't cheese. It's the ghost of cheese, a facsimile of cheese, a cheese-like substance which is a lot cheaper than cheese, and they put a crust around that which is equally unreal in that it is not made from anything that has grown in the ground or walked on the earth. Then the marketing geniuses design a bright little plastic package for it and they call it the Blue Cheese Donut Delight! Ha! Okay?

WADE: Are you . . . ?

WALLY: I'm in the cattle business. Real food. Meat. (*Ann looks for Cross.*) I was telling a white-haired gentleman about it before.

ANN: That's my husband. He must be inside.

WALLY: He ain't! (*She goes in anyway. He watches her leave, follows to the door, looks in.*) Uh, oh. (*Sayer starts out. Wade puts distance between them.*)

SAYER: (*Half in, half out.*) THE MOST IMPORTANT DEATH OF ALL IS MINE. IT IS IN FACT THE ONLY DEATH. IT IS MINE IN SOLITUDE, AND THE ONLY ONE.

MARTIN: (*Inside.*) SHUT THE DOOR, Sayer. (*Sayer does so.*)

WALLY: What I was trying to tell you before, Sayer, about electricity—

SAYER: That wasn't you, that was Bint.

WALLY: That was me. Bint doesn't know anything. The power, the electricity, is sucked out of the flow of water, out of the air, out of the little worlds and big worlds, sucked out, drained, and grounded as waste into the Earth.

SAYER: Time is running out, running out into the walls, into the machinery!

WALLY: That is to say, the flow of electrons, with vibration, movement, currents, waves, is channeled into the machinery and then dumped as waste into the earth.

SAYER: THE MOST IMPORTANT DEATH OF ALL IS MINE. IT IS IN FACT THE ONLY DEATH. IT IS MINE IN SOLITUDE, AND THE ONLY ONE.

WALLY: Good, Dr. Sayer!

SAYER: (*Shouting, to Wade.*) What is the Sun? Come on!

WADE: The Sun is a star.

SAYER: No! The Sun is a hole! Come on! What is the moon?

WADE: The moon is a planet.

SAYER: No! The moon is a rock! Come on! Where is the earth?

WADE: The earth is between.

SAYER: Right! Between a hole and a hard place! Ha! Come on! Don't you find this entertaining?

WADE: Sure, Dad.

SAYER: Come on! Why are people round?

WADE: Are people round?

SAYER: Well, they have a round shape. And all the microbes are equally round. What do you make of that?

WADE: I don't understand where the competition comes from then.

WALLY: Good point, Wade! Ha! (*Enter Cross.*)

SAYER: Best get back to the meeting, Wally.

WALLY: Yeah, yeah, rock and roll . . . RAP . . . OP-ER-RA . . . (*Goes.*)

MARTIN: (*Inside.*) DON'T SLAM THE DOOR.

SAYER: Hell of a meeting, Mr. Cross.

CROSS: Is my wife in there?

SAYER: For example, cocaine is a product, right? Opium is a product. It's a product. It comes out of the ground, it's a flower. It's a pretty flower, right? So where do we draw the line? What's going on?

CROSS: Are they talking drugs now?

SAYER: How can you not talk about drugs? You can't not talk about drugs anymore! You got a group of guys running the coke trade, you got others running the opium, you got the marijuana business. Ain't it the same with sugar? Ain't it the same with tobacco? I mean, where is the difference there? And what about alcohol? It's not good for ya, either. It's an abused substance fer chrissakes! So you got these fucked up economies, right? You got these populations out of control. You got these huge debts. They owe us money! These people owe us a lot of money! And we got this huge demand here. We got an America with an insatiable appetite for drugs. And these people are supplying the demand. And they owe us money. You see what I'm saying?—you look at it clean and there ain't no difference. These agricultural products are meeting a market demand. I mean, what is it we are doing? Let us leave the market be and get our money back, with interest! (*Pause.*) Ha!

CROSS: Ah.

SAYER: (*To Wade.*) How'd you get here? COME ON! DID YOU WALK? DID YOU DRIVE?

WADE: I'm okay, Dad.

SAYER: DID YA RIDE OVER IN A CAR? (*Wade doesn't answer. Sayer stares at him. Wheeling, to Cross.*) What's a CANCER CLUSTER, Cross? Come on!

CROSS: No.

SAYER: I still have a bone to pick with you, Sir, about speaking and oratory.

CROSS: My mother was schizophrenic and abusive; my brother is schizophrenic and retarded; my sister is so shy she's in a convent in Ohio; and I got a great Aunt left in the family, but she's had a series of strokes and is losing her mind. Ha.

SAYER: Ha! Back into the fray now, Mr. Cross! (*At door.*) Watch out for ol' Ginnie, for she is in a foul mood! (*Goes in.*)

WADE: Ginnie's his friend.

CROSS: Ah.

WADE: She's conservative.

CROSS: Ah.

WADE: I think about suicide a lot.

CROSS: (*Dismayed.*) Why?

WADE: I don't know. I have thoughts. He's very creative. He's an entrepreneur.

CROSS: Who?

WADE: My father.

CROSS: True.

WADE: It's hard to live with a man like that. (*Cross sighs.*) She pulled up my big sister by the hair and threw her around the room, against the walls.

CROSS: Who did?

WADE: My mother. My sister has problems.

CROSS: Everybody, Wade. Everybody in that room's got problems.

WADE: Oh, yeah, sure, I see what you're sayin'. Thank you. I feel better talkin' about it.

CROSS: You don't have to thank me.

WADE: Okay. (*Wally comes half-way out, hesitates.*)

BILL: (*Inside.*) I don't have a stake in this fucking country and at my age and you got nothing but contempt for that! I can see it on your face as you go farting through the K -Mart!

MARTIN: (*Inside.*) Fuck you!

ANN: (*INSIDE.*) Did you hear uh, uh, . . . that Doctor . . . ? His talk was of angry children . . . ? That was his theme. That the children are angry, because of all the abortions. When the child is killed in the womb, then the soul of the murdered child is made angry. And they come back, they come back as the newborn, as angry children! (*Cries.*)

GINNIE: (*Inside.*) It's all right, honey. There, there. Just a theory. Don't take it all to heart.

MARTIN: (*Inside.*) CLOSE THE DAMN DOOR, Wally. (*Wally goes back in, closing the door.*)

CROSS: That was Ann.

WADE: Oh. Is that your wife? (*Cross nods.*) She seems nice. (*Cross nods.*) Oh. I forgot to tell you, she was looking for you.

CROSS: Thank you. (*Of the bandage.*) Hurt yourself?

WADE: Yeah, I had an accident, I guess. (*Cross stares.*)

CROSS: When I was your age I was blasting away at myself, blasting away, like a miner, like a saboteur, like a terrorist. I wasn't investing in my future, I was trying to smash a loop into the sublime.

WADE: Oh, that's good!

CROSS: You're thinking, "That old fart, he's difficult to get along with." Naturally, you don't think it'll ever happen to you. I see what I've become and I can't do anything about it. Time and experience wear you out. I've lived five lifetimes already.

WADE: I don't think like that.

CROSS: You don't?

WADE: I'm sorry.

CROSS: Come on!

WADE: I cruise in the City of Commerce. I live alone in rooms. He drove right into a trailer. He drove right into a truck. He drove right into the Bay. He killed himself. He took a hike. That's how I think. The black guys out there take advantage of me. I don't know why.

CROSS: You don't?

WADE: Yeah, I do.

CROSS: What do you do for fun?

WADE: I like music, I guess. (*Cross stares.*) I drive a lot. I don't like to drive, but I do a lot of it. I don't understand where everybody comes from or where they're going. I just wanna crash it. (*Cross stares.*) Everybody's angry. It's not my fault. They all had mothers. They're psychopaths, alcoholics and addicts. When I'm thinking about it, I'm thinking about smashing her. (*Cross stares.*) Do you drive?

CROSS: I'm new here.

WADE: Oh, I see. That's it, then. Do you . . . uh . . . teach?

CROSS: History. Ancient.

WADE: Bitchin'. (*Cross stares.*)

CROSS: It's the most amazing thing: a school in the valley, a house with a porch . . .

WADE: Yeah . . . I wanted to love her. I was an innocent child.

CROSS: (*Not hearing him.*) I should have been a filmmaker.

WADE: Really?

CROSS: I keep having this vision. I see this image. It's a film image, a sequence in black and white. A woman, wearing a shawl, a wanderer, is approaching. She is dark, in her forties, greying, still beautiful. Very sad. She is coming for her allotment, her allotment, on a street. The sky is background, a sunset. It is near the sea. The woman approaches, staring at the street. She knows the people in this place, who will provide her allotment, her portion. She is one of those . . . one of those upon whom vengeance has been taken, and she's saying, "Have you seen my man? Have you seen him? I was just hoping you'd seen my—my husband, he's vanished."

WADE: It's sad. Is that how it ends?

CROSS: Yeah . . . I want a drink. I want a smoke. I want to check out.

I'm okay and you're okay. I feel crowded. I'm gone. (*Walks away.*)

WADE: Where you goin'? (*Cross doesn't answer, wanders off. Shatter appears, way off, calls out.*)

SHATTER: Wade! Wade! (*Wade steps back.*) ARE YOU ANGRY? ARE YOU ANGRY, Wade? COME ON! (*Wade takes another step back. Shatter withdraws. Ann comes out, searches.*)

ANN: (*Seeing Wade.*) Oh!

WADE: Hi.

ANN: I'm looking for my husband. Have you seen my husband?

WADE: (*Shocked.*) Well. . . .

ANN: (*Distraught.*) Oh, where is he? What's wrong?

WADE: He's coming back, I guess. (*Ann looks at him.*)

ANN: What kind of a kid are you?

WADE: I'm a beastie boy and a bum, I guess.

ANN: Oh, God!

WADE: Did I say something wrong?

ANN: Nothing. Never mind.

WADE: What's the matter?

ANN: Oh, I don't know. (*Pause.*) I don't know what they think about me. I'm embarrassed how much I care what they think about me.

WADE: They maybe don't think about you at all, I guess.

ANN: Oh, how would you know! You won't even attend the meeting! There's a woman in there who hates my views! Why don't you even go inside!

WADE: Do you think I should?

ANN: (*Distraught.*) Oh, God! What's the matter with you? They're trying to help!

WADE: Well . . . I don't say what I have to say because I don't know. I don't know what I have to say.

ANN: But you can't act as though nothing's happening! It's possible to become monstrous!

WADE: Actually, I have nothing to do with it.

ANN: God. I need a break. (*Wade walks away, leaving his boom box. Yelling inside. Ann wipes the tears from her eyes. Ginnie comes out.*)

GINNIE: Hi.

ANN: Hi.

GINNIE: I didn't mean to insult you. You weren't the target. (*Pause.*) I agree that we should all save money on nuclear arms now. I just hope they don't put it into social programs. Makes for a weak country.

ANN: What about Health Care?

GINNIE: Nobody has to pay for health here. You just have to know what to do. People come here and live off the fat of the land. Like the Mexicans. (*Ann bursts into tears.*) All right, all right. Listen to this. I heard a chiropractor the other day, she's talking about the new age: people will live a thousand years, they won't get to puberty till they're a hundred, they'll be as calm as clocks and clear-minded. She's got the idea that billions of years of accident and cosmic debris are in the body. Health is detoxification of enemy vibrations from the past life of the Earth. Ha! That and the realignment of entities. As I understand it, an entity is anything that moves. Everything that moves is from the Divine Will toward Being, the explosion of space into space, the first endless moment. All is and isn't, as the Masters say, for in the beginning was Nothing. (*Laughs; off, the Screamer screams.*)

ANN: Who is that person?

GINNIE: You get used to it. You get used to everything.

ANN: (*Cold.*) Thank you.

GINNIE: Don't thank me. Self-reliance is what makes a country strong, honey, and violence is a part of that. It's the struggle for life. It's competition. Violence is the key, violence is the mode. What's good for me may not be what's good for you. Should we treat people like children and take care of them? Sex is violent. Eating is violent. Should we stop killing animals for food? At least we don't burn them alive, like in the old days, for the gods and spirits. Politics is violent because that is its nature. Power means violence. It does not mean civility. Civilization means amenities for the powerful, for the ones who can afford it. Culture is an amenity, a way to occupy the mind, to pass the time. Otherwise you work, eat, sleep, fuck and die. In any event, you die. Working is better than not working. Working is for the morally fit. To lay around, to do nothing, to indulge, to want to be taken care of—this is a life unworthy even of insects. (*Ann walks away from her.*) What are we supposed to do, give up our energy? Our light and heat?

ANN: We're gonna bring the whole thing down, them and us! Take the very breath out of the atmosphere!

GINNIE: What difference does it make? Old age and death are curses enough! Earth is nothin' but a pain factory! It will bubble up, when the time comes, with a new set of employees!—Insects, probably! (*Shatter has appeared on the periphery, listening in.*)

SHATTER: Were you talking about incest?

GINNIE: No. Insects.

SHATTER: I thought you were talking incest.

GINNIE: Insects.

SHATTER: I could say a few things.

GINNIE: Of course, dear.

SHATTER: But I won't!

ANN: Excuse me. I . . . I'm looking for my husband. (*Walks off.*)

GINNIE: Your brother's around, Shatter.

SHATTER: Yeah.

GINNIE: And so's your father, dear.

SHATTER: All over the nation men are hurting women, husbands are killing their wives and getting away with it.

GINNIE: So what do you want from me?

SHATTER: Ginnie! (*Cries.*)

GINNIE: Oh, fer cryin' out loud.

SHATTER: Ginnie! I'm livin' in this house. I'm livin' in the back room. Right here in the Valley. The father, he hates his job, he beats his wife and he screws his daughters! Then he wants me to listen to his troubles and feel sorry for him and pay his goddamn rent!

(*Martin steps out, disgusted.*)

MARTIN: (*To Ginnie.*) I have a choice—I have one choice—I can maintain my fuck you attitude to the bitter end or I can turn myself around and start a new life.

GINNIE: What do you think it'll be, Councilor?

MARTIN: I don't know—it's late in the day—and I like fighting and I love revenge—so it's a tossup as far as I'm concerned—I could go either way—there's something very appealing about goin' out with my shit intact to the last—let's go for a ride, Ginnie.

SHATTER: Hey! We're talkin' here! My father kicked me out! They put me in a hospital and gave me drugs! If people stopped taking drugs this whole country would turn to shit! You got that? I'm protesting!

MARTIN: (*To Shatter.*) Talk! Talk! Rock and Roll!

SHATTER: I drink and I smoke. I know that. I don't feel good about that. I'd like to talk about it. At least Wade doesn't drink, doesn't smoke. Wade's clean. He is now. He had enough of the City of Commerce and he went home. People pickin' on him in the City of Commerce. Gross shit. Scared lil white boy. Call him a mushroom. What's he to do now? At least he's a poet.

(*Ann approaches the door, looks in.*)

MARTIN: (*To Shatter.*) Get adjusted! That's the trouble! Nobody makes an adjustment! Move away! Find a home!

SHATTER: (*Singing wildly.*) They'll always negate you
    Prosecute and hate you
    Humiliate and screw you
    Sacrifice and fool you—!

GINNIE: Stop that!

SHATTER: I'M GONNA KILL SOMEONE!

MARTIN: HEY! CAN YOU DO NO WRONG? ARE YOU A SAINT? WHO ARE YOU TO JUDGE? OBEY THE LAW AND WATCH YOUR ASS! YOU SHOULD GET OUT OF BED IN THE MORNING AND SAY THANK YOU A THOUSAND TIMES YOU WOKE UP IN AMERICA!

(*Ann opens the door.*)

SAYER: (*Inside.*) Something is going to happen—worse than AIDS. A plague, a virus, it's in the works now. It's being prepared. Somewhere, in the womb of the earth, in the atmosphere, is being prepared an antidote to man. The catastrophe is here, but the correction awaits us. Floods, famine, drought, the burning of the forests. Massacres. Planes falling out of the sky. We have despoiled the chain of existence. But these are ticks, these are spasms, signs and portents. The fulsome planetary shudder is yet to come. I don't think it will be nuclear, no—it will be just as total, but more subtle: atomic, viral. A virulence never seen on earth, because we are so many. And the poison in the chain—no, the lawful results of the poisoning of the chain—will destroy all but a few: the renaissance man, the enlightened, the fit to live. I won't be here. I am neutral. I am interested in the science of it, in the laws. I won't be around. I will have met my Maker, the Initiate of Laws, who regards his Work with sublime neutrality from a higher world. His Will be done. Let the survivors remember what happened here—if there are survivors. I couldn't say. This is only an opinion. It could be indiscriminate. It's possible. The fit could die with the unfit.

GINNIE: The sonofabitch is reading! He's making a prepared speech!

(*Ann steps back as Bint comes out.*)

MARTIN: (*Of Sayer.*) Who is he?—Who does he think he is?—He doesn't make a dime!—Nobody pays attention to him!—Nobody votes for him!—Nobody puts his name in the fuckin' paper anymore!—Fuck him!

GINNIE: He read from a text!

SHATTER: I can't stand it! (*Attacks Bint and beats him. Music. Sayer and the others come rushing out.*)

WALLY: OH, SHE'S A SPITFIRE SHE IS!

(*Sayer pulls Shatter off of Bint.*)

SHATTER: (*To Wally.*) DROP DEAD YOU SCUMBAG!

SAYER: (*To Shatter.*) HAVE YOU BEEN DRINKING?

(*Bint starts crawling off. The Screamer screams. A HUGE, SHATTERING CRASH, close by. Cross comes running in, finds Ann and takes her in his arms.*)

WADE: (*On boom box tape.*) You talk as though you don't know and maybe you don't, but maybe you better express your feelings because time is wearing out your sneakers and fiendish darkness is wearing out your welcome. (*Pause.*) You don't have to smile when I smile and I don't give a shit if you know or you don't.

SHATTER: Wade?

WADE: (*Tape.*) The Earth will bounce its axis and momentum like the snap of a ball and shake off the slugs and everything else on it into oblivion which is a long fall past the moon deader than absolute nothing and meanwhile I'm hanging here figuring things out responsibly like I know what to do, going from here to there on my rump and saying things with my mouth.

SAYER: (*To Cross.*) Where? (*Cross points, Sayer rushes off. Martin follows him.*)

WADE: (*TAPE.*) What I want to do is come alongside with my wheels on straight and eyes level with things as they are and have the knives out for people who bother me—because if you don't win, you lose around here, pal—but my head feels like a tired tree with old leaves in the smog and my chest is like crusty with like 32 years of agent orange and I wish it would rain.

ANN: (*Upset, to Cross.*) What happened?

CROSS: He crashed, honey. Let's go home. (*Leads her off.*)

WADE: (*Tape, continuing.*) I want to be left alone to die but by the same token I don't. Of all the moments gone and coming how many would be shaken out into the void like dead leaves when the big shake that's on its way is here? Like a ball, like a towel, like a rug—SNAP.

(*Ginnie turns off boom box. Blackout.*)

END

CITIES
OUT
OF
PRINT

BY
SUSAN
MOSAKOWSKI

Cities Out of Print was commissioned by BACA Downtown in 1988 where it was presented as a work in progress. It was then further developed and presented at the Padua Hills Playwrights Festival in 1989. It premiered in New York at the Manhattan Theater Club in 1990. The Padua Hills cast was as follows:

He	John Diehl
She	Shawna Casey
Director	Susan Mosakowski
Lighting Design	Jason Berliner
Sound Design	Susan Mosakowski

THE LANDSCAPE:

At the edge of the stage, as if taking a curve, is the skeleton of a crashed car. Assembled from wrecked car parts, the twisted body appears as if the front end is making a turn while the back end trails behind in a cartoon-like image of speed. At the furthest point upstage center, stands an isolated door hinged to a door post. Spinning freely around itself, it is always opened and alway closed. A perpetual in/out. Right of the in/out, an elevated billboard features a vista of an open road in forced perspective; the dotted line receding to the horizon. In front of the billboard is a table and chairs, sometimes making the billboard seem like an overlooking window. Down left of the in/out, are vertical lockers spray painted with drawings of animals, people, and names of cities. A glass specimen case, a table, old car parts, and disembodied car seats haphazardly complete the scene.

THE INHABITANTS:

HE
Sometimes known as JFK, Jackson Pollock, Roland Barthes, Frank O'Hara, Hank Williams, General George Patton, T.E. Lawrence, Josef von Sternberg, Alex (*A Clockwork Orange*), Jeffrey Beaumont, and Frank (*Blue Velvet*), Travis Bickle (*Taxi Driver*), George Raft (*They Drive By Night*), and Vaughan (from J.G. Ballard's *Crash*).

SHE
Sometimes known as Jayne Mansfield, Isadora Duncan, Grace Kelly, Bessie Smith, Jessica Savitch, Marlene Dietrich, Dorothy (*Blue Velvet*), Ann Sheridan (*They Drive By Night*), and Catherine (from J.G. Ballard's *Crash*).

Included in the text are inserts from the films: *Blue Velvet, They Drive By Night, Taxi Driver,* and *A Clockwork Orange.* Additional inserts are from J.G. Ballard's novel *Crash,* General George S. Patton's speech on D-Day, Jeffrey Potter's *To A Violent Grave: An Oral Biography of Jackson Pollock,* and Frank O' Hara's poem, *The Eyelid Has Its Storms.*

Day Zero (the prologue)

Bright lights up revealing He and She vigorously polishing the car. She rubs and rubs. He rubs and rubs.

HE: Are ya getting a shine?

SHE: I'm working on it.

HE: It's gonna sparkle!

SHE: It's gonna light up!

HE: Yeah.

SHE: Yeah.

(Rub rub rub . . . rub rub.)

SHE: It's gonna shine like a mirror careening down the highway.

HE: The green lights are gonna beam off the windshield like a spaceship in the night.

SHE: It will see everything like a huge eye penetrating the galaxy.

HE: Yeah.

SHE: Everything.

HE: Yeah.

(Rub rub rub . . . rub rub . . . she looks into the bumper . . . she rubs rubs rubs . . . she looks into the bumper . . . she breathes on the bumper and rubs and searches for her reflection. Nothing. He stops rubbing. He watches her as she frantically breathes and rubs, breathes and rubs.)

HE: If you keep rubbing like that you'll put a hole in that bumper.

SHE: WHAT'S WRONG WITH THIS BUMPER!

(He looks into the bumper.)

HE: It's shining . . . but it's not picking you up.

(She leans closer to the bumper, her eyes search the bright surface.)

SHE: It's shining . . . but it's not picking you up.

(*They turn to each other, their expressions fall from their faces, leaving them like two empty masks.*)

(*Blackout.*)

Day 1

(*The sound of soaring winds . . . then lights up. She walks towards the front of the car. At the specimen case, he waits, holding a long blond wig in his hands. She yanks a squashed high heel from under the front tire, and finds the other lying in front of the car. She slips them on and walks to the waiting wig. He fits the wig over her head. She turns to him and he places a license plate under her arm as if it were a clutch purse. He drops a set of car keys into her waiting palm and leaves through the in/out. Strains of Bernard Herrman's score for* The Day the Earth Stood Still *come up. Her spikes hit the floor as she moves to the car. Headlights beam on. She sits at the wheel as the voluptuous and very blond Jayne Mansfield. She tosses her license plate on the hood and kisses her 2D cardboard dog, Chou Chou, and places him on the dash. She gives it the gas and peels out. The simulated sounds of tires screeching blast on cue from the car. She drives her car. She drives a stationary wreck of twisted metal. She takes the curve, the wheel vibrates and throbs in her hands. In apparent simulation, automobile sound effects continue. Little Richard's* Lucille *blasts from the car radio.*)

> **Lucille, please come back where you belong.**
> **Oooohoooohoyaahhha please come back where you belong.**

(*Rocking and rolling to Little Richard . . .*)

> **I give it to ya baby please don't leave me lone.**
> **Well I woke up this morning Lucille was not in sight,**

(*The car screeches along . . .*)

> **I asked my friends about her but all they did was laugh.**
> **Lucille, baby satisfy my heart.**

(*The car CRASHES throwing her forward onto the steering wheel.*)

> **Lucille . . .**

(Car crash soundtrack off. He turns on his portable cassette, the voice of Travis Bickle from Taxi Driver *seamlessly interfaces as the new soundtrack. Cued to the soundtrack, he assumes the identity of Travis Bickle, and she drops the Mansfield act. She pulls off her wig and kicks off her shoes. As Travis Bickle, he opens locker after locker until he finds his revolver. He practices his pistol technique. Finishing, he slams the lockers shut one by one.)*

> **May 10th, thank God for the rain which has helped wash away the garbage and trash off the sidewalks. I'm working long hours now, 6 in the afternoon to 6 in the morning, sometimes even 8 in the morning 6 days a week sometimes 7 days a week. It's a long hustle but it keeps me real busy. I can take in three, three fifty a week, sometime even more when I do it off the meter.**

(Leaning against the front fender on the passenger side of the car, she waits for him to finish his routine. He enters through the in/out to the melodic strains of the Taxi Driver *theme.)*

SHE: Wrong! *(He snaps off the soundtrack.)* I'm set up for Jack.

HE: Were you just doing Mansfield again?

SHE: Yeah, I lost my head.

HE: Where's the dog?

SHE: In the ditch.

HE: Perfect.

(Simultaneously they burst into peals of forced hysterical laughter. Their laughter comes to a dead stop. He turns on the soundtrack. She opens the imaginary rear door for him. He gets in the back seat. She takes her place at the wheel. He snaps off the soundtrack.)

SHE: Jack? . . . .

HE: Jacked in.

SHE: Alright. Where to?

HE: Dallas. Get in the back.

SHE: Listen baby, I can't drive and be Jackie too.

HE: Just drive.

SHE: You got it.

HE: Hit the fucking road.

(*She hits the drive button. The simulated sounds of the car peeling out blasts from the car. She drives as he waves to the imaginary crowds lining the Dallas street.*)

SHE: Here it comes baby . . . .

(*Four high-powered rifle shots are heard. He lurches forward, his body contorting with each shot. His head ricochets from side to side. She crashes the car again. Soundtrack off.*)

SHE: You were good . . . real good.

(*He snaps upright.*)

HE: Yeah, 'n the shots came right on time.

(*He snaps on his portable cassette; the soundtrack from* Taxi Driver *comes on again. On cue with the soundtrack, he assumes the identity of Travis and gets out of the car.*

> *All the animals come out at night.*
> *Whores, skunk, pussys, buzzards, queens, fairies, dopers,*
> *junkies—sick . . . venal.*
> *Someday a real rain will come and wash all the scum off*
> *the streets.*

She throws him a crowbar. He wields the crowbar at times like a Kendo warrior, then as a street fighter, then as an angry man trashing a city street. He lunges with ripping and tearing motions, lashing out as if he could carve the space around him. She pulls a knife from the trunk and edges her way past him. He rushes to her as if he were going to strike her with the crowbar, catches himself, and turns the attack into a violent embrace as he hooks her neck with the crowbar and draws her close . . .)

HE: Goodnight Kid.

> *I go all over. I take people to the Bronx, Brooklyn,*
> *I take em to Harlem, I don't care.*
> *Don't make no difference to me . . . . it does to some,*
> *don't make no difference to me . . . .*

(*He exits through the in/out. She places the crowbar in the specimen case and removes a black wig. She reclines in a bucket seat near the specimen case. She snaps on the soundtrack from the film,* Blue Velvet. *She puts on the wig, she listens, and lip-syncs the lines of Dorothy as played by Isabella Rossellini.*)

> *Get out of there! Get Out!*
> *Put your hands up . . . on your head!*
> *Do it!*
> *Get on your knees. DO IT!*
> *What are you doing? Who are you?*

(*From the in/out he emerges carrying hubcaps and his cassette player. Puccini's aria ("O mio babbino, caro") from his opera,* Gianni Schicchi, *blasts from his recorder in counterpoint to her soundtrack. He presents her with a hubcap. She ignores his offering. He throws it at her feet.*)

> *What's your name? What's your name?*
> *Jeffrey.*
> *Jeffrey what?*
> *Jeffrey nothing.*
> *Give me your wallet.*

(*He offers another, she ignores him, he throws it at her feet.*)

> *Give me your wallet. Give me your wallet.*
> *Jeffrey Beaumont . . . what are you doing in my apartment*
> *Jeffrey Beaumont?*

(*The ritual is repeated again. The hubcap is hurled and crashes at her feet.*)

> *I wanted to see you.*

(*He stops and pulls a bra from his pocket. He places the bra over her breasts.*)

> *Are you kidding? Who sent you here?*
> *Nobody.*

And what did you see tonight? Tell me.

(Frustrated with being ignored, he snaps off the aria.)

HE: Give me the keys.

(She turns off the Blue Velvet soundtrack and lifts the bra from her breasts.)

SHE: Where'd ya get this?

HE: In a glove compartment of a Chevrolet. It's for Mansfield.

SHE: Jayne's not here.

HE: I know.

SHE: I'll give it to her.

HE: Give me the keys.

(She hands him the keys. He sprints to the car.)

SHE: Vaughan!

(He stops dead in his tracks.)

SHE: Vaughan?

(Transformed into Vaughan.)

HE: Where to?

SHE: The Road Research Laboratory . . . where the cars are cracking into the concrete target blocks.

(He places a trashed car seat opposite her for an erotic reverie.)

HE: Yeah, I can see it in my head . . . playing over and over like a slow-motion film . . . IMPACT!

SHE: Yeah, I can see it in my head . . . WHIPLASH!

HE: ROLL-OVER!

SHE: ECSTASIES!

HE: HEAD-ON!

SHE: Sometimes when I'm cruising alone I see myself at the controls of those impacting cars. The concrete target block rushes down the runway head-on over and over and the moment of impact lasts forever and ever and the skin breaks and breaks and the glass tears open the air and the glass tears open the air . . . .

(To break her repetitious fixation with tearing glass, he brays in a cockney accent as Alex from A Clockwork Orange:)

HE: How about loaning me a quid and the Jag? *(She tosses him a derby and cane. He dashes to the car.)* We were all feeling a bit shagged, fagged, and faished, it having been an evening of some small energy expenditure . . .

(He turns on the car tape featuring tires screeching and Rossini's The Thieving Magpie.)

HE & SHE: . . . Oh my brother . . .

(They begin their riotous routine. He takes the curves, the wheel throbs under his fingers, and the simulated sounds of tires screeching blast on cue from the car. His driving becomes more reckless. Suddenly, she hurls herself in front of the car as the crash victim. She tries to crash on cue with the screeching soundtrack. On the second try she makes it. She hits the road, a twisted wreck. He turns off the tape. She comes to life.)

SHE: So we got rid of the auto . . .

(As he pulls her up from the ground and she takes his arm.)

HE & SHE: . . . and stopped off at the Corova for a nightcapper.

(They exit through the in/out. She re-enters and immediately is aware of the absence of a taped soundtrack. She waits, not knowing what to do or how to continue. Uncomfortable with the silence, she turns the car tape back on. The Thieving Magpie, again blasts away, and features tires screeching. The car crashes. He appears in the doorway.)

SHE: Where'd ya go?

HE: Checked out the tree on 466.

SHE: What are you, some kind of dog hanging around that tree?

HE: Don't talk about Jimmy Dean's tree that way or you'll find yourself at the end of a fast moving scarf. It's my totem pole, baby.

(*He revolves round and round in the in/out. She joins him.*)

SHE: It's nothing but scars . . .

HE: Get the typewriter. I'm doing an action poem on Jimmy.

(*She emerges from the in/out and is aware that he is acting as Frank O'Hara.*)

SHE: Frankie, it's gone, you ran over it the last time you got worked up. The guts were crashed.

HE: Screw it! O'Hara has it up here with immediate transmission to the digits. I don't need a typewriter. I'll scratch it out in the sand . . . It will be born as it dies . . . I see the sand stretching before me . . .

(*He drops to his knees, then splays himself out in the sand. She drops beside him and playfully knocks on his head.*)

SHE: Frankie . . . Frankie . . . are you there?

HE: Hmmmm . . .

SHE: Jimmy's poem will go with your "Lana Turner Has Collapsed" poem.

HE: Yeah. Next time out it's Old Fireplace Road to check out Jackson's tree. You must know my poem to Jackson, "The Eyelid Has Its Storms."

SHE: Some other time, Frankie.

(*He begins finger snapping to the beat. She joins in as they beat it out.*)

HE: "The Eyelid Has Its Storms." "There is the opaque fish-scale green of it after swimming in the sea and then suddenly wrenching violence, strangled lashes, and a barbed wire of sand falls to the shore."

SHE: That's beautiful . . . now let's get back to Alex . . . (*In cockney.*) How about some supper Alex?

(They dash to the trunk and do an inventory of cassette tapes.)

HE: What have we got?

SHE: We got . . .

(As he reads the titles, he throws the cassettes over his shoulder. She catches the rapid media fire.)

HE: *Blue Velvet, Drugstore Cowboy, Blowout, Roger and Me, A Clockwork Orange, Patton, The Blue Angel, Taxi Driver,* the news, *They Drive by Night, Lord of the Flies, Mondo New York, Blade Runner* . . .

(She halts the media fire.)

SHE: What'll it be?

HE: The news.

(They hoof it, double-time, to the table as if they were doing a comic vaudevillian shuffle. They immediately sit. She grabs a nearby waste basket and dumps it over. Broken crockery hits the table. In unison, they put on safety glasses.)

SHE: Stand by, GO.

(He hits the cassette player which broadcasts the news. They both listen and lip-sync:)

> *Orders from big ticket factory goods had their sharpest increase in fifteen months in December. It capped the best year for manufacturers since 1984. At least thirty three Mexican miners . . .*

(He snaps off the broadcast and picks it up live:)

HE: At least thirty three Mexican miners are feared dead after an explosion and fire in a coal mine near the Texas border. Some one hundred forty men were inside the mine. An unprecedented global summit on AIDS is underway in London, health officials from a hundred fifty countries attending. One expert predicted one million cases by 1991. Now this:

(On cue, she repeats the same newscast. Midway she forgets her lines; he feeds

her a line to keep her going. She continues to lose her place and stumble and break down.)

SHE: At least thirty three Mexican miners are feared dead after an explosion and fire near . . . near . . .

HE: The Texas border.

SHE: Some one hundred forty men were inside the mine. An unprecedented . . .

HE: Global summit.

SHE: Global summit on on on.

HE: AIDS.

SHE: AIDS . . . Good evening . . . I'm I'm I'm I'm I'm I'm I'm—

HE: Jessica!

(He smashes the crockery with a hammer.)

HE: DRIVE!

(She grabs the keys from the table and thrusts her hand forward as if there were a waiting ignition.)

HE: DRIVE!

(She thrusts the keys forward again in the empty space.)

HE: DRIVE!!!

(Her arm arcs overhead and slowly lowers the dangling keys into her open and waiting mouth.)

(Blackout.)

Day 2

(He stands at the table with a baseball bat. He turns on a cassette player featuring crowds cheering. He steps to the plate. Up at bat he misses the first two pitches, hits the third pitch, runs the bases and skids home. She snaps off the cheering crowds. He freezes on his back in mid-skid. She turns on

Puccini's aria ("Un bel di vedremo") from Madame Butterfly. *Fanning herself with a dismantled fan blade from a car radiator, she kneels above him as the tragic heroine. She quotes a passage from Ballard's* Crash.)

SHE: "Before his death Vaughan had taken part in many crashes. Two months earlier I found him on the lower deck of the airport fly-over after the first rehearsal of his own death. I saw him through the fractured windshield of the white convertible. Vaughan sat on the glass-covered seat, studying his own posture with a complacent gaze. His hands, palms upwards at his sides, were covered with blood from his injured knee-caps. I tried to lift him from the car, but his tight buttocks were clamped together as if they had seized while forcing the last drops of fluid from his seminal vesicles."

HE: I can't hold this any longer . . . what happens? What happened!

SHE: I'm only up to page 10.

(*He breaks the mid-skid freeze and snaps off the tape, leaving her kneeling. He transforms to Josef von Sternberg.*)

HE: Put on your costume.

SHE: What are you talking about?

HE: Lola, my angel, sing.

(*She gets up and straddles a chair between her legs. A cigarette loosely hangs from the corner of her mouth. She sings:*)

SHE: It's not cause I couldn't. It's not cause I shouldn't.
     And you know, it's not cause I wouldn't.
     It's simply because I'm the laziest gal in town.

SHE: Josef, are we shooting this scene?

HE: Yes my dove . . . I want you to sing like a siren, mysterious, magical, so that men like moths will be drawn to your light, to your heat.

SHE: I haven't had any rehearsal.

HE: Would you like a cigarette?

SHE: I'd like a lipstick.

(*He produces a lipstick, and applies it to her lips as if he were putting the crowning touches on his masterpiece.*)

SHE: Josef, who do I look like?

HE: Marlene.

SHE: Do I really look like her?

HE: No one but you could look like her.

(*She savors this thought, then abruptly, as if she were on the movie set, she gets down to business.*)

SHE: Where's the professor?

HE: Jannings' practicing his cockcrowing for the final scene.

SHE: Why does he have to break down like that . . . humiliated, dishonored, emptied . . . it's sadistic.

HE: Some must be emptied so others can be full. Now sing.

SHE: I can't.

HE: You can and you will.

SHE: Don't pull that director act. Without me this picture would be nothing!

HE: Without me you'd still be with Ziegfield.

SHE: Hang on to your crown jewels Josef, because I know that your real name is not von Sternberg.

HE: Don't push me.

SHE: Are we close to the edge?

HE: You're fired!

SHE: Impostor! Pseudonyhmbo! Who are you? What's your real name?

HE: Who wants to know? (*Covering his left eye.*) Marlene? or (*Covering his right eye.*) Marlene?

(*He exits through the in/out. Her "Marlene" identity drops and for a moment she stands alone and lost. She picks up a knife from the table as Dorothy from* Blue Velvet. *Sensing him behind the door:*)

SHE: Get out of there! Get out! (*He enters with a vacuum cleaner and drops it on her command.*) Put your hands up! On your head! Do it! Get on your knees! Do it! What are you doing? Who are you? What's your name? What's your name?

HE: Jeffrey.

SHE: Jeffrey what?

HE: Jeffrey nothing.

SHE: Give me your wallet. Give me your wallet!

(*He produces his wallet.*)

SHE: Jeffrey Beaumont . . . what are you doing in my apartment, Jeffrey Beaumont?

HE: I wanted to see you.

SHE: Are you kidding? Who sent you here?

HE: Nobody.

SHE: And what did you see tonight? Tell me.

HE: I saw you come in, I saw you talk on the phone . . .

SHE: And then??????

HE: I saw you get undressed.

SHE: Get undressed. I want to see you.

(*He starts unbuttoning his shirt, then abruptly breaks and heads for the specimen case. Grabbing some paint cans he heads for the car.*)

SHE: What are you doing? Where are you going? You're not going to paint?! Jackson! Who the hell do you know who understands your picture? People understand the painting, the dripping, the splattering, the action, but who really knows the picture? . . . the contents?

(*He piles paint cans in the backseat. She takes them and returns them to the specimen case.*)

HE: Knowing isn't in the head crissake! Knowing, the real knowing is inside. A lot of these guys play it safe. A limb can get awful shaky if you're alone out there and the corner you get pushed in, not by them, but by that horseshit art world that belongs to dealers and those young ass-kissers coming up. Some days I feel big, real big, which is why the corner is getting tight. When a car keeps breaking down, they fix it, but me——

SHE: You're in no condition to drive.

(*He climbs on top of the hood. She plants herself against the front bumper.*)

HE: When you've done it, turns out you're done for . . . in yourself you're nowhere and no one. You're caught, only nothing's holding you. You got to go somewhere, to the edge of something, but there's no edge . . . crissake!

SHE: Then you must be falling. The edges are out there. I see them all the time. They just keep moving, so you have to keep moving.

HE: I have an edge dream, off and on . . . I'm sort of way out there on my own, moving slowly to the edge but not to a cliff, and it's not a void either. What it is, what it feels like, is just more me, on and on. Give me the Olds. (*She tosses him keys.*) These are to the Rover 3500. (*He tosses them back to her.*)

SHE: Then I must drive. (*She slips on a pair of dainty white gloves.*) Moving to the edge . . . to the cliff . . .

HE: Grace, don't go there!

SHE: And closer . . .

(*He grabs her. She reacts as if they were doing a love scene, and that he was about to kiss her.*)

SHE: . . . and closer . . .

HE: Cut it out!

(She stops, and looks around bewildered, then, as if she came to her senses:)

SHE: Tell the Prince I'm going shopping.

(Like a vacuum cleaner salesman he demonstrates the virtues and smooth handling of the vacuum.)

HE: It goes anywher,e anytime, and it's great on palaces.

SHE: I'll take it.

HE: Good.

(He takes the keys from her hand, she snaps back to her old self. They pause as if they don't know who they are or how to continue. She drops the vacuum and drifts from place to place as he paces nervously. Then, with an effort she begins:)

SHE: Where'd ya find it?

HE: Back seat of a Cadillac.

SHE: See anyone driving?

(She opens the vacuum cleaner and with a knife cuts the vacuum bag which has consumed a perfume atomizer, a toothbrush, bottlecaps, dirt, dust, and debris from modern life.)

HE: Nah. Nobody drives anymore, they look for parking spaces . . . idling in and out . . . in and out . . . then they turn off the ignition and vanish inside the mall. Once they go in it's all over . . . they just shop and shop and shop and then they die. It's a funeral parlor out there, nobody drives.

(She mists herself with the perfume atomizer. He catches a whiff of perfume and begins breathing heavily. He makes his way to the specimen case and puts on a breathing mask as he transforms to Frank in Blue Velvet. *He breathes . . . she waits . . . he breathes . . . she tranforms to Dorothy.)*

SHE: What are you doing? Who are you? What's your name? What's your name? *(He continues to inhale deeply through the mask as he turns to her.)* Frank . . . hi baby.

HE: Shut up! It's Daddy, you shithead. Where's my bourbon? Get the fucking bourbon.

(She runs and gets an empty can of Coca Cola and offers it to him. He smashes it out of her hand. She recoils in terror.)

HE: That's not the fucking bourbon. Can't you fucking remember anything?! Don't you look at me! *(She whips her head the other way. He grabs a pair of scissors from the table . . .)* Don't you fucking look at me!

(He sits down . . . then transforms.)

HE: How about a trim?

(She takes the scissors and begins cutting his hair. Pulling playing cards from the deck as if they were from a Trivial Pursuit game, he reads the questions.)

HE: Blue. How many tennis players play tennis?

SHE: All tennis players.

(They burst into hysterical laughter.)

HE: Green. Why do dogs lick their balls?

SHE: Because they can.

(They burst into hysterical laughter.)

HE: Yellow. What's the name of a cold South American country?

SHE: Chile.

(They burst into hysterical laughter.)

HE: Red. How many U.S. presidents have been assassinated?

SHE: Not enough.

(They burst into hysterical laughter.)

SHE: How we doing?

HE: Get the crowbar.

(Blackout.)

Day 3

(He sits in a trashed bucket seat next to the specimen case practicing the dialogue from Taxi Driver *along with the movie soundtrack.)*

> *Listen you fuckers, you screwheads,*
> *here's someone who would not take it anymore,*
> *who would not . . . let . . .*
> *Listen you fuckers, . . . you screwheads,*
> *here's a man . . . who would not take it anymore,*
> *a man who stood up against the scum, the cunts, the dogs,*
> *the filth, the shit . . .*
> *Here is someone who stood up.*

(She comes in through the in/out. She carries a rust-corroded car muffler. She presents it to him as an offering. He ignores it. Determined to make him respond, she exits and enters again. She presents the same muffler again. She offers it lovingly. His obsession with Taxi Driver *continues. In anger, she throws the muffler at his feet. He ignores the crashing sound. She stands over him. He ignores her deliberate presence. She hits the stop button.)*

SHE: Give me the keys.

(He tosses her the keys and punches the tape player back on. She walks aways then suddenly turns back to him. She hits the stop button and throws the keys back to him.)

SHE: Not the BMW, I want the Bugatti.

(He gives her the same set of keys and punches the tape player back on. She hurries towards the car then suddenly breaks into dance and returns to him. She snaps off the tape player.)

SHE: Forget about the screwheads. Hold this. We're going to the cliffs.

(She flings a long scarf into his hands and winds one end around her neck. She assumes the identity of Isadora Duncan as she dances towards the car. She gets in the car and peels out taking the curves at breakneck speed. Little Richard blasts from the radio, "She can't help it, the girl can't help it." He stands next

to the car flapping her scarve in the breeze. He suddenly yanks the scarf—her neck snaps back—the simulated sound of a car crash—her head falls limply from her neck. He plays the traffic cop. She plays dead.)

HE: Pull over. You drive too fast. Show me your licence . . . Isadora Duncan. You were good, you really know how to move.

(*She snaps back to life.*)

SHE: Yeah.

HE: Get out of the car.

(*She gets out of the car, then stops as if lost, not knowing what to say or how to continue. She turns to him, he has dropped the cop routine and stands staring into space. She manages to speak.*)

SHE: You said to get out of the car.

HE: Yeah.

SHE: I'm out of the car. (*No response. She shouts:*) I'M OUT OF THE CAR!

(*Jolted from his suspended state, he mechanically feeds her an opening line which snaps them into a George Raft/Ann Sheridan routine from the movie,* They Drive by Night.)

HE: That's some classy chassis you got there, sister.

SHE: Yeah and it's all mine, all paid for.

HE: I wouldn't mind making a down payment.

SHE: You couldn't afford the headlights.

HE: Whata ya got around here that ain't poison? How about a cup of java?

SHE: How about a pair of shoes . . .

(*She produces two shoes.*)

HE: Whose are these?

SHE: Albert's.

HE: Albert who?

SHE: Albert Camus.

HE: Where did ya find them?

SHE: On the gas pedals of a Vega. Tag'm.

(He takes them to the specimen case and ties a name tag to the shoes. She exits through the in/out and returns with more shoes. She announces the names of their owners.)

SHE: Jayne, John, Travis, and Vaughan.

(He picks up their shoes as he speaks of each person.)

HE: First there was Jayne, Jayne met John, then came Travis and Vaughan.

(She returns with more shoes:)

SHE: Alex, O'Hara, Jessica, von Sternberg, Marlene.

HE: Followed by Alex, O'Hara, and Jessica. Jessica met von Sternberg and von Sternberg met Marlene.

(She returns with more shoes:)

SHE: Dorothy, Jackson, Gracie, Frank, Isadora, Bessie.

HE: Then came Dorothy, and Jackson. Jackson met Gracie, Frank and Isadora. Then there was Albert. Albert met Bessie, and Bessie met Hank, Roland and Patton. Then there was Lawrence, followed by . . .

(With all of the shoes piled in his arms, he continues the sequence of the litany as he drifts through the in/out.)

HE: . . . Jeffrey and George and Ann and Catherine . . .

(She enters, as if she were a performer making an entrance on stage, acknowledging the presence of the audience. She walks to the specimen case and examines the contents:)

SHE: You find in police museums collections of items under glass cases. If you move into a house that hasn't been properly cleaned up, you find strange unrelated items.

(*She breaks out in a blues song in the style of Bessie Smith.*)

> A pen and a hairclip, a copy of a poem,
> that's all I need . . . that's all I need,
> ta see all da folks that once lived in this house.
> I got da empty house blues, got da empty house blues,
> list'nin all night ta empty stomping shoes.
> And now I'd like to introduce my good friend, Hank Williams.
> Come on out here, Papa.

(*As Hank Williams he joins her with a cassette player cradled in his arms like a guitar.*)

HE: Howdy Bessie.

SHE: Howdy Hank.

(*He sings:*)

HE: A pen, a hairclip, a copy of a poem,
> that's all I'll ever need,
> to know all the folks that once lived in this house . . .
> that's all I'll ever need.

(*She sings:*)

SHE: I got the empty house blues.
> I got the empty house blues.

(*She leans in the doorway as he continues:*)

HE: And now I'd like to do a special number for you it's called: "I'll Never Get Out of This World Alive".

(*He turns on the soundtrack of Hank Williams' "I'll Never Get Out of This World Alive". He stands holding the cassette player and smiling as his foot taps the beat. The smile slowly leaves his face as the song plays. His foot stops tapping. Suddenly his eyes snap shut,.and the song is cut off.*)

(*Blackout.*)

Day 4

He sits at the table writing, his pen poised in the air. She stands behind him quietly with her hand on his shoulder. They remain in this still tableaux throughout the day.

SHE: What are you writing?

HE: Shish. I'm thinking.

SHE: I thought you were writing.

HE: I was writng, now I'm thinking.

SHE: What are you thinking about?

HE: Origins, the beginning of the beginning.

SHE: It will never fit in a book. Listen Roland, lighten up.

HE: I thought you liked my piece on the *New Citroen* and *The Pleasures of The Text* you said was titillating.

SHE: It set my cerebellum on fire. What are you doing now?

(Nothing has changed.)

HE: Writing.

SHE: It looks like you're thinking.

HE: They both look the same.

SHE: Roland, there are only letters on this page.

HE: Yes.

SHE: Roland, where are the words?

HE: I don't know. I'm lost in the letters . . . the space is eternal.

(In unison, they speak as his pen is drawn slowly to meet the paper.)

HE: Out out out out out out out out out out out out!

SHE: In in in in in in in in in in in in in in in in in!

(His pen finally reaches the page.)

HE: Listen, the mute are speaking and the babblers are silent.

SHE: Roland, what is this place?

HE: It is the place where one waits.

SHE: Roland, are we waiting?

HE: Yes my swan.

SHE: Roland, open the door.

(Blackout.)

(Lights up. Firmly, loudly, agitated:)

SHE: Roland, open the door.

(Blackout.)

(Lights up. She casts herself to the floor, screaming and pleading:)

SHE: ROLAND, OPEN THE DOOR!

(Blackout.)

Day 5

He marches through the in/out as General George S. Patton with a riding crop under his arm. She sits in the front seat of the car with her head and face covered in Bedouin garb.

HE: We're not going to just shoot the sons-of-bitches, we're going to rip out their living goddamned guts and use them to grease the treads of our tanks. We're going to murder those lousy Hun cocksuckers by the bushel-fucking basket. War is a bloody killing business . . .

(She snaps open her face flap:)

SHE: Georgie, cut it out!

(Closing the face flap.)

HE: Rip em up the belly. Shoot em in the guts!

(*Opening the face flap:*)

SHE: Let's go for a drive.

(*He strides to the car and takes the back seat.*)

HE: Where to?

SHE: Cairo.

HE: Cairo, I was stationed there for two years.

SHE: Georgie, you were never there.

(*He transforms into T.E. Lawrence.*)

HE: The year is 1914, the desert is stretching before me.

(*He hands her the riding crop.*)

SHE: I see, it's Lawrence, isn't it?

HE: Orance is what the Arabs call me . . . we're taking the Blue Mist.

(*She snaps the crop against the side of the car.*)

SHE: Start it up, Orance. We'll pick up some shieks along the way and
we'll rip up the dunes!

HE: We'll bring the Arab revolt to full glory!

(*She beats the side of the car.*)

SHE: Start it up, Orance . . . Orance! . . . Start it up!

(*He tries to start the car, it won't start.*)

HE: Revolutions don't just start like that. They take work and
planning, planning planning planning. We need to regroup.

(*She hands him back the riding crop. They begin again. He enters as Patton
and she assumes the role of the Bedouin escort:*)

HE: We are advancing constantly and we are not interested in holding
on to anything except the enemy's balls. We are going to twist his

balls and kick the living shit out of him all the time. We are going to go through him like crap through a goose . . .

(*She snaps open her face flap:*)

SHE: Cut it out Georgie! D-Day's next week.

(*Closing the face flap.*)

HE: . . . Like shit through a tin horn!

(*Opening the face flap:*)

SHE: Let's go for a drive.

(*He strides to the car and takes the back seat.*)

HE: Where to?

SHE: The Pyramids.

(*Again he transforms to Lawrence.*)

HE: Cairo, the year is 1914, the desert is stretching before me.

SHE: Lawrence.

(*He rises and moves to the driver's seat. She slips the riding crop from his hands.*)

HE: Orance is what the Arabs call me . . .

SHE: I know.

HE: We're taking the Blue Mist.

SHE: This is the Blue Mist.

(*She moves from the front to the back. Standing on the back seat, in slow motion, she delivers blows to his back with the riding crop as he speaks:*)

HE: A herd of wild ostriches crossed my path on the way here, beautiful, wild; running in furious packs their large toes kicking up the dust in vaporous clouds. My Bedouin escort fled after them to make a capture. He raced on his camel alongside the herd and for an instant the herd seemed suspended in the air, running so fast that their legs were pulled tight under them as if they were in a never-ending leap. Released from the ground their plumage flared, their necks were stretched taut and their nostrils were inhaling the sky, and all the while their eyes were wild as they watched the Bedouin disappear in their dust . . . and in the distance the sun was setting like a red mosque on the desert floor and for a moment they were racing toward this red dome and it was impossible to believe that these magnificent creatures could ever bury their faces in the the sand and that they couldn't really fly.

(*She discards the crop.*)

SHE: Start the car, Orance.

HE: Orance has left.

(*Perplexed that he is not playing along, she tries to lead him to a new character.*)

SHE: Then get Jimmy to start it.

HE: Jimmy's not around.

(*He shakes his head no to each name.*)

SHE: Alex . . . Vaughan . . . Frankie? Somebody has to start it. You start it. Take the Pontiac.

(*She hands him a set of keys from a pile of car keys. He tries to start the car. No luck.*)

SHE: Try the Impala.

(*She hands him another set of keys. He tries again.*)

SHE: Falcon.

(*She hands him another set of keys. He tries again.*)

SHE: T Bird?!

(*She hands him another set of keys. The car still won't start. She abruptly stands.*)

SHE: We'll wait . . . We'll drive by night.

(She walks to the table, puts on an apron, and plays Ann Sheridan playing a lunch counter waitress in They Drive By Night.*)*

SHE: Steak's up.

(He sits in the car, not responding. She hits a cassette player: The dialogue between George Raft, Humprey Bogart and Ann Sheridan from the movie score plays. She as Ann Sheridan, repeats her lines. He doesn't pick up on his lines.)

TAPE: Hey Red, this steak's tough.

SHE: Your line.

SHE & TAPE: You can't send it back now you already bit it.

TAPE: I'll be back.

SHE: I'll be back. Your line.

SHE & TAPE: Thanks for the warning.

TAPE: Another cup of java

SHE: Another cup of java. Your line.

SHE: & TAPE: You must like our coffee.

TAPE: It stinks.

SHE: Your line. This is your second cup. My line.

TAPE: I like your sugar.

SHE: I like your sugar. Your line.

TAPE: Give me a cup of coffee.

SHE: The other guy.

TAPE: Yeah, what else ya got that ain't poison?

SHE: Yeah, what else ya got that ain't poison? Your line. Come on Baby, YOU HAVE TO EAT!

HE: We were all feeling a bit shagged, fagged, and faished, it having been an evening of some small energy expenditure . . . oh my brother.

SHE: Now you're cooking.

(*Pleased that he is going along, she sits at the table and deals cards as if he were going to join her.*)

HE: Are you talking to me? You must be talking to me. Spread your legs. There isn't anybody here you must be talking to me. Get me the fucking bourbon! At least thirty three Mexican miners are feared dead after an explosion. You talking to me? I'll go anywhere anytime . . . listen you screwheads . . . WAR is a bloody killing business. Here's a man who stood up. Who are you? Welcome to the OK Club. Who are you? How about a cup of java? What's your name? That's your line. You're not Jeffrey Beaumont, I'm Jeffrey Beaumont. Call me Alex. Make that Jimmy. Forget about Jimmy, it's Hank, gimme my guitar. It's not Hank . . . it's Albert. It's not Albert. I'm not French! It's John, long gone, that's right Gracie . . . I mean Bessie! . . . Jessica! Forget it! It's Lawrence. That's it! Blasted! And Jackson, he dripped off the road, and then there's George crapping up the highways and then Vaughan, yeah, he cracked and cracked. It's Travis, my name is Travis. He stayed on the road. They all stayed in the vinyl seat. They kept driving. They crashed driving right up the middle. Now the freeways are jammed like used car-lots. What happened?

SHE: What's this from?

HE: I'll tell you what happened . . . an intersection appeared. It took us left or right instead of cutting down the middle. Left and right the intersection took us to the shopping malls. We were swallowed up! . . . and our cars were abandoned in the parking lots. We stopped driving. Then we turned on our TVs and went to sleep watching the TV thinking we were watching the world and we talked into our telephones while we were making dinner and we were already taking out the trash and washing our faces getting ready for grid-lock the next day. And we continued to sleep. And in sleep we started our cars. In sleep we were moving in and out of traffic passing each other and I began to dream . . . and I whizzed past my father and his father and tailgated his children and their children and I knew my position as I sped along in perfect harmony. In my dreams, the gas pedals were always down. In my dreams, the motor purred, the headlights worked. I knew where I was going.

Everyone had the green light. No red lights, no caution, no stopping, no grid lock, no stopping, no getting off, no left, no right, no wrong direction, just a clean cut down the middle. Get the knife. Your line.

(Silence.)

(Blackout.)

Day 6

Terminally bored, he sits tossing cards in the air. She turns on a tape of Bessie Smith . . . listens, shuts it off, fast forwards at random, play on, stop, play on at random, stop, fast forward at random, stop, play, stop, play . . .

HE: Whatsa matter, got the blues?

(She nods her head and continues . . .)

HE: Write a song.

SHE: Don't feel like singing.

(She continues to fast forward at random, play, stop, fast forward, and rewind. The tape crackles and speeds crazily along, almost impossible to bear.)

HE: Now there's a tune . . . stop listening to your old songs.

SHE: They're not my songs, they're Bessie's.

(She continues to play at random, he has to shout to be heard.)

HE: Then write your own.

SHE: Can't.

HE: Then can it! Play something else.

(She turns on a different cassette, then another and another until all the tape players are going. All playback, a babble of noise. In defiance she brays:)

SHE: HA HA HA HA HA HA HA HA HA HA HA HA HA HA HA
    HA HA haha ha ha ha

ha ha ha HA HA HA HA haha haha haha haha aaaahhhh

(*Trying to form the words of a song, she blurts out a phrase, then repeats it, then starts at another place in the song, then starts again and returns to another place. Her continuity is gone, much like the tape players.*)

SHE: Hahahaha aaaaaaa DA DA da da da da da DA dada da da ha da da I got da da da dadadadada   I got da da dada . . . listen . . . listen . . . I got I got I aaaaa da da em em em empty, I got empty, dada da da da da da da, all night all night I got da da dadadada . . .

(*Physically, she begins breaking down and smashes the crockery on the table with the hammer. Trying to restore sanity he turns off all the cassettes. Silence. Then in an outburst, she brays:*)

SHE: SOB . . . SOB . . . SOB . . . SOB . . . SOB . . . SOB . . .

(*He closes her mouth gently, the braying stops. All sound ceases. They begin dancing, cheek to cheek in silence.*)

SHE: I hear footsteps.

HE: They're yours.

(*Blackout.*)

Day 7

He sits in the back seat, she sits directly ahead of him in the front seat. Both stare at the horizon.

HE: From now on it's you and me, baby.

SHE: Right, just you and me.

HE: Blank tape.

SHE: Tabula rasa . . .

HE: Right.

(*Delayed response.*)

SHE: Right.

(*Delay . . .*)

HE: Our thoughts will be the only sounds, so if anything comes up
we'll tape it.

(*Delay . . .*)

SHE: Right.

(*Blackout . . . then lights up.*)

HE: So if anything comes up let me know.

(*Delay.*)

SHE: I heard you the first time.

(*Blackout . . . then lights up.*)

(*Their heads, in exact unison, slowly pan from side to side scanning the
horizon from east to west and then back again. Midway . . .*)

(*Blackout.*)

Day 8

*He sits at wheel, she at his side. He drives, taking the curves. A small
household fan set up on the dash, blows and whips its wind through their hair
and clothes. Their eyes are fixated on the road. They begin to lean to the side,
she grips the dash.*

HE: We're coming up on a hairpin curve.

SHE: Get ready.

(*They break the simulated action. They leave the car and move to the table. He
sits down. She stands behind him. The ritual begins: he hands her
fingerprinting equipment and lifts his hand. She presses his fingers into an
inkpad and then presses them to paper. She walks to the specimen case and
places the fingerprints in a baggie. He picks up scissors. She sits in the chair.
He cuts a lock of her hair. He walks to the specimen case and places the hair in
a baggie. She gets up from the chair and engages a syringe. He sits in the
chair. She places the needle in his arm and draws blood. She walks to the
specimen case and places the syringe in a baggie. He gets up from the chair*

and picks up a wooden tongue swab. She sits in the chair and tilts her head back. He takes a throat culture. He walks to the specimen case and places the swab in a baggie. She begins speaking. The sound of cars screeching and crashing get louder and louder.)

SHE: Vaughan died yesterday in his last car-crash, Albert died yesterday in his last crash, Jayne stopped, Jack stopped, Hank stopped, Bessie stopped, Isadora . . . stopped, Jackson . . . stopped, Jimmy . . . stopped. Everybody stops . . .

HE: Here it comes.

(They break and race to the car and jump into the front seat. He grabs the wheel, she grips the dash, and they both lean into the curve.)

SHE: Step on it!

(They suddenly lurch forward and ricochet back into their seats and stop dead. A red bubble light revolves, flashing light in circular patterns.)

SHE: The sun is hemorrhaging.

HE: No. It's the revolving red light of the ambulance.

SHE: Blackout.

(Blackout.)

Day 9

Standing face to face, she places a tape recorder between them and hits the record button. She signals him to start. He begins to breath deeply and loudly. She conducts him as if she were a maestro. He reaches a crescendo. They stop.

SHE: Perfect!

(She turns to the specimen case and removes a lipstick. She walks to the back bumper. He lifts the specimen case and places it in the back seat. He then places the tape recorder on the dash and plays back the breathing tape. The loud sounds of inhalation and exhalation fill the air. She leans close to the bumper to apply her lipstick and rubs the vapor from her breath off the bumper to see her reflection.)

HE: Are ya getting a shine?

SHE: I'm getting a shine . . . and I'm picking you up.

HE: It's time to get out of Dodge.

(The soundtrack of a rocket countdown swells, ten, nine, eight, seven, six, etc. He takes off his driving glove and places it on the steering wheel. She tosses the lipstick in the car. They leap up onto the ledge of the billboard and stand in front of the image of the open road. The countdown approaches zero.)

HE: Where to?

SHE: Just drive.

(The rocket blasts off in a deafening crescendo.)

(Final tableau: They stand on either side of the painted road, facing each other. They lean closely into the billboard, lining up their gaze with the point where the road vanishes into the horizon. Strains of Hank Williams' "I'll Never Get Out of This World Alive" come up:)

>   *No matter how I struggle and strive*
>   *I'll never get out of this world alive.*

(Fade out.)

END

STORYLAND

BY

JOHN

STEPPLING

Storyland was first performed at the 1990 Padua Hills Playwrights Festival with the following cast:

Bat	Rick Dean
Phyllis	Laura Fanning
Conrad	Mick Collins
Daniel	Alexis Steppling
Eric	Demosthenes Stathigiannopoulos
Wanda	Kathleen Cramer
Parks Dept. Man #1	Nick Flynn
Parks Dept. Man #2	Thomas George Carter
Pinocchio Narration	Bob Glaudini
Director	John Steppling
Assistant Director	Adelaide MacKenzie
Set Design	Laura Carter
Lighting Design	Jason Berliner
Stage Manager	Hillary Fox

This play, ideally, is conceived for on site production. Outdoor locations such as nursery schools or children's parks could easily transform to Storyland.

The Pinocchio narration is from Mr. Collodi's book. The passages chosen are left to the discretion of the director.

—J.S.

"Waitin' on midnight
    when death comes slippin' in the room."

—Blind Willie Johnson
    from "You're Gonna Need Somebody on Your Bond"

SET:

The playing area is part of a small "children's park" in a large city park. We see a cement whale, painted, with Pinocchio on top. There is a speaker next to the whale, etc., from which we hear the *Pinocchio* story. Everything is run down.

Scene 1

In dark: sound of cheap speaker hissing, then warped tape starts—the story of Pinocchio.

After a few moments tape stops—breaks. Still in dark.

BAT: Shit.

(Lights up slowly: Bat is in mid-30's—with thick glasses. One lens is yellow—his blind eye—and he wears a worn powder blue suit with white piping and tux shirt and bowtie. He is greasy and unshaven. He shuffles over to speaker and unscrews the back, trying to fix the tape.)

BAT: *(To himself.)* Cocksucker.

(After a moment he resumes trying to repair the tape. The tape starts again and we hear the Pinocchio *story as Bat leans back, sitting on grass. He lights a cigarette and looks around.)*

(Lights fade out.)

Scene 2

Lights up slowly. We see a couple of small children posing in front of "whale" for photo. A man, Conrad, is looking through viewer of cheap 35mm camera. He has on cheap suit. A woman, Phyllis, is standing off to side talking to the kids. Pinocchio story fades out.

PHYLLIS: Hold still. *(To Conrad—irritated.)* Take it—*(Beat.)* Take the picture.

(He snaps flash.)

PHYLLIS: They moved.

(She steps over and re-adjusts the kids.)

PHYLLIS: Now. Hold still. *(Beat.)* Still.

(Conrad re-focuses. Phyllis moves aside. He snaps flash.)

PHYLLIS: *(To Conrad.)* That ok?

CONRAD: Wha. . . ?

(They look at each other . . .)

CONRAD: The picture?

PHYLLIS: Was it ok?

CONRAD: Yes. Yes.

(The kids run off yelling.)

PHYLLIS: Hey . . .

(She starts after the kids but stops. She turns and looks at Conrad. Long silence.)

CONRAD: How about a picture of you. *(Pause.)* Ok—ok. In front of the whale. *(Beat.)* Come on. *(Beat.)* Come on.

(She doesn't move.)

(Lights fade out. Pinocchio story resumes.)

Scene 3

As story fades; lights come up slowly.

(Wanda sits on bench listening to story. As it ends she nods to herself, sighs, and stands. She wears expensive and conservative clothes. The "light" on Pinocchio goes out. Wanda comes out of her reverie. Bat shuffles out. They look at each other. Silence.)

BAT: We're closing. *(Beat.)* Storyland is closing.

(They continue to look at each other. Silence.)

(Lights fade out. Story resumes.)

Scene 4

Lights come up slowly as story fades: Phyllis and Conrad. Conrad sits untying shoe and taking it off—then as he speaks he rubs his foot.

CONRAD: The humidity—makes your feet swell.

PHYLLIS: You won't be able to get your shoe back on.

(*Pause as he rubs.*)

CONRAD: This kind of weather, ought to have sandals, something of that sort.

(*He keeps rubbing. Phyllis watching. Silence. He trys to put his shoe back on but has difficulty.*)

PHYLLIS: See —

(*Pause. She watches.*)

PHYLLIS: What did I say?!

(*He has shoe on, but doesn't tie laces.*)

CONRAD: You need the right clothes—this kind of humidity.

(*Phyllis turns away and paces a bit. Pause.*)

CONRAD: A man needs to know how to dress. This is what distinguishes a man, his attire—his shoes. (*Pause.*) The appropriateness of his dress.

(*He looks over at Phyllis. Pause.*)

CONRAD: Of course having the money, having the income to dress correctly, that's always a factor. (*Pause.*) I've never been able to really dress myself the way I like. (*Beat.*) Phyllis.

(*She turns and looks at him. He fingers the lapel of his jacket.*)

CONRAD: This kind of "off the rack" thing, this doesn't really drape the way it should. You get what you pay for. You just can't fake quality. (*Beat.*) Can you? You can't fake quality. (*Beat.*) Baby?

PHYLLIS: Tie your shoe.

(*Conrad slowly stands, without tying shoe. Pause.*)

PHYLLIS: You seen the kids?

CONRAD: Have I seen the kids?

PHYLLIS: Uh huh—the kids—you seen 'em?

(*Conrad gives her a look.*)

(*Lights fade out. Story resumes.*)

Scene 5

Story fades as lights come up slowly. Wanda stands looking at the whale. Bat enters.

WANDA: I brought my niece today. Jenine.

BAT: We'll close early today. We got repairs to make.

WANDA: You close at six.

BAT: Some of the storybook characters need repair.

WANDA: It's a wonderful story, Pinocchio, an Italian story.

BAT: Today is different, today we gotta fix some stuff. I told you
    already.

(*Silence.*)

BAT: This is a park for children. We're closing at four o'clock. (*Pause.*)
    I'm the man in charge. (*Pause.*) What I do for a living: I'm the man
    here at Storyland. The man you want to see at Storyland. (*Pause.*) I
    run the gift shop there, I do it all.

WANDA: Pinocchio's arm is broken. His arm is missing.

BAT: The children are rough on things. (*Pause.*) I work here—that is
    exactly all I do.

WANDA: An Italian story. The original. Pinocchio is a story by a man
    named Collodi. (*Pause.*) A carpenter gives Gepetto a piece of wood
    that laughed and cried like a child. There is a talking cricket. There
    is the inn of the red crawfish where Pinocchio is corrupted. The cat
    and the fox, they corrupt the puppet Pinocchio. There is a child
    with blue hair who rescues the puppet from assassins. They must
    call in three doctors to see if he is alive or dead. (*Pause.*)
    Somewhere in the story there is the part about him telling a lie and

as a consequence his nose grows longer—that's a very well known part of the story, the lying and the growing nose, that's the part most people know about—if you asked them, that's the part they'd tell you about.

(Bat nods. Bat starts to walk off, stops.)

BAT: The parks department is who pays me.

(Lights fade out. Story resumes.)

Scene 6

As story fades: lights up slowly . . . Phyllis sits on bench. Bat stands holding broom and dust pan. Story ends.

(Long silence.)

BAT: This tape has gotten old.

PHYLLIS: The tape?

BAT: The Pinocchio story.

PHYLLIS: I don't feel well.

BAT: Resting is good.

PHYLLIS: My husband is with the kids. *(Pause.)* My son and his friend like to come here. We came on my son's birthday. We came today because we didn't want to drive all the way to the zoo.

(Conrad enters, slowly.)

PHYLLIS: This is Conrad.

(Conrad stops, looks at Bat. Silence.)

PHYLLIS: The kids playing?

CONRAD: Yeah.

(Conrad goes to other bench and sits.)

CONRAD: Terrible humidity, isn't it?!

BAT: It's like this every day. *(Beat.)* You don't need weather forecasts, because every day is like this.

CONRAD: All just like each other huh.

BAT: In summer.

CONRAD: In summer?!

BAT: Through summer.

CONRAD: *(Nodding.)* Uh huh.

BAT: Eighty percent humidity. At the least.

(Conrad exchanges look with Phyllis.)

BAT: And every summer it's the same. Since I've been here, always the same.

CONRAD: Always follows the same pattern does it?

BAT: Yes, it does, yes it does.

CONRAD: How long have you been working here?

BAT: Seven years.

CONRAD: Quite awhile.

BAT: I didn't expect to be here that long.

CONRAD: That happens.

BAT: This is the suit they gave me my first day—this same suit.

CONRAD: Maybe they should give you another one.

BAT: I think so. *(Laughs—then stops as he sees nobody else is laughing.)*

(Pause.)

PHYLLIS: The suit has lasted pretty well—for seven years.

BAT: I certainly never expected to be here for seven years—if you'd told me that then, I would never have believed you. Never.

CONRAD: One day you wake up—and what, it's seven years. *(Beat.)* That can be how it comes on you, that can be exactly how it happens—you wake up, look at yourself in the mirror—and you're not young— and you're surprised. *(Beat.)* It's a surprise. A surprise. *(Beat.)*—Let me tell you, ok, so you can get prepared, ok, because it's not a surprise you want to look forward to. It's not that kind of surprise.

(Conrad stands, a little agitated. Silence.)

PHYLLIS: *(To Bat.)* Do you like this job?

BAT: It's fine.

CONRAD: All jobs are fine—right.

PHYLLIS: Being with children, well, that must be nice.

BAT: Children, yeah.

PHYLLIS: And being out in the fresh air, I suppose that's nice.

BAT: I like being outside.

PHYLLIS: Hmnn. Well, . . . of course.

(Phyllis and Conrad looking at each other.)

CONRAD: I'm gonna go get the kids.

(Phyllis stands . . .)

PHYLLIS: Alright, yeah . . .

(Conrad exits . . .)

BAT: My first week here, I almost lost my job. *(Pause.)* I was cleaning up, and back then, they had this long driveway—where everyone parked, sort of—and I'd have to go out with this big bag slung over my shoulder and a long stick with a nail at the end—see, and I'd stab the paper cups and litter, and put them in the sack. And it was hot—it was very hot, and the man from the city, from the parks department drove up in his truck, a city truck and he started yelling at me—telling me how I'd missed all these papers and I just got mad and it was so hot, and I threw his stick at him—

like it was a spear.

PHYLLIS: What happened after that?

BAT: It bounced off the top of the cab you know—it didn't hit him. *(Pause.)* They yelled at me later but I was allowed to stay on. *(Pause.)* They changed that driveway later, and then—when the park got a little bigger they hired a guy, a Mexican, to do the outer area, to clean up out there after closing.

(Bat puts both broom and long-handled dust pan into one hand.)

BAT: I still clean up a bit here inside.

PHYLLIS: Yes.

BAT: A couple of times a day. Inside Storyland itself.

(They look at each other.)

(Lights fade. Story resumes.)

Scene 7

Lights up as story fades. Phyllis and Daniel.

PHYLLIS: You have to use the bathroom? *(Pause.)* Daniel? *(Pause.)* Are you mad with me? *(Pause.)* Is there something else you want to do? *(Beat.)* Are you mad? Tell me, Daniel, tell me if you are. *(Pause.)* You sure you don't need to use the bathroom? *(Longer pause.)* Daniel?

DANIEL: Leave me alone.

(Silence.)

(Lights out. Story resumes.)

Scene 8

Lights up on Wanda and Bat. Story fades.

WANDA: My husband left—now he dates a girl I knew from work, a girl who had once dated one of the Blue Angels. *(Pause.)* I don't know anything about that, what it was like or anything. *(Pause.)* Brittany is her name, she works with retarded children or something, at some agency. *(Pause.)* I cheated on Brian twice—over five years.

(Pause.)

BAT: I believe they're going to repair Pinocchio soon.

WANDA: That's good. They'll fix his arm. That's **very** good.

BAT: Repaint him.   George says all the figures will be repainted.

WANDA: The Blue Angels are some sort of jet plane pilots, they work air shows.

BAT: I know.

WANDA: Does this place make any money?

BAT: *(Pause.)* It's not trying to make money. *(Pause.)* It's a city-run facility, and the parks department maintains things—same with the pony rides down there.

(Silence.)

(Bat sits.)

BAT: I can't stand for too long.

WANDA: You're young.

BAT: I'm thirty-two.

WANDA: I'll teach high school. As a substitute, a variety of subjects.

(Bat nods. Silence.)

WANDA: So many people are killed at air shows.

BAT: They don't pay teachers enough. *(Beat.)* Do you think they get paid enough?

WANDA: *(Pause.)* No, not nearly enough.

(Bat stands with effort.)

BAT: I have a hernia.

(He shuffles off a few feet, stops. Silence.)

WANDA: When I was a child I saw my father urinate in a public park, at night.

BAT: Was he drunk? Probably . . . ?

WANDA: I was about six or seven. I don't know if he was drunk. I'm glad Jenine has a good family. Jenine is six.

BAT: The others here resent me. That work here, those others resent me. Because I have ambition, and I don't think I will work for the parks department for that much longer. *(Beat.)* Fuck them, I don't give a shit—one way or the other.

(Wanda stares at him. Bat turns and moves a few feet further off . . .)

WANDA: Do you want to hear the story about how I cheated on Brian?

BAT: What did Brian do—for a living?

WANDA: Brian did a lot of things. Brian is not a man of great strength.

(Silence.)

BAT: What's Brian's last name?

WANDA: He worked for other people. *(Pause.)* He was always just Brian to everybody. *(Beat.)* I always called him Brian. I still do.

(Bat walks back toward her, stops. Silence.)

WANDA: What happened to your eye, Bat?

BAT: The nurse put in too much silver nitrate.

(Bat sits down next to her. Pause.)

BAT: She was a nurse trainee or something. She quit when she found what she'd done.

WANDA: It takes great will—don't you think, to do most things.

BAT: I don't know.

WANDA: Most anything. *(Pause.)* Most anything at all—it's a very definite struggle.

(Pause.)

WANDA: I just don't want to pretend as though I care when I don't. I'm not a pretender.

(Silence.)

BAT: There are other older people who come here. People who have no children or grown children. They come alone and they usually sit on the benches and later they leave.

(Bat stands slowly, with effort.)

WANDA: I won't come here anymore. Not after today. I don't think I should.

(Lights fade out. Story resumes.)

Scene 9

Lights up slowly: Conrad sits. After a moment Wanda enters—they look at each other. Story fades.

CONRAD: Pretty empty.

WANDA: Yes. *(Beat.)* You're speaking of the park here?

CONRAD: It is, isn't it? I think our kids are the only ones here.

(Wanda goes over to whale, touching it.)

WANDA: Do you understand this story?

CONRAD: Lady—which story are we talking about?

WANDA: Pinocchio? We are talking about Pinocchio!

(Conrad nods, incredulous.)

CONRAD: Ten-four.

(Wanda caresses whale.)

WANDA: *(Pause.)* I would describe it as "upsetting".

CONRAD: It's a kid's story. I can't even remember the fuckin' Pinocchio story.

WANDA: This is the last time I come here.

CONRAD: Phyllis' boy—Daniel, and his friend . . . Eric— they like to come here.

WANDA: I would have liked it as a girl.

CONRAD: Daniel is my step son.

(Wanda nods. Pause. Conrad stands.)

CONRAD: I better find them.

(Pause. Wanda stares at him a moment.)

CONRAD: You find it restful, coming to, what is it? Storyland?

WANDA: Restful? No, I don't think that.

CONRAD: No? *(Pause.)* But you come a lot don't you?

(Pause.)

CONRAD: That's right isn't it—? I bet you come here two, three times a week?!

WANDA: It's a great help to learn when it's time to leave a place or a person alone.

CONRAD: Is it?

WANDA: I was very beautiful once.

CONRAD: You're still beautiful.

WANDA: But not the same—not beautiful the way it can be when you're twenty—I walked into a restaurant once and people stopped and applauded as I passed.

CONRAD: Were you by yourself?

WANDA: No. I was with a man—an older man, grey haired, very rich. He liked it when they applauded.

CONRAD: Did you sleep with him?

WANDA: Sometimes.

CONRAD: *(Pause.)* I have to find Phyllis.

(Pause.)

WANDA: It's a mean-spirited story in many ways.

(Wanda turns her attention back to the whale. Conrad watching her . . .)

CONRAD: Yeah.

(Slowly Conrad gets to his feet . . .)

CONRAD: Find Phyllis, find the boys—guess I better go on do that. *(Beat.)* Sort of thing I do . . . go get them, all of us go get into our car, Phyllis' car, the Honda. Then we'll go on drive back, like always, stopping at Eric's house first—wave to his mother, then we drive over to this Chink place for take out—Phyllis and Daniel like this place, this Chink food. And we'll take it back to Phyllis' house, our house, and we'll get out plates and forks, and we'll turn on television and we'll eat and open our fortune cookies, and make some jokes, you know, about everyone's fortune.

(Silence.)

CONRAD: But it could be different. One time it could all be some other way. *(Pause.)* What would it take for things to change like that? *(Pause.)* It might cause things to happen—just thinking about it, could cause things to happen.

(They stare at each other. Conrad steps closer to Wanda, speaking quiet and intense.)

CONRAD: It's scary, isn't it—that we might do something—be in the middle of something, something that'd be whipping around us. In the center of something we could never forget. *(Pause.)* I can feel the pull of that. *(Beat.)* I can feel the pull.

(They stare at each other. Conrad backs away . . .)

(Lights fade out. Story resumes.)

Scene 10

Lights up slowly. Story fades: Wanda and Phyllis.

WANDA: An older bachelor. In his early forties. He was never married—no children. A man who lived outside the system. No bank account, nothing like that. *(Pause.)* He'd come over to see my sister. *(Pause.)* Jenine is my sister's child. *(Pause.)* He'd come from Vancouver—he was Canadian. He came to L.A. to be an actor. But he didn't want it bad enough. I told him that, last time I saw him. *(Pause.)* Is Conrad with the children?

PHYLLIS: Of course he's with the children.

WANDA: It's after five. It's getting dark.

PHYLLIS: They went to get hot dogs and have a pony ride.

WANDA: Jenine doesn't really remember her father. *(Pause.)* My sister loved him. She told me the ways he felt, and how beautiful his hands were. *(Pause.)* I thought his hands were exceptionally large. I think I found them beautiful too. *(Pause.)* They've gone to the pony rides.

PHYLLIS: Yes. Conrad took them for hot dogs. Hot dogs, soda, and then to the pony rides.

WANDA: Jenine rarely gets to go out with me. *(Pause.)* Jenine is six.

PHYLLIS: Six.

(Bat appears behind them. Silence.)

WANDA: Does Daniel like the pony rides?

PHYLLIS: *(Pause.)* I think he does. Conrad, he usually takes the boys to the pony rides.

WANDA: My sister tells me that Jenine loves pony rides. *(Beat.)* She loves the merry-go-round also. *(Beat.)* Her father left—there is really no man in her life, in Jenine's life. *(Pause.)* They were going to close at six here today.

PHYLLIS: Conrad loves Daniel.

(Bat moves closer. Silence.)

WANDA: Jenine has only her mother and myself.

PHYLLIS: *(Pause.)* You and your sister must be close.

WANDA: Without a man—without that physical strength, that presence, I'm afraid Jenine will become too much of a princess.

(Pause.)

WANDA: For a boy it's even more important, don't you think?

PHYLLIS: *(Pause.)* Yes. Yes, Conrad loves Daniel.

WANDA: I think you'd have to be concerned about a son becoming a "mama's boy" *(Pause.)* I think you'd have to keep a close watch on that, wouldn't you say—keep an eye peeled—keep on the lookout.

(Silence.)

BAT: Everyone has gone home.

(Wanda nods. Neither woman looks at Bat.)

(Lights out. Story resumes.)

Scene 11

Lights up: Bat and Conrad downstage. Conrad's shirt is pulled out of his pants, there's dirt on his hands—he looks a little out of breath. Bat stands nearby . . . Story fades out.

BAT: It's six-thirty.

CONRAD: Huh? Yeah—yeah . . .

BAT: Your wife and another woman, Wanda, went to look for you.

CONRAD: Got worried huh.

(Conrad sits. Pause.)

CONRAD: I have an older brother. His name is Anthony.

(He and Bat stare at each other.)

CONRAD: He left his wife. He has a lot of different women now. Cheryl still sleeps with him—his wife, they're not divorced. She fucks him whenever he wants it. (Pause.) I've gone over there, to Anthony's, do up a little coke, and there'll be three, four women there—good-look'n women. Do some coke, watch the porn tapes he's got. Big Mama Jama—this 300-pound black woman—Big Mama Jama, you ever seen her?

(Bat doesn't respond.)

CONRAD: Some of it's in black and white. Anthony likes watching blow jobs—he likes watching two broads working a guy—suck'n the knobski—see, while one licks his balls.

(Conrad stands, moving closer to Bat as he speaks . . .)

CONRAD: You ever had that? Someone licking on your balls?—And the one broad can stick her finger up your ass—then you come in the other broad's mouth. (Beat.) You like to watch porno, Bat?

(Conrad tucking his shirt in, getting himself together . . .)

CONRAD: It embarrasses you, me talking to you this way?

BAT: (Shaking head "no.") No.

CONRAD: Some guys don't like blow jobs—they think it keeps them from getting hard later on, you know. (Pause.) I never had that trouble, throw'n a hard-on—it's not one of my problems. (Pause.) Amber Lynn—ever see her? Huh? Amber Lynn—ok, Candy Samples, huh? Some of my favorites.

(Silence. Conrad edgy, still breathing a little hard.)

CONRAD: You can get a broad really hot—watching fuck films. Get 'em really hot—some very hot pussy. (Beat.) Put your hand down there—feel that wet. Huh!

(Silence. Bat steps back from him. Conrad looking around . . .)

CONRAD: *(To himself.)* Fuck. *(Beat.)* Yes. *(Pause.)* I don't get over to Anthony's much. I don't have that kind of cash, to throw around on broads. *(Beat.)* The rich get richer. *(Beat.)* These are good-look'n women I'm talking about. Youngsters—in their twenties.

(Pause. Conrad looking around.)

CONRAD: A lot of the lights are off.

BAT: Yes.

(He points up at the only remaining light.)

BAT: This is the only light left on.

(Conrad nods.)

(Lights out.)

Scene 12

Lights up: same as before except Wanda and Phyllis stand behind Conrad. Bat stands to side. Silence.

CONRAD: *(Not looking at them.)* What?

(Silence.)

CONRAD: *(Louder, without turning around.)* What?

(Silence.)

CONRAD: I hit him. *(He left-hooks empty space. Long pause.)* Caught him on the cheek. Broke his cheek I think.

(Conrad turns and looks at Bat. Silence.)

WANDA: Is Jenine with them?

CONRAD: I don't know where any one of them are. *(Pause.)* Right at the pony rides, that's where it was—I think Daniel is the one *(He left-hooks again.)* I hit. *(Beat.)* I hit him fuck'n hard.

(Lights out. Story resumes.)

Scene 13

Lights up slowly: Bat seated. Wanda stands. Story fades out.

WANDA: Bat? Can you tell me about these horses? Where do they get those horses?

BAT: Which horses? *(Pause.)* I don't know anything about it.

WANDA: For the pony ride. *(Beat.)* They look old, those horses.

BAT: *(Pause.)* I don't want to go home tonight. *(Pause.)* I'll sleep here, up at the gift shop. *(Beat.)* I've done it before.

WANDA: Jenine is with my sister now.

BAT: I would be afraid to go home right now. *(Pause.)* It's still warm out.

(Pause.)

WANDA: When my mother died I refused to attend the funeral. They had this priest, and he didn't know anything about what my mother was like. I didn't want to listen to him lie about her. Was that wrong of me?

BAT: I don't think so.

(Bat stands. Silence.)

WANDA: Can I stay out here for a while?

BAT: Yes. *(Beat.)* Sure. *(Beat.)* I don't care.

(Bat starts off toward gift shop. Wanda lays down on bench.)

(Lights fade out. Story resumes.)

Scene 14

Lights up slowly: Parks Department Men enter far upstage. One (#2) carries shovel, cigarette in mouth. The other (#1) follows behind. Story fades out. Bat enters from gift shop area. He has stick with nail and big bag slung over his shoulder.

PARKS DEPT. MAN #1: You sleep here, Bat? *(Beat.)* Huh?!

(Bat stops, looks around, sees the two men.)

MAN #1: Bat? Huh?! Man, you look like you slept here. *(Pause.)* You fuck, you dumb fuck, you can't do that, man.

BAT: Alright.

MAN #2: *(To Man #1.)* Come on, man.

MAN #1: We have a little problem here yesterday? Is that right?!

(Bat says nothing. Man #1 moves closer . . .)

MAN #1: Did I hear that right? Bat? *(Beat—with edge.)* Well, did I?

(Man #1 shoves Bat . . .)

MAN #1: Huh?! Tell me about it—come on you stupid fuck.

(Bat shoves his arm away . . .)

MAN #1: *(Angrier.)* I heard the police came—is that correct?

MAN #2: Leave him alone . . .

MAN #1: *(To Man #2.)* Shit. This asshole pisses me off.

MAN #2: Fuck him.

(They start moving off. Man #1 stops, turns back to Bat.)

MAN #1: Clean the fucking grounds, man.

(Bat watches them exit. Pause. Bat starts picking up papers with nailed stick and putting them in sack. He stops, lights a cigarette.)

(Lights very slowly fade out, as Blind Willie Johnson's recording of "You're Gonna Need Somebody On Your Bond" comes up.)

END

Theory

of

Miracles

by

John

Steppling

Theory of Miracles was first performed at the 1989 Padua Hills Playwrights Festival with the following cast:

Richard	Murray Mednick
Man	Nick Flynn
The Doctor	Mick Collins
Woman #1	Rachel Powell
Mr. Benvenuto	Gill Gayle
Woman #2	Taylor Donlan
Man with Guitar	Jack Slater
Woman with Chickens	Kathleen Cramer
Director	John Steppling
Assistant Director	Elizabeth Iannaci
Set Design	Erica Birch
Lighting Design	Jason Berliner

This play is meant to be performed outdoors, although it is possible to create the appropriate small pageant atmosphere indoors. There should be small Christmas lights and candles placed throughout the audience. RICHARD should sit on a plain straight-back chair atop a small platform, separate from the other characters. The WOMAN WITH CHICKENS needs to enter with live chickens. If no chickens are available, find some other type of livestock.

—J.S.

Scene 1

Spot up on RICHARD.

RICHARD: By the border . . . (*Pause.*) some place, down near the border, south of Juarez—ten miles and the first suggestion of morning. (*Pause.*) I felt I had driven eight, nine hours, driven through the night. (*Pause.*) I felt I had come to receive one of the seven gifts. I couldn't, at that time, remember all seven—there was a clairvoyance, which was what I wanted. There were kinds of healing—the laying on of hands . . . And there was something, too, with prophecy. The rest, I didn't know—didn't remember.

(*He stops. Spot fades.*)

(*Lights up on MAN and WOMAN #1.*)

MAN: Hollywood. I live up on Argyle—right up on the hill there. (*Pause.*) My roommate—Jim—a nice guy—but he's real into religion—into this very fundamentalist shit, right?!

WOMAN #1: Uh huh, okay.

MAN: You're very pretty—very . . . uh . . . very "simpatico."

(*He smiles. Pause.*)

MAN: Jim is against abortion—against a number of things, but, well, he's a nice guy.

WOMAN: Sure.

MAN: Jim? Sure—very nice—and what he believes is his business.

WOMAN: (*Nodding vaguely.*) Yeah.

(*Man lights cigarette. Silence. Lights fade.*)

(*Spot up on RICHARD.*)

RICHARD: I had been told to give up everything—all that I owned, all my possessions. At that time, the sky getting lighter—I was behind the wheel—and I was shaking. I looked in the rear view mirror and I could see I was very pale. Very pale—white, and I was shaking. (*Pause.*) I could tell that the day would be hot. Then I thought about the motel room in San Antonio where I'd been staying the previous four or five nights. The hotel was pink on the outside, faded, with green lettering over the entrance. My room overlooked the alley and I thought that perhaps it had been a mistake to leave there. Sitting in the front seat of this '71 Ford LTD—shaking—the color drained from my face—I wished I was in San Antonio—in my room—in the hotel.

(*Spot fades.*)

(*Spot up on MAN, THE DOCTOR, and WOMAN #1.*)

THE DOCTOR: There's always someone worse off than yourself. If all you got is potatoes, you can be sure someone will be following after you picking up the peelings. (*Laughs.*) You know, the bible isn't the only holy book—no, no, there's plenty of holy books, plenty. There are hundreds of books that one could call holy—"Sacred" (*Laughs.*) —Sacred books, holy books, books written by wise or holy men with special callings, special gifts.

(*Silence.*)

THE DOCTOR: The people of dark complexion—throughout the world—those people with dark or muddy skin tones are the possessors—or you might, to put it better, say they are the caretakers of the secondary books of holiness. The books of which I speak— and to which I access.

(*Lights fade.*)

(*Spot up on MR. BENVENUTO, WOMAN #2.*)

MR BENVENUTO: You have to find the place—that is first.

WOMAN # 2: Of course it would be.

MR BENVENUTO: To sense the next spot—the cutting edge, no, beyond, or prior to the cutting edge—the place that is the vortex— some unknown corner of the world—a hidden isolated little area where the next wave of change will come from—the place that is never found out—the place that gives birth to the cutting edge—as it were.

WOMAN #2: Fascinating.

BENVENUTO: You'll know it when you find it.

WOMAN #2: I would imagine so, yes.

BENVENUTO: I was born speaking another language.

(*Lights fade.*)

(*Lights up on THE DOCTOR, MAN, WOMAN #1.*)

THE DOCTOR: There is no hiding place.

MAN: Hiding place?

THE DOCTOR: Down here—you've got no hiding place.

MAN: Yeah?

THE DOCTOR: I got lots of information may be useful to you. (*To WOMAN #1.*) Secrets—teachings, practices, disciplines. (*Pause.*) I got lots of information.

MAN: You a real doctor?

THE DOCTOR: Am I what? Am I a real doctor?

MAN: Are you a real doctor?

THE DOCTOR: They call me Doctor—that's what they call me.

(*Silence.*)

THE DOCTOR: (*To WOMAN #1.*) I can be of great assistance—I'm a very valuable ally.

MAN: What are you selling here exactly?

(*THE DOCTOR looks at MAN, then back to WOMAN #1.*)

THE DOCTOR: The fallen angels—their wills bent, their sins forever attached to their being. These angels, their hearts, which in the beginning were the purest, the highest in nature—these hearts now beat with the dark blood of transgression.

WOMAN: (*Pause.*) Do you believe in angels?

THE DOCTOR: (*Pause.*) Yes, oh yes, I do.

(*Lights fade.*)

(*Spot up on RICHARD.*)

RICHARD: There was a small rock formation to my right. Smoke trees and ocotillo to my left. I recall a jackrabbit had crossed in front of the car—maybe an hour before, but I only just then gave it any thought. (*Pause.*) It was light now, but I left the headlights on. I had not eaten since San Antonio. I am pretty sure that I felt no hunger. I tried to remember all the Spanish words I knew, all the phrases. I didn't know many, not many at all. I felt that what I was doing had importance. I was waiting—I had made the decision weeks before, in Michigan, in a small room at the halfway house in Jackson.

(*Spot fades.*)

(*Lights up on BENVENUTO, WOMAN #2.*)

BENVENUTO: The air is foul—(*Pause.*) it fouls our breath.

WOMAN #2: Yes, it seems to.

BENVENUTO: The road to heaven is preceded by the purification of the air.

WOMAN #2: I read, somewhere, in my school—a girls' school—it was in the desert, in Nevada,—and I read how Christ had put the hook into Leviathan's nose and led him around.

BENVENUTO: Yes. (*Pause.*) Christ did not destroy the demons, you know this of course?

WOMAN #2: Of course.

(*Silence.*)

BENVENUTO: One of the weapons used against the demons was the saving breath. You must blow on demons—but your breath must be clean—the air must be clean.

(*Silence.*)

WOMAN #2: Saint Hilerion heard demons as crying babies—he heard women crying, the crying of the mothers—and he heard the cattle in his yard moan as if in sexual ecstasy.

(*BENVENUTO nods. Lights fade.*)

(*Lights up on: THE DOCTOR, MAN, WOMAN #1.*)

THE DOCTOR: (*To WOMAN # 1.*) You travelling alone?

WOMAN #1: Yes, alone.

THE DOCTOR: (*Smiles.*) You've got to be careful. A young woman, alone. (*Pause.*) What do you think about that—about the dangers that lurk everywhere—the forces that creep up on you, and can destroy your will?

WOMAN #1: I am very careful.

THE DOCTOR: (*Smiles.*) Well, good, good. I am relieved to hear that, I am.

(*THE DOCTOR turns and indicates MAN.*)

THE DOCTOR: This man here, he might be just what you're looking for. A strong, able fellow—alert, aware. It's possible, don't you agree?

WOMAN #1: It's possible.

THE DOCTOR: The dark angels can enter your body—but not your mind. Did you know that?

WOMAN #1: No, I didn't.

THE DOCTOR: Angels live in the air—the ether—the upper air just below heaven.

WOMAN #1: I see.

THE DOCTOR: But they move to earth on occasion. There are demons or fallen angels, and there are the righteous angels of light. There is also a third class—the evil angels or watchers, who have fallen from grace because of the lust for mortal woman.

(Silence. THE DOCTOR looks back and forth between MAN and WOMAN #1.)

THE DOCTOR: The watchers contaminate the physical plane—they circle the lower air, in search of those who travel alone, alone and unprotected.

(Lights fade.)

(Spot up on RICHARD.)

RICHARD: As it became more hot the surrounding landscape changed. I began to see new things, and I experienced an ever increasing anxiety. My eyes hurt from the glare and my ears rang with a continuous explosion of sound. I was occasionally gripped with a shortness of breath but I never let panic take hold and so the fear would pass—and my breathing would, for a while, return to normal. *(Pause.)* I don't remember the particulars—the details of that day. I can remember a few images; a bird circling above possibly a hawk. The wind blowing small clouds of dust against the windshield. By afternoon, the hills far off to my left had slowly started to move closer—they turned toward purple by sunset, and I recognized them as malevolent. *(Pause.)* I believe it must have been very hot inside the car, but I didn't think to move, or to open the windows. I sat and felt that I must remain prepared. That I must not miss what I had come for.

(Spot fades.)

(Lights up on BENVENUTO and WOMAN #2.)

BENVENUTO: Of all gifts, the discernment of spirits is the most important. The man who is able to distinguish the good spirit from the harmful is a man in much demand. He is one that in past times may have been the oracle, or the sage.

WOMAN #2: Are there such men alive today?

BENVENUTO: It is impossible to know.

(Pause.)

WOMAN #2: There's to be a pageant here, that's what the concierge told me.

BENVENUTO: Yes—a small pageant, small and without hope.

(*Lights fade.*)

(*Lights up on MAN, WOMAN #1 and THE DOCTOR.*)

MAN: Should be a nice little pageant this year. (*Pause.*) You ever been here before?

THE DOCTOR: Me? Oh, yes, I've been coming here for years.

MAN: Should be a nice one this year—that's what I've heard, that's what I've been told.

THE DOCTOR: Yes—well—the pageant is always nice. It's a nice little pageant.

MAN: Yeah—a little one, though—I mean, it's not very big, this pageant. It's on the small side—wouldn't you say?

THE DOCTOR: It's a matter of one's perspective.

MAN: Things should kick off here pretty soon. Isn't that right? It's about time for the festivities to start. Time for things to liven up.

THE DOCTOR: Have another drink. Relax.

MAN: Yeah—good idea. I'll do that. I like you, Doc—you're an alright guy. Relax—and wait for it all to begin.

(*MAN WITH GUITAR enters. Pause. Everyone looking at one another . . .*)

MAN: You know "Bes-a-may-mucho?"

MAN WITH GUITAR: (*Pause.*) That a favorite of yours?

MAN: I like the shit out of that song, yeah.

MAN WITH GUITAR: It's a favorite song with lots of people.

(*Pause.*)

(*MAN sings a few bars. Pause. MAN looking around.*)

MAN: How does this work? I mean, is this a good table? Am I missing something?

MAN WITH GUITAR: (*Pause.*) Here . . .

(*Strums a single chord.*)

MAN WITH GUITAR: In Mazatlan I used to play at the bar next to the bullring. (*Pause.*) They'd cut up the dead bulls and sometimes they'd hand the meat out—to the poor people—right outside of the bar I was playing.

THE DOCTOR: Savage sport—bullfighting.

MAN WITH GUITAR: (*With weariness.*) I used to sing cowboy songs there—in English—they loved me.

(*Pause.*)

MAN: You been doing this for a while, huh?! (*Pause.*) Hell of a thing. (*Pause.*) I think the hotel had some bad information, that's what I think.

(*Lights fade.*)

(*Spot up on RICHARD.*)

RICHARD: At some point I found myself outside the car—on my hands and knees. The ground beneath me was caked hard with small little rocks that cut into my palms. It was sunset and I could see the shadows lengthen. (*Pause.*) I was terribly thirsty, I could feel my throat tighten but at that time I did not think about it. I thought—instead—about the movement of the earth, about our revolving movement through space and how immense everything was. In the distance I saw the headlights of another car, or a truck. I wondered who it might be, and on what road they were. Where would they be going; who was travelling with them?

(*Spot fades.*)

(*Lights up on BENVENUTO, WOMAN #2.*)

BENVENUTO: Dancing . . . one of the reasons I come to this event is that they always let me dance.

WOMAN #2: You're a wonderful dancer.

BENVENUTO: Yes—it's something I do quite well. I think not only do they let me dance—they actually "welcome" my dancing.

WOMAN #2: Yes.

BENVENUTO: For years I felt I couldn't dance—without ridicule—but when I discovered that here I was appreciated—I knew I would return again and again.

(*Lights fade.*)

(*Lights up on MAN, THE DOCTOR, WOMAN #1.*)

WOMAN #1: My luggage, at least most of my luggage, was lost. Or possibly it was stolen. I was warned that theft was an ever present danger. I believe it was stolen. I believe someone stalked me—and then in a moment of distraction they moved with great quickness and stealth and they took my bags, I say they, there may only have been one, a solitary little thief. I can see his eyes— eyes alive with the death wish—liquid and impenetrable— predatory. His hands gnarled with premature arthritis—his feet cold and disconnected from his body. (*Pause.*) He runs along the alley, my bags under his arms. He knows exactly where he is— despite the total utter darkness through which he runs. I've refused to report this theft—I have two pieces of luggage remaining—more than enough. There is music here that drifts up to my window at night—or carries across the black fields as I return to my hotel from the nightclub. (*Pause.*) This is some kind of holiday—a holiday marking a birth or a death—or a miracle. I like to think that this was the location of a miracle—one that has been forgotten—and that whatever shrine was here was left to decay—that people stopped believing in the miracle. Perhaps nobody even remembers what the miracle was, or who was involved. I may be the only person alive who is aware that there was a miracle—and someday—when I die—it will be utterly forgotten.

(*Lights fade.*)

(*Lights up on WOMAN #2 and BENVENUTO.*)

WOMAN #2: All those people outside . . . Mister Benvenuto?

BENVENUTO: Yes?

WOMAN #2: Are they from here? (*Beat.*) Of course they are, they would be, naturally.

BENVENUTO: They've come for various reasons, I suppose . . . their own reasons.

WOMAN #2: It is very difficult to get past them. (*Pause.*) Mister Benvenuto? It's quite difficult to get past them, quite difficult.

(*MAN WITH GUITAR enters, playing . . . .*)

(*Lights fade.*)

(*Spot up on RICHARD.*)

RICHARD: By the following morning, as the sun rose high—I knew I would not be leaving. There was no water. (*Pause.*) My legs twitched—my heels digging into the hard ground. My wrist swelled around my watchband—and in many places I could feel my skin crack and split. (*Pause.*) I could no longer hear sounds— I stared for a long time at the tires of the Ford. A small lizard crept along the outside tread of the front right tire. I had not received clairvoyance—(*Pause.*) I do not remember feeling disappointment—but I do remember thinking that nobody would worry that I was missing—there would be no record of my having come here. I left as I arrived—without attention, without concern.

(*Spot fades.*)

(*Lights up on WOMAN WITH CHICKENS.*)

WOMAN WITH CHICKENS: It was the the man with the crutch. He spoke of being a man lost. He had a single crutch, and I adored him. I was a child . . . I was 16. I was a child, I was very fragile. (*Pause.*) A lost and crippled man spoke English, but he spoke Spanish and other languages also. I never knew where he was born, except he longed to go home. He came to me because he could not go home. (*Pause.*) I did not feel violated. (*Pause.*) He believed in practices, cures and alchemy, the possibility of changing one's life. He had lived as a thief and he told me that was why he could not be healed. (*Pause.*) After they took my father away, my mother asked for a miracle. She continued to expect a miracle. As I became older, I became more ill. I too asked for a miracle. (*Pause.*) But I no longer expect to receive one.

(*Lights fade.*)

END

BALL

AND

CHAIN

BY

KELLY

STUART

Ball and Chain was first performed at the 1990 Padua Hills Playwrights Festival with the following cast:

Bernice	Roberta Wallach
Dale	James Oseland
Ray	James Storm
Sylvia	Diane Defoe
Joey	Demosthenes Stathigiannopoulos
Baby	Isabella Glaudini
Director	Kelly Stuart
Lighting Design	Jason Berliner
Stage Manager	Hillary Fox

The Scene

The yard of a nursery school: Upstage right is a giant smiling cut-out of a frog, painted bright green. It's about seven feet tall, and wide enough to serve as an offstage area. Upstage left is a brightly painted playhouse. Upstage center is a bright yellow chair.

Calliope music plays, and the actors stand upstage center in a tableau, as the audience enters. They remain frozen until the audience is seated. Then the actors move downstage, using an exaggerated character walk: Dale lurches, Ray uses huge clown steps and somersaults, Bernice moves rigidly, Sylvia walks as if she were dragging hundreds of pounds. The Boy runs. They form another tableau center stage. The music stops. Then everyone takes their place: Ray and Sylvia go offstage. The Boy comes down center and plays with a rock. Bernice stands near the playhouse. Dale approaches her.

DALE: I've tried so hard to make this a place. A wonderful place where children can come. That's why mother left it to me. She knew I love children. Children are wonderful. The parents don't bring them in like they used to. They've taken them away. I don't like that. Things have run down here Bernice. Enrollment is down.

(Bernice walks away from him and stands protectively over the Boy. Dale follows and stands opposite Bernice.)

DALE: You're silent a lot. I enjoy that. I enjoy a woman who is full of long silences.

(Bernice takes the Boy and leads him to the chair. On the chair is a white plate full of green food, and a large wooden spoon. Bernice hands the plate and spoon to Dale. Helps the Boy into the chair. Dale feeds the Boy.)

DALE: My mother did a very great service to me. A very great service. She simply insisted on a very simple act. She stuck to her guns. She insisted calmly, consistently, but surely, that I eat all the food that was placed on my plate.

(Bernice grabs the plate away from Dale and feeds the Boy a few bites. Dale walks downstage and continues to speak. While he's speaking, Bernice sneaks off behind the playhouse and scrapes the remaining food off the plate.)

DALE: I was trained to swallow food, any food, though it may have seemed repugnant. Raw garlic and Brewers yeast mixed with plain yoghurt. This is healthy, very very healthy food. And I was made to swallow it, like it or not. At times I vomited under the table. She remained compassionate. Compassionate but firm. Stern as she stood there and held the silver bowl. She held it as I vomited then heaped more on my plate. She did this discreetly with a great deal of charm. I could not protest. There was never a point. There was simply the food that I hated before me and I ate it as always, given no choice. And because of that, I've been given great freedom. Today I am free, from like, and dislike. I am utterly free. I can swallow anything.

(Dale turns, sees that the plates are empty. He picks them up and carries them into the playhouse.)

DALE: It's a great gift to have. A great gift to have been given. And I have her to thank.

(Ray enters from the audience stage right. Bernice doesn't see him. He walks quietly, and watches her.)

BERNICE: Give me the money that's in your pocket. The money your mother gave you for Dale. Give it to me. Don't be afraid. We're going to tell Dale that the money was lost. It fell out of your pocket. It's not your fault. It's lost, all right? You lost the money. It's lost. Okay? Now give it to me.

(Bernice grabs in the Boy's pocket and comes out with a wad of money. She stuffs it in her bra. Sylvia enters. She's dragging a baby carrier covered by a blanket, and a diaper bag.)

SYLVIA: You never help me! You're selfish. Selfish!

(Bernice notices Sylvia and Ray, changes her tone.)

BERNICE: You've been so good. Such a good boy. Bernice is going to buy a surprise. You're quiet . . . You're quiet and good. Aren't you.

RAY: Is Dale around?

BERNICE: DALE!

(Dale comes out of the playhouse.)

RAY: Sylvia said I should come to you. Ask you. I've been laid off my job as a standup comic.

SYLVIA: Work has been slow for him.

RAY: But something will happen. Something is bound to come up soon. We're being optimistic.

SYLVIA: With a little request.

RAY: Sylvia said I should come to you.

SYLVIA: He's short of money. It's a temporary thing. And I thought since you were family, his family . . .

RAY: Sylvia said I should ask you for a loan.

DALE: You were my favorite cousin Ray.

RAY: I'm sorry you know, how I used to beat you up.

DALE: That was just children. Children are cruel.

RAY: I've changed since then. Grown up. Sylvia, she just had a baby.

DALE: Babies are worth a lot these days.

RAY: And they cost a lot to raise.

DALE: People don't throw them away like they used to.

RAY: I guess not.

DALE: And you know how to make them.

RAY: Sure, that's easy.

DALE: Not if you're alone. I don't have a partner.

RAY: You'll find one.

DALE: And you'll find someone to give you a loan.

SYLVIA: We thought you could do that.

DALE: I don't make loans.

RAY: Could you make it a gift?

DALE: I feel very close to you, Ray. You're my favorite cousin.

RAY: I know you've got the money. You've got lots of money. We can't pay the rent. That's all we need. It's nothing. Just money.

SYLVIA: Here. Look at the baby.

(Sylvia unwraps the blanket of the carrier. The Baby is not there.)

SYLVIA: Shit.

RAY: Where'd you leave it honey?

SYLVIA: Shit shit shit shit!!!!

(Sylvia exits.)

RAY: Give us the money.

DALE: No.

RAY: Why not?

DALE: I don't want people to walk on me, Ray.

RAY: Just like a cockroach.

DALE: I don't want to be a cockroach, Ray.

RAY: Why not. It's something you're good at.

(Dale gestures to Bernice, in the playhouse.)

DALE: Bernice and I are going to have a family but she doesn't know it. I tried to tell her in my own way. In fact I told her several times. I just can't get it through her head. Would you help me? Teach me to boogie?

RAY: You want me to teach you to fuck? Is that it?

DALE: I'd like it better if you'd use the word seduce. I'll pay you. How much is your rent?

RAY: Seven hundred dollars.

(Dale counts out the money.)

RAY: Could you make it a thousand?

(*Bernice comes out of the playhouse. She takes the Boy by the hand and leads him inside the playhouse.*)

DALE: Look at that woman. She's perfect. Isn't she.

RAY: Yep.

DALE: Do you like her?

RAY: She's good enough to practice on.

DALE: This isn't practice, it's the real thing.

RAY: Really?

DALE: Yes.

RAY: She's just another blow job mouth as far as I'm concerned. Introduce us.

(*Ray moves towards Bernice. Dale grabs him, stops him. Sylvia enters with the Baby in a chest carrier. Ray doesn't see her. She stands there watching.*)

DALE: Take that back.

RAY: What?

DALE: What you said about her mouth.

RAY: Why?

DALE: You talk like a pig. I don't allow pigs at my nursery school.

RAY: Fuck you.

DALE: Give me back my money.

RAY: Here, you can have it.

(*Ray holds the money over Dale's head.*)

DALE: Give it to me!

RAY: Jump for it.

(*Dale jumps, he can't get it. Ray knocks him down.*)

RAY: I'm going to show you something funny, okay? But don't laugh yet.

(*Ray throws the money on the ground. Dale scrambles to pick it up. Ray finally notices Sylvia. She's shaking. She takes out a bottle of aspirin.*)

RAY: Honey.

(*Sylvia flips the cap off the aspirin bottle and gulps several pills at once.*)

RAY: You've got to stop taking those aspirin honey.

SYLVIA: Why? Did he give you the money?

RAY: He wanted it back.

SYLVIA: I'm going to kill myself.

RAY: Who will take care of the baby?

SYLVIA: You will you bastard. You're the one who wanted it.

(*Sylvia exits.*)

RAY: I'm sorry you had to see that Dale. It's tough at home, now you see how it is. That's why sometimes things just come out of my mouth. Don't take it personally, Dale. I apologize.

DALE: I forgive you.

RAY: Could you give me the money?

DALE: All right. You'll have to wear a clown suit, and I want it happy. Happy happy happy. Positive Positive. Therapeutic.

(*Ray exits to behind the giant frog. Bernice and the Boy come out of the playhouse.*)

BERNICE: We have something to tell you.

DALE: Oh?

BERNICE: Go on. He's not going to bite you.

DALE: What's the matter? Cat got your tongue?

BERNICE: He's lost his tuition . . . again.

DALE: Call his mother.

BERNICE: She'll be very very angry.

DALE: That's the third time, you were careless again.

BERNICE: He's just a little boy.

DALE: Little boys have got to learn. (*Dale takes the Boy and sits him in the yellow chair.*) There once was a blue tin horse that I wanted. We passed it in a window, my mother and I. And always I stopped to stare at the horsie. And one day she asked, "Do you want the horsie?" She bought it immediately. The horse and I played together all day long. And finally she took it and threw it in the fire. And while I watched she said, "See, you've been tricked. The creature you thought was a horse is just a lump of tin. See how easily we can be fooled?" And then she pulled it out with a pair of tongs. I didn't want to look at it. I didn't have the strength. But she made me look until I understood. She made me see how I had been fooled. Today, I am grateful I had such lessons.

(*Sylvia marches onstage, looking for Ray. Ray, now in his clown suit and makeup, springs out at her from behind the frog.*)

RAY: He gave me a job.

SYLVIA: I'm a terrible person.

RAY: No you're not.

SYLVIA: Terrible. I've ruined your life. Haven't I? Haven't I? Ruined it! I promise I'm not going to ruin it anymore okay? That's a promise. I'll make a fresh start. And that's not easy for a worthless piece of shit. I'm not going to let that get in my way.

RAY: That's good.

SYLVIA: You've been very supportive. Very supportive. All my life you've been very supportive. But all I can do is just SMASH YOU IN THE FACE! I'm sorry for that. It isn't intentional. I'll make it up to you honey, okay? I'll go clean the house. I'll clean it. I'll clean it, okay? I'll clean it.

(*Sylvia exits muttering "I'll clean it, I'll clean it." Bernice come out of the playhouse. Sees the clown.*)

BERNICE: What's that?

DALE: We're going to have a party.

BERNICE: No thanks.

DALE: You look good.

BERNICE: Thank you.

DALE: You have a nice figure. It almost looks like you stuff your bra.

BERNICE: No, I don't.

DALE: You are very demure . . . .

(*Dale notices that the Boy is staring at them.*)

DALE: Look Joey, we got you a clown.

(*Dale slinks off to behind the frog. Ray looks slyly at Bernice, then he sings and speaks in pseudo French.*)

RAY: La Lune, et la montan . . . et le petit wazo cest magnifique—

(*Etc . . . ad lib. Ray circles around her. Suddenly he stops, speaks in English.*)

RAY: Actress? Or model.

BERNICE: What?

RAY: Which is it? Actress? Or Model?

BERNICE: Neither.

RAY: What are you?

BERNICE I'm a nursery school teacher.

RAY: I was with the Cirque Du Soleil for ten years. Not like this—

(*He gestures to his clown suit.*)

RAY: This isn't me, although I make a pretty damn good living doing parties. No, I was an animal trainer. I've traveled the world for the last ten years.

BERNICE: I've never been anywhere. Just here.

RAY: You must love children. Children are wonderful.

BERNICE: Do you have any of your own?

RAY: No. Uh . . . My wife was a tightrope walker who worked without a net. She . . . one day she . . .

BERNICE: I'm so sorry.

RAY: That's why I quit the circus.

RAY: You're spiritual aren't you. You have very special eyes. Mind if I look closer?

BERNICE: No.

RAY: Don't look away.

BERNICE: Don't look at me up close. I don't like that.

RAY: Why?

BERNICE: You might see something loathsome.

RAY: You're boyfriend doesn't think so.

BERNICE: There is no boyfriend.

RAY: Why is that?

BERNICE: Who would want me?

RAY: Dale wants you. He wants you a lot.

(*Bernice screams.*)

BERNICE: Go away.

RAY: Give him a chance.

BERNICE: I'm sick of Dale and his fucking clowns. Where does he get you? You're all alike.

RAY: Is that why you steal?

BERNICE: Shut up.

RAY: Why do you steal?

BERNICE: I'm 39 and I've never had sex.

RAY: Do you have a hot pussy?

BERNICE: Nope.

BOY: When is my mother coming back?

BERNICE: Maybe she's not. How does that feel. (*Bernice turns back to Ray.*) I used to feel guilty but now I just hate. I love to hate. It's my hobby.

(*Bernice exits into the playhouse. Dale enters from behind the frog.*)

DALE: Do you think you got her in a partyin' mood?

RAY: She has very strong feelings for you Dale.

DALE: She'll talk to you.

RAY: When you have a sense of humor, it greases the wheels.

DALE: Maybe I should try and joke with her.

RAY: Leave that to me.

DALE: I want to listen, see how you do it.

(*Sylvia enters at a dead run. Stops right in front of Dale.*)

SYLVIA: Can I ask you a question? Did you pay him?

DALE: Yes. He's been compensated.

SYLVIA: Why didn't you give me the money? Why? Have you spent it? You spent it already?

RAY: No.

SYLVIA: But you're going to spend it. Aren't you. Not on the rent. I can feel that. You've probably got something better in mind. Like a microphone.

RAY: What's wrong with that?

SYLVIA: Sodomize yourself. Why don't you sodomize yourself!!!

RAY: Don't talk like that. Why do you want to act like that?

SYLVIA: You don't care about me.

RAY: Yes I do.

SYLVIA: You don't even know I exist.

RAY: Yes I do . . . I dream about you.

(*Sylvia looks suspicious, Dale is watching curiously.*)

SYLVIA: What do you dream?

(*Ray illustrates his dream with several grandiose physical gestures.*)

RAY: I dream that . . . you're in a pool of water swimming in the moonlight. I feel you're in danger . . . dark dark flowers. You smell like them now. This mysterious fragrance. And then I see you floating away. I jump in the water. You're floating downstream and then you disappear. You're deep in the rapids. I see you once slip under the water. The roaring is ominous. Piranhas at my feet . . . . And I have this overwhelming feeling of despair. I feel so afraid. Please, don't hurt me. That's what the dream means.

SYLVIA: I would never hurt you. Don't you know that? Never never never . . . .

(*Sylvia exits muttering "never never". Ray watches her go, then claps his hands, leaps and exits to the frog. Bernice comes out of the playhouse.*)

(*Dale decides to try this technique he's learned from Ray. He tells her his dream and uses many of the same gestures Ray used, but they backfire.*)

DALE: I had a dream about you. You were vacuuming the playroom. It was dark. And you cut yourself on a piece of glass. You weren't wearing shoes. And then you screamed. Your clothes fell off.

(Bernice moves away from him. She marches in a large circle to escape him.)

DALE: I brought you a robe. I stood in the door and I covered my eyes, but you just kept vacuuming, vacuuming away. Then you went outside and the vacuum broke. I couldn't find you. I followed a trail of your blood. I bandaged your foot. Then the wild dogs came. I saw you devoured by wild dogs. I ran away. *(Dale comes close to Bernice.)* Please, don't hurt me.

(Bernice slaps his face. He runs into the playhouse. He comes out immediately.)

DALE: Why is the nursery school safe wide open?

BERNICE: You left it unlocked you stupid schmuck.

(Bernice's shirt is cut low. Money can be seen hanging out of her bra.)

DALE: So you steal from me!

BERNICE: Yes.

(Dale turns to Ray, who's been watching from behind the frog.)

DALE: What should I do?

RAY: Forgive her first, then give her a raise. A woman likes a generous man.

DALE: That's me, all the way.

(Ray snickers. Ray and Bernice share a look.)

DALE: Go entertain the children. Go on. Go play with the kids.

(Ray walks over to the Boy, stands near him sheepishly.)

DALE: I'd give you money. You don't have to steal. Please smile. I am just a human being. Aren't you afraid of losing your job?

BERNICE: I am a good person. Children are my life.

DALE: I could call the police. Does that scare you? Don't be scared. I guess I've never paid you enough. You can keep what you've stolen, would that be all right?

BERNICE: Thank you.

DALE: See? I'm not so bad. Right? You are very demure. May I pay you a compliment? You are aging, so beautifully. Did you steal enough money to take care of yourself? I'll give you more, you just have to ask.

BERNICE: No, this is enough for now.

DALE: Let's have a party.

BERNICE: I'd like to go early.

DALE: But I've already hired the clown.

BERNICE: I'd rather . . . I'd like to go early.

DALE: I'll need you to stay until his mother comes.

BERNICE: She's always late.

DALE: I've given you a pretty good bonus there, haven't I. That ought to cover it . . . . Am I right? Don't make me put on my businessman's face.

BERNICE: I've worked here ten years and I've never left early.

DALE: You've got nothing else better to do.

BERNICE: I do. I have something very important.

DALE; You never said sorry.

(*Bernice walks away from him defiantly and crosses her arms.*)

DALE: All right. Dismissed.

BERNICE: What?

(*The Boy runs across the stage, hides behind Bernice, clinging to her skirt.*)

DALE: Dismissed. I don't need your services. I've got the clown. You're dismissed.

BERNICE: What does that mean?

DALE: It means the sack is getting full. Go on, dismissed. You want something from me?

BERNICE: No.

DALE: Then go home.

BERNICE Am I being replaced?

DALE: That's up to you . . . . (*To the Boy.*) Go with the clown.

BERNICE: He hates clowns.

DALE: Now he has a chance to overcome his hate. Go with the clown. Go on. We got him for your birthday. Happy birthday.

BOY: It's not my birthday.

(*Bernice drags the Boy to the Clown.*)

BERNICE: Jesus Christ, just pretend it's your birthday.

(*Bernice plants the Boy in front of the clown. A beat.*)

RAY: I'll bet your folks pay through the nose. Pay through the nose to send you here. So that they don't have to play with you.   That's MY job. I'll play with you, sure.

(*Ray hands the Boy a balloon and then deftly pops it right in his face.*)

BERNICE: Well, that was unprofessional.

RAY: It's a joke.

BERNICE: It's not funny.

RAY: Then why did he smile?

BERNICE: He doesn't smile.

RAY: All kids smile. Go on. Show him how you smile.

BERNICE: He won't smile.

RAY: I'll make him smile.

BERNICE: You can't.

RAY: Yes I can. Okay? There was this man and wife eating dinner in a restaurant see . . . and the wife starts choking. Choking on a piece of meat. She's choking to death, and her husband yells HELP! SOMEBODY HELP! So this Texan runs over and he pulls down her pants. Do you know what you're doing? the husband asks. Of course, says the Texan, and he starts licking her ass. WHAT THE HELL DO YOU THINK YOU'RE DOING her husband yells. And the Texan looks up and says: THE HEINY LICK MANEUVER. Ha ha ha. The heiny lick maneuver. Get it?

BERNICE: You don't do things like that to a little boy.

RAY: What do you do?

BERNICE: You take care of him.

RAY: How?

BERNICE: You pay attention. The main thing to do is to pay attention. Children need lots and lots of attention. That's what they need. They need it. Attention. That's what's wrong with the world today. Nobody pays attention to their kids.

BOY: When is my mother coming back?

(*Bernice ignores the Boy.*)

BERNICE: You'll be a lousy father I'll bet because obviously you can't pay attention to a child.

BOY: When is my mother coming back?

BERNICE: Be quiet now Joey, we're trying to talk.

RAY: I never had a father. Maybe that's why.

BERNICE: I never had a mother.

RAY: My stepfather drank.

BERNICE: My father used to stick me with pins.

RAY: My mother smashed all of my toys.

BERNICE: I never had toys.

RAY: I never had shoes.

BERNICE: My stepmother poisoned my favorite dog.

RAY: My stepfather stabbed my mother in the heart. And you look just like her.

BERNICE: Really?

BOY: When is my mother going to come back?

BERNICE: Don't interrupt. It's not polite.

(*The Boy crosses to Dale, sits down sadly.*)

RAY: My life has been tragic.

BERNICE: I never had a life.

RAY: You've been a good girl, that must count for something.

BERNICE: I'm solidified.

RAY: What?

BERNICE: I'm hard as a rock.

RAY: I could break you.

BERNICE: That wouldn't be appropriate.

RAY: All right.

BERNICE: Where are you going?

RAY: I respect your feelings.

BERNICE: I don't have any feelings.

RAY: Of course you do.

BERNICE: Where?

(*Ray walks towards her; grabs her as if he's going to kiss her, but instead he rubs his face against hers, smearing clown makeup across her cheeks. They stare at each other. Pause.*)

RAY: Don't look at me like that, unless you want to fuck me.

BERNICE: Not till I'm married.

RAY: I'll marry you. I promise I will. Really. I promise. I will, I promise.

(*Ray backs her into the playhouse. They lay down. All we can see are their feet sticking out. Sylvia enters. She's wearing rubber gloves. She has a plate in one hand, a hammer in the other. Dale comes down center stage. He's staring at the playhouse with a distraught look on his face.*)

SYLVIA: Where's Ray?

DALE: He's in there.

(*We see Ray and Bernice's legs moving around. The sound of Ray having an orgasm can be heard. Then silence. Sylvia stares at the playhouse.*)

SYLVIA: I was trying to do the dishes but then I had this terrible feeling, this feeling in my head that I try to stuff down. One of those feelings the therapist says is just a bad tape that plays in my head. But it wasn't a tape. That's what I discovered. Has everyone been lying to me? About these tapes? Are these tapes in my head are they telling the truth? Answer me. ANSWER ME!

DALE: I don't know.

(*Sylvia breaks the plate with the hammer. Then exits. Ray comes out of the playhouse.*)

DALE: You weren't supposed to do that, Ray.

RAY: Had to.

DALE: That was a breach of contract, Ray.

RAY: So what.

DALE: That was a bad bad thing.

RAY: You know how it is when your wife just had a baby.

DALE: No, I don't. I guess I never will.

RAY: Sure you will. Don't worry. You will.

DALE: There is not going to be any hope.

RAY: There's hope. Just give it a chance.

DALE: Don't lie to me.

RAY: I'm telling the truth.

DALE: Then why did she do that?

RAY: She did it to make you jealous, that's why.

DALE: Think I'm stupid or something?

RAY: Just trust me.

DALE: No. Not anymore.

RAY: She really likes you Dale. She wants to shlong you.

DALE: Then why'd she let you?

RAY: Promise not to tell?

DALE: Okay.

RAY: Don't tell her I told you, but I had to break her in.

DALE: What do you mean?

RAY: She's a virgin, Dale, and it hurts the first time. I had to hurt her. I hurt her a lot. I did it first because you shouldn't have to. You should have it nice . . . nice and romantic.

DALE: I don't know how to be romantic. I don't know how to do that.

RAY: You've got to be yourself. Be yourself and nothing will hurt you.

DALE: You mean I'd be impervious?

RAY: Absolutely.

(*Dale goes to Bernice, who's just starting to emerge from the playhouse.*)

DALE: Bernice, I have something very important to tell you. The time has come. If we could just start fresh with a new born life. Bernice, you won't say anything, will you? No. You don't believe that we could start fresh. We could just start fresh with a newborn life. But the choice does not reside with me. The choice is yours. The choice is with you. And you know what? That drives me crazy. In all other matters I have freedom of choice, but not with this. No, no valid choice. Open your mouth and say what you want. Open it. Just say what you want. I'm looking at you, just open your mouth. (*Referring to Ray.*) He takes you for granted.

BERNICE: That's your opinion.

DALE: You deserve better.

BERNICE: That's nice of you to say.

DALE: He calls you THE BLOW JOB MOUTH. That's what he said. That Blow job mouth. I'm not seeing any kind of progress from you.

BERNICE: I can't have intimate relations with you.

DALE: Intimate relations. Is that what you call it?

BERNICE: Yes.

DALE: That's not what I'm asking for.

BERNICE: Sexual intercourse.

DALE: Again. That is not what I want. The stakes are quite a bit higher than that. I've been talking to you. What have you heard?

BERNICE: You said a lot of things.

DALE: What?

BERNICE: About your mother, and self reproduction.

DALE: Science hasn't found a way for me unassisted.

BERNICE: I already told you I don't want to fuck you.

DALE: Wrong. Wrong wrong wrong. That's wrong wrong wrong WRONG.

BERNICE: I'm serious. I don't want to do it.

DALE: That wouldn't be necessary.

BERNICE: What then? What?

(*Dale runs to the playhouse. He comes back with a jar of cloudy fluid.*)

BERNICE: What's this?

DALE: It's for you. Don't drink it.

BERNICE: It's what. This is what?

DALE: What does it look like?

BERNICE: Oh my god.

DALE: You take this. You know what to do with it. You'll do it. You know where to put it.

BERNICE: This is sick.

(*She shoves the jar to him, he shoves it back at her.*)

DALE: No. It's for you. It was always for you. Tell me you'll do it.

BERNICE: I don't want it.

DALE: It's for your own good.

BERNICE: Get it out of my sight.

DALE: Just look at it. Consider it.

BERNICE: NO.

(*She drops it, it spills.*)

BERNICE: Oh god.

DALE: Why did you do that? I know that you want it.

BERNICE: The normal way. Not like that.

DALE: That's perfectly fine. We can do it the normal——

BERNICE: Not with you.

DALE: Why not?

BERNICE: Do you have to ask?

DALE: Yes.

BERNICE: Okay . . . A person like you should have died at birth.

DALE: I know I'm not a perfect ten. You're looking at me, but you don't see.

BERNICE: Sure I do. You're nothing but a geek. You should work for the carnival biting chickens' necks.

DALE: I could take you by force if that's what I wanted. If that's the kind of person I was.

BERNICE: Why not Dale. Why not try?

DALE: Because I believe in the power of persuasion.

(*Sylvia enters with the Baby. The Baby is wrapped in a blanket.*)

SYLVIA: Do you know who I am?

BERNICE: No.

DALE: That's Ray's wife.

SYLVIA: Is that it? Is that who I am? What's my name?

RAY: Sylvia . . . .

SYLVIA: That's not my name.

(*Ray speaks to Bernice.*)

RAY: Go back in the playhouse now.

BERNICE: No.

DALE: He's got a partner. He doesn't need you.

RAY: SHUT UP!

SYLVIA: Is that THING the best you could do?

RAY: Get in the playhouse.

BERNICE: No, I won't.

RAY: This will all work out. It will work out okay.

DALE: That's his baby. He doesn't need yours.

SYLVIA: I'm not who I thought I was, not anymore. I'm not a mother.

RAY: Yes you are, you're a fine mother . . . .

BERNICE: You lied to me.

RAY: No. I was telling the truth.

(*Sylvia starts to walk away.*)

RAY: Wait!

SYLVIA: Why?

RAY: I did it for the money. I did it for you. I sacrificed myself. (*Ray turns to Bernice in an aside.*) This woman is crazy, I don't even know her.

BERNICE: You lied to me.

RAY: But I won't anymore. I'll leave her.

SYLVIA: Ray—

BERNICE: Go home and eat bon bons, you stupid bitch.

RAY: Sylvia, this will work out, I promise.

SYLVIA: I am no longer Sylvia now. Okay?

RAY: Yes, you are. You've just had an attack. Go on home and pay the rent. Go pay the rent. This will all work out.

SYLVIA: No, the house has burned down.

RAY: What!

(*Dale moves closer to Bernice.*)

DALE: We're exactly alike . . . .Bernice? You deserve a man like me.

(Dale tries to put his arms around her. She throws him off with a violent scream and stomps towards off stage. Ray sees her, and follows, although for a moment he's torn between her and Sylvia. He yells after her but she walks quickly like she never wants to see him again. The actors may ad lib as they exit. When they get to the perimeter of the playing area, they freeze.)

(Sylvia takes her baby and gently places it on the ground. She stands over it.)

SYLVIA: You are just like me. You are just like me. You are just like me. And I HATE myself.

(Sylvia stands back a little from the baby, looks at Dale.)

DALE: Give me your burden. Do that for me. Give me your burden. You don't want to keep her.

(Sylvia exits, the opposite direction as Bernice did. Just before she goes offstage, she freezes in mid-stride.)

(Dale picks the baby up and cradles it. He sings a lullaby.)

DALE: Bye baby bunting.
           Daddy's gone a-hunting.
           To get a little rabbit skin
           To wrap his baby bunting in.

(Dale takes the baby inside the playhouse. The Boy comes down center stage and looks at the audience. After a long pause, calliope music comes up and Sylvia, Ray, Bernice and Boy exit.)

END

Biographies

Susan Champagne has been associated with the Padua Festival since she was a student in 1981. Her published plays include *Honeymoon* (which premiered at the Magic Theatre) and *Take A Picture* (for which she received an L.A. Weekly Award). Other plays include *Walkin' Me Home* (for which she received a Drama-Logue Award), *Bondage, Winter Soldiers*, and *Song of Songs* (which played at the last Padua Festival).

Martin Epstein's published plays include *The Man Who Killed the Buddha, Autobiography of a Pearl Diver, Mysteries of the Bridal Night, Three Variations on the Theme of Pain* and *How Gertrude Stormed the Philosopher's Club*. His other plays, *Your Back Yard and My Back Yard, Possum Song, Charles the Irrelevant, Off Center, Vera*, and *The Ordeal of Nancy Fergusson* have been produced at Padua and other theatres. *Vera* has also aired several times on NPR. Epstein is a 1985 Rockefeller grant recipient and is currently teaching at the Tisch School of the Arts at NYU.

Maria Irene Fornes is the author of more than two dozen works for the stage. Among them are *Promenade, The Successful Life of 3, Fefu and Her Friends, Eyes on the Harem, The Danube, Mud, The Conduct of Life, Abingdon Square, What of the Night*, and *Enter the Night*. She is the recipient of seven Obie Awards, one of which was for Sustained Achievement. She is also the recipient of a Distinguished Artist Award from the National Endowment for the Arts, Honorary Doctor of Letters Degree, Bates College, Lewiston, ME, a Distinguished Directors Award from the San Diego Theater Critics Circle and an award for Distinguished Achievements as an artist and educator from the Association for Theater in Higher Education. She has received grants and fellowships form the Rockefeller Foundation, The John Simon Guggenheim Memorial Foundation, CINTAS and NEA, among others. At present she is recipient of a Lila Wallace Reader's Digest Award.

Julie Hebert has directed plays throughout America and in Japan. In 1985 she was an NEA Directing Fellow. Her career as a playwright began at Padua with the writing of *True Beauties*. The Magic Theatre production, directed by the author, was honored with the Critics' Circle Best Play of 1987 and six Drama-Logue awards. Her other plays include *Almost Asleep, In the Privacy of Strangers, Ruby's Bucket of Blood* and *Burning Dreams*, an opera composed by Gina Leishman with libretto co-written by Hebert and Octavio Solis, commissioned by Meet the Composer, AT&T/NEA, produced by San Diego Rep. From 1989 through 1993, Hebert served as Artistic Director for the Contemporary Arts Center in New Orleans, during which time she received a grant from the NEA's Inter-Arts program for her collaboration on Heiner Mueller's *Medeamaterial*. The work was further honored with a cover story in American Theatre magazine. Hebert wrote the screenplay *Female Perversions* for Susan Streitfeld and FP Productions, adapted from the book of the same name by Louise J. Kaplan. She recently completed a new play, *The Knee Desires the Dirt*, commissioned by 7 Stages in Atlanta through the Rockefeller Foundation.

Leon Martell, originally from Vermont, (B.A. from the University of Vermont, MFA from the University of Iowa) in 1975, co-founded the comedy group, "Duck's Breath Mystery Theatre." With the "Ducks," he performed live across the country for sixteen years, as well as writing and performing series for National Public Radio, Fox Television, and specials for PBS. He joined the Padua Hills Playwrights Festival in 1982 as both writer and actor. His Padua plays include *Hoss Drawin'*, *Guys at the Spunk Hole*, *1961 El Dorado* (co-written with wife Elizabeth Ruscio), *Brick Time Stories*, and *Kindling*. His one-act *Feed Them Dogs* was produced in '91 by Theatre of NOTE. The Audrey Skirball Kenis Theatre has produced readings of his *Mooncalf*, *Kindling* and a workshop of *The Admiral of Bolivia*. *Mooncalf* was produced by The Road Theatre Company, winning four Drama-Logue awards in '93. Martell is a charter member of the Wilton Project and currently a member of the Mark Taper Forum's "Mentor Playwrights Project."

Murray Mednick founded the Padua Hills Playwrights' Workshop/Festival in 1978, and remains its Artistic Director. He was formerly Artistic Co-Director of Theatre Genesis in New York. Plays since then include *Iowa* and *Blessings* (for the PBS series "Visions"), *The Coyote Cycle*, *Taxes*, *Scar*, *Heads*, *Shatter 'n Wade*, and *Joe and Betty*. He has been the recipient of two Rockefeller Foundation grants, a Guggenheim Fellowship, an OBIE, several Drama-Logue and Bay Area Critics Circle Awards. His play *Scar* (starring Ed Harris) recently received a critically-acclaimed and sold-out run at the Met Theatre in Los Angeles. His play *Fedunn* received a workshop production by the Skirball-Kenis Theatre at UCLA. Mr. Mednick received a 1992 Ovation Award from the LA Theatre League Alliance for his outstanding contributions to Los Angeles Theater.

Susan Mosokowski is the Co-Artistic director of Creation Production Company. Her plays include: *Eclipse, White/Black, Chromatic Spectacles, Circuits, The Commie Stories, Ice Station Zebra, The Bride and Her Extra-rapid Exposure, The Rotary Notary and His Hot Plate, The Bachelor Machine,* and adaptations of *The Cabinet of Dr. Caligari* and *The Inferno.* Her work has been presented in theatres and museums in the U.S. and Europe. She has been the recipient of three Northwest Area Fellowships for her interdisciplinary trilogy based on Marcel Duchamp's *Large Glass* which was presented at the Philadelphia Museum of Art as part of their Duchamp Centennial, an NEA Playwriting Fellowship, and a Rockefeller Foundation Fellowship. Her plays for Padua include *Cities Out of Print* and *The Tight Fit.*

An original founding member of the Padua Hills Playwrights Festival, John Steppling is currently co-artistic director of the Circus Minimus Lab in L.A. His plays include *The Shaper, Sea of Cortez, Standard of the Breed, My Crummy Job, Deep Tropical Tan* and *The Dream Coast.* His work has been performed in L.A., San Francisco, New York and London. He has received four NEA grants for writing and directing, as well as a Rockefeller Fellowship. He is the father of a twelve-year-old son and lives in L.A. with actress/dancer Priscilla Harris.

Kelly Stuart is a founding member of the theatre group Heliogabalus, which produced her first plays, *The Secret of Body Language* and *Taxi Dance,* at the Cast Theatre. *The Woman Who Tried To Shout Underwater* and *The Interpreter of Horror* were produced at the Taper, Too in their Festival of New Works.

The 1989 and 1990 Padua Hills Playwrights' Festivals were made possible in part by grants from the Irvine Foundation, LA. Cultural Affairs, the Rockefeller Foundation, and the California Arts Council.

Best of the West, 2nd Edition, was made possible in part by the Audrey Skriball-Kenis Foundation and the Board of Directors of the Padua Hills Playwrights Workshop/Festival: Kathy Baker, John Bunzel, Kathy Heller, Nick Love, Amy Madigan, Paul Mayersohn, Nancy Mette, Murray Mednick, Scott Paulin, Cheryl Slean, and Julie Warner.

Editors:	Murray Mednick, Bill Raden, Cheryl Slean
Design:	Julie Williams
Additional Design (2nd edition):	Cheryl Slean
Typesetting:	Kristin Conradi
Scanning & Color Separations:	Icon West
Special Thanks to:	Amy Madigan, Kathy Baker, John Orders, Media Logic, Inc., Rhythm & Hues, Inc., Shawn Davis, Gina Kaufmann, Cheryl Bianchi, Anna Roth, Georgia Davis, Chris Mednick, Tim Robbins, and Cal State Northridge.

Also available from Padua Hills Press:
The Coyote Cycle, Seven Plays by Murray Mednick